THE BRIDES AND GROOMS OF CHRIST

Vol.1: The Chosen Elect Lady
Vol. 2: World Wide Conspiracy

THE BRIDES AND GROOMS OF CHRIST

Vol.1: The Chosen Elect Lady
Vol. 2: World Wide Conspiracy

by
Valetta Johnson

Gotham Books

30 N Gould St.
Ste. 20820, Sheridan, WY 82801
https://gothambooksinc.com/

Phone: 1 (307) 464-7800

© 2025 *Valetta Johnson*. All rights reserved.

No part of this book may be reproduced, stored in a retrieval system, or transmitted by any means without the written permission of the author.

Published by Gotham Books (February 12, 2025)

ISBN: 979-8-34851-759-5 (H)
ISBN: 979-8-88775-756-8 (P)
ISBN: 979-8-88775-757-5 (E)

Because of the dynamic nature of the Internet, any web addresses or links contained in this book may have changed since publication and may no longer be valid.

The views expressed in this work are solely those of the author and do not necessarily reflect the views of the publisher, and the publisher hereby disclaims any responsibility for them.

Table of Contents

Acknowledgment vi
Preface vii
Introduction xi
Chapter 1 1
Chapter 2 39
Chapter 3 64
Chapter 4 97
Chapter 5 138
Chapter 6 153
Chapter 7 169
Chapter 8 190
Chapter 9 208
Chapter 10 244
Chapter 11 250
Chapter 12 269
Chapter 13 287
Chapter 14 315
Chapter 15 325
Chapter 16 333
Chapter 18 398
Chapter 19 451
Appendix 500

Acknowledgment

I would like to thank God for giving me the direction that he gave, to show me in his word, that his word was like a manual for our life's and without him or his word, this mission never would have been completed. I also appreciate the fact that he manages to resolve the issues with my mother, and she eventually became the mother that I could call on. God was my mother, when there was nowhere else to turn. And first and foremost, my Lord and Savior Jesus Christ, who died that all people would experience the grace that would allow all women a better chance at preparing for their family.

Preface

When this author's tumultuous journey led her life through a couple of rapes and a justifiable homicide, not to mention other encounters her life survived, she felt as Moses once did and became. Yet she was determined to live a normal life even though the author wanted nothing more than to live a normal life. The world was watching and waiting to hear her testimony since she was triumphant in her will to rise above the odds. She stayed busy as an entrepreneur and workaholic. Even though she had always wanted to share her experience, she didn't know when or where it would happen. Since it was such a sensitive matter, the author decided to move on in life.

Many that knew of the author suspected she was a spiritual person because of the crosses she would wear, thinking they were her good-luck charms, but the author had a deeper relationship with God than most people knew, including herself.

It wasn't until she realized that God was calling her into the ministry and understanding what a calling was made her thankful to God for a chance to fulfill her destiny in him. When she answered the calling on her life is when everything began to make sense, and she realized how she lived through the good and the bad things in life to help others to find their strength in God as she had.

The author wasn't open to share everything in her life… until she ended up going to a church where she had to confront the abortion issue, opening another can of worms. Now this meant she would have to face the demons that called abortion murder as well, and this meant she would have to dig up her past and find peace with the abortion she had. That made it even more difficult to share with others openly.

Since others knew of her battles, and others were just curious, she knew she had to set the records straight and give the Lord the glory. This is how the book came into play.

As she attempted to write the book, reservations arose as she contemplated sharing about the abortion and how she started to name the book "Sin for a Season," yet it wasn't her intention to glorify sin because most of us are in situations where sin has dominated our lives, and her life was no different than others.

After coming to terms on sharing about the abortion, the author felt the truth would set her free, and she would have to depend on the leading of the Lord since she also felt the abortion was a blessing in disguise because the pregnancy would've been untimely.

As the author struggled for acceptance in the church, she knew it wasn't going to happen unless she lowered her standards and agreed with the hypocrites of the world. Nevertheless, it wasn't an option; the author couldn't agree with the traditional churches, and she opted to separate herself from that church doctrine and sought the face of God directly.

Her journey through the Bible fascinates her. As she dissects the Bible, her awareness unveils the deepest, darkest secrets of the Bible and exposes the Antichrist. And then she stumbles upon a book that reaches out and touches her, with only a revelation that she can reveal: Second John, "The Elect Lady." As she reads this book, it becomes evident that she is this lady, and the book was written for her.

Suddenly, her life is an open book before the actual book is written—as the government precariously watches and guards her every move, until her life is everything but normal. She knows now that she must save many with her testimony before it's too late. The spirit of the Antichrist has filled the world with lies and deception, but the truth will come through the Word of God and her testimony.

Throughout the Bible, the author is inspired as she identifies with the Ethiopian daughter's testimony and imagines herself as this lady, yet the Antichrist is trying to come against her at her job, home, and the church of Satan. Now the author knows that, for such a time as now, her life has been preserved to expose the Antichrist and save the world from ultimate doom.

While the presidents ignored her warnings, the judgment of God swept over America, and it may not be over yet. It took the author three years to write the book because she didn't start writing the book until she answered God's calling on her life and her refusal to believe that the abortion issue had to be dealt with by the entire world. Then it took fifteen years to get the book published because many refused to believe the truth in God's Word. After the pandemic in 2020, the book was revised because it put an entirely new spin on the book.

Introduction

An autobiography that took a utopia turn, this book is written in the third-person form by the author, and the names have been changed to protect those identified in the book, especially the author.

A young lady struggled in her teen years to find herself established and independent before making a commitment to God while growing up in a dysfunctional family environment. She knew nothing was going to be given to her on a silver platter, and she would have gladly worked for it.

Despite her desire to become independent, she held her own in God as she attempted to be a witness in a worldly way. Some thought she was a child prodigy until she proved that she was much more, after buying her first home after high school, only to encounter numerous burglaries. However, after her life was threatened by a rapist, the author was forced to purchase a gun. Most people would have moved long before the rape, but even then, she was determined to hold on to a home, which she never had as a child. And after moving from one place to another growing up, she was determined not to let them drive her away from her home.

Nine months after the first rape, another attempt on her life proved deadly for another rapist as she defended herself and killed the rapist on his way out the door.

She becomes a local hero despite knowing that she did nothing herself, but God's strength and courage pulled her through. Even though the author realized that God alone had carried her through the countless trials her life had already experienced, she still couldn't come to terms with going to church, knowing that she didn't want to be a hypocrite; she prayed and studied about God in her own way.

Eventually, the enemy lured her sister into the drug world and cost her sister her life. Being extremely close to this sister, it became the straw that broke the camel's back since it was her sister's husband's drug involvement that led the author down the wrong road as well. After the burial of her sister, the author's life was resurrected.

Finally, her decision to join the church took on an adventure and fun-filled journey as she committed to the things of God, and she then realized what a calling was. She became the living testimony that she had prayed her sister would be. Directions into prison ministry led her to minister to the man that killed her sister, and he began to preach in the prison.

Her life became full of church activities. As she taught the four- and five-year-olds, she was teaching herself as well. It was a need in the church everywhere she turned; missions and joining the choir had the author busy from sunup until sundown until her growth was stumped, then magnified, by the abortion issue. It seemed like her passion to know and love God made her question another phase of the church that encouraged pregnant girls to adopt out their babies to the church.

The author didn't feel condemned by the abortion she experienced at the age of seventeen; as a matter of fact, she felt thankful that they had legal abortion at the time, and she didn't want to be a hypocrite with the issue, especially since the church had become a welfare system promoting sin.

Also, the minister saying malicious things about abortion to try to condemn women from having one made the author leery. Since the minister was single, he knew that a lot of women were there for him, and the author also sensed he was trying to flirt with her. For that reason, she let the man of God know that if God ever called her to minister in the abortion area, the only thing she could do was pray that God would direct their decision.

After the author informed the minister of her views on abortion, she was glad that she got it off her chest, and she was ready to move on, but it wasn't that easy. One thing led to another, and before she knew it, it seemed like the signs were leading the author to defend women that needed an abortion; however, it wouldn't be at the church she was at since they wanted to kick her out of the church after the letter the author wrote and all the other things, she did prove to her point.

Obedience was the furthest thing on her mind when she realized how many would oppose her. Even the women's movement was annoyed by her when she tried to stand by the Word of God. Finally, her only defense was the Bible as the author studied to show herself approved, rightfully dividing the Word of God. More evidence in the Bible proved that the false teachers had misled the churches and that the government might have helped them.

As she stood by the Word of God, amazingly, near the end of the Bible, John wrote a book to the elect lady. To her surprise, it seemed like the book bore witness with her spirit. She began to feel an awesome connection with the book, especially since her name tied in with the book. The author knew the word *children* also referred to all the believers that agreed with this truth, but the scary thing about it was John warned her that those opposing the choices for women were the Antichrist.

Now the author knows that some people don't know they are the Antichrist, and she needs to show them in the Bible. One book led to another book titled: *"Forbidden Fruit"*. The author would like to challenge the atheists and help people understand the scriptures and how to read the Bible.

Ironically, John also wrote, in 3 John, to Gaius, a disciple of Jesus Christ, how to beware of the opposer of Christ. He described in this book exactly what happened at the first church that the author attended; even the minister's name was identified in this book as an arrogant and stubborn leader of the Gospel. John warned Gaius, for the love of God, not to take anything from the Gentiles because he needed to teach the people the right way of truth.

The author believes that these two books at the end of the Bible prove that the abortion issue has been around for a long time, and mostly all the books in the Bible refer to it one way or the other. However scary it may seem, when God talked about illegitimacy in the Old Testament, and then also in the New Testament, he didn't change his law, yet our society has polluted the world with a different standard, creating a diversion on the face of the earth. Yet God has blessed our country with the diversity of many offspring, but truth must prevail. When we see what's going on in China, and our country still seems ignorant to the pure facts, it's time to get real.

Chapter 1

Trials of Growing Up

The crackling whispers sounded, and the aroma of fire sizzled as the parents alerted the others that something was terribly wrong.

Papa Joseph Johnson raced through the house, grabbing the little ones as the older daughter gathered herself and ran out the front door where Mother was waiting with high hopes that all would be saved.

Papa Joseph, scorched and battered, came out with the two youngest girls in his arms while James, the oldest, had the two younger boys. Josie, the eldest girl, had clinched on to Mother. Now they all huddled together as the firemen came. You could hear the sirens blast in the distance.

All six children were accounted for and at the nick of time; it seemed like the roof was caving in from the fire, leaving the house in utter ashes as the neighbors gathered around to offer their help. At 2:00 in the morning, it was a bit cold.

The January cold had settled in, in Northern Oklahoma. It was not always a sunny climate, and when it was cold, it was cold. Mother and Father held each other in despair, knowing their problems would be easier to deal with since they were together.

Just then, the firemen arrived and began to finish what was left of the smoldering fire. While Papa gave a report to the police officer, one of the neighbors offered Mother and the children a place to camp until it was over. It looked like all of them got out with just the clothes on their backs, and that was about it. They would have to start over, from having a place to stay to having clothes to put on their backs, but it seemed better just knowing they were family.

After Papa came in from talking with the officer, he told the others that the police officer suspected someone caught the house on fire because of the evidence they found in the back of the house. Mother was upset, wondering who could have done this and not caring about the family.

As they pondered on what enemies surrounded them, they just grew weary and decided to give it to God, knowing that he would protect them from all harm. Papa still had a job and needed it more than ever now, so he didn't sleep much that night, but a wink here and there.

At daybreak, Mother and Papa were agreeing on what they had planned to do that day since they knew they didn't want to burden the neighbors any longer than they had.

A family of eight was now without shelter, clothing, and food. Papa had planned on going to work and asking about getting some time off because of this situation. Papa had a sister who was dear and near to him, and she was always able to help, and Mom's mother was always there to extend a helping hand. Papa worked at the City Refuse Department, and even though it was hauling trash, he was glad to have a job to support his family.

That evening, Papa came home with good news—his job took up an offering, and the church where they attended frequently did the same thing. Papa had already started looking for another place to live. It seemed like offerings and services were pouring in, and clothes were donated as well. Papa's sister worked at a laundromat, and she found a lot of clothing that was left behind. She knew the lost-and-found was never claimed most of the time, and if someone came back looking for anything, she would just tell them they were donated. Within a week, the family had settled in their new place, and the donations and offerings as well as those that gave to the cause, were blessings they could thank God for.

The Johnson were no more than the typical American family that struggled in a society that often neglected the needs of the poor people, but the community pulled together and helped one another. As a strong tower rose, they rose to the occasion, and now, the kids were back in school, and Mother tended to the younger ones at home until they were able to attend school.

Even though Papa's grandfather was a street preacher, it was Mother who was adamant about taking the children to church. Now that the older children were back in school, Mother kept herself busy with the two younger girls, Candi and Babe. As they played together, it seemed like they fussed more than anything. As Babe went around singing and praising the Lord, Mother had a feeling that she would be the one that would enjoy church. Babe was very impressionable, and it seemed like she liked to think that God and his angels were always looking after them. Mother couldn't remember exactly if it was when the house burned down when Babe habitually started talking about the Lord.

Babe's obsession to know God and be about the church business also came because of Mother being involved in the Pentecostal Church while she was pregnant with Babe. Babe was the last of seven children, although the oldest brother wasn't from the same mother. Now the Johnson attended a more traditional church, but they switched over to Baptist after Babe was born. Babe found herself in church even when others had no desire or interest to attend.

Babe had such a tear-jerking experience when a preview of Jesus's Crucifixion was shown at the church. She wanted more than anything, to be involved with the church's Easter pageant.

She felt that it was her way of giving something back to Jesus. After Babe asked her mother if it was okay, with Mother's approval, Babe received a speech from the director of the pageant. Babe studied and recited it; she was overwhelmed with joy to be able to participate.

All eyes were on Babe as she stepped up to the microphone and loudly proclaimed her love for the Lord Jesus and denounced sin in her life as she would live for the Lord. At the tender age of seven, Babe didn't know what sin was, but she knew that was what her speech said, which she had remembered. As she exited the stage, all stood for a standing ovation, and at the reception, Mother was proud to see her little angel perform as well as she did.

It seemed like Babe was fondest of the church, and it wasn't long before she signed up for water baptism. Papa was too busy working, but the other children were there to witness, even if they didn't feel compelled to follow her leadings, and it never was pushed on any of them because Mother felt that she couldn't force such a decision on her children.

But with Babe, it seemed natural. As Babe bubbled around with her newfound faith, her brothers were always there to defend her. They all tried to look after their sisters, but by now, everyone in school was struggling with something since Papa and Mother never completed high school themselves. It took some real studying to overcome the obstacles and challenges that school was bringing. James and Josie as well as Martin and Joseph Jr. (who was called JJ since he was named after Papa) were busy at studying for school and helping with the family chores.

Josie combed Candi's and Babe's hair and cared for the two girls after Mother found a job at a department store. It seemed like the busier Papa and Mother stayed working to put food on the table, the more distance took over, which slipped right in, and separation issues became so settled because everyone was busy in their own world.

By now, Candi and Babe were in school, and that gave Mother a chance to find a job and help with the family responsibilities; it also gave the kids more time to get involved in mischief after school, which would eventually cause trouble.

After school one evening, while everyone was taking turns riding the only bike they had, JJ offered to take Babe for a ride—that way, she didn't have to wait as long. They had learned how to saddle up with Babe on the handlebars while JJ peddled. JJ had taken a liking to cruising down Roosevelt Hills, a hilly elite district with lots of trees and shrubs. As they struggled up the hills, JJ knew that downhill would be a breeze because he had done it several times. Down the hill, he peddled at first, but then the speed was so enormous he didn't have to peddle at all. It seemed like they automatically glided at an increasingly high speed while the wind pushed them forward. The breeze kept them refreshed until, suddenly, JJ forgot the stop sign, and it would've tossed Babe overboard. Yet the car coming from the opposite direction couldn't avoid the crash that threw Babe in a hedge of bushes while for JJ, screeching brakes couldn't save him from the impact of the car crashing into him.

As the couple got out of the car, Babe was dusting herself off the pile of leaves she had fallen into. The couple was amazed at how she didn't show any signs that she was hurt, but it was obvious that JJ was, as they scrapped their bike off the side of the curve. They gently picked up JJ, but it seemed like the only thing wrong was his leg was broken. They immediately gathered them both in their car and proceeded to go to the hospital, where they called their parents while JJ got his leg casted.

Papa and Mother were there about the same time JJ finished getting his leg casted. The couple was nice enough to wait and meet the parents, and boy, was Mother upset. She wanted to start whipping JJ there, but since he had a cast on his leg, she held off, but she promised him a good whooping after he recovered. She didn't even have to ask how Babe got there since JJ was the oldest. But she was thankful that Babe didn't have a scar on her from the accident. After that incident, it seemed like Papa and Mother just knew Babe was a trooper and God had his hands on her.

School wasn't a big hit in the Johnson family. Babe wasn't crazy about school like her other brothers and sisters; she struggled with studying. Babe ended up being put in special education while she was in elementary school, but for some reason it was just to guard her from being bullied. Nevertheless, Babe's teacher saw some potential in Babe even when she didn't study. Babe's teacher wanted her to sign up for the spelling bee. Babe didn't really want to, but she was elected anyway.

Babe never studied for it, and she didn't even look forward to it, maybe because no one in the family showed any interest. The teacher was upset with Babe when she missed a simple word like *chimney*. She couldn't believe it, but Babe tried not to take it personally when she lost because she didn't want to enter, but the teacher made her. Then the teacher realized that Babe wasn't getting enough encouragement from home, but she knew that she couldn't follow her home.

As Babe began to blossom her baby fat got in the way of her maturity, and with Josie wearing a bra now, Babe thought that she needed one also. Her baby fat left her chubby and jolly. Babe tried on Josie's bra. She could tell it was kind of big, but she didn't care; she just wanted to cover herself up. That evening, Babe was anxious to go to the store with Papa, and boy was he surprised to see Babe in a bra. Papa joked about her rushing things as he looked down at her bra. Babe still only in the third grade explained to Papa that she was too fat, and she thought she needed a bra. Papa explained that it was only baby fat. Babe was still awfully bashful, and that night, when they returned from the store and before she went to bed, she remembered praying to God: "Please, God, don't let them get too big."

Babe and Candi both struggled with baby fat, and Candi worried that she would be a diabetic. She would remember everything she had eaten that day, and at the end of the day, she would ask James, the oldest brother if eating all she had eaten would make her a diabetic, and James would assure her that it wouldn't. Yet they continued growing like normal girls, and while the others prepared for high school, others were held back in school because of lack of understanding. Out of the six children, three were held back while the others barely made it through the system.

Despite the setbacks in the family, they still managed through life even though some were held back a year because the teacher noticed some deficiencies in their ability to learn. It made Babe study a bit more, but it seemed like there were still things that kept her from focusing.

It became more apparent when Papa and Mother began to fight more and stories of infidelity hit the surface, next came the divorce. It seemed like Josie and James were more prepared for it than the others; they had taken on the role as the oldest, and they knew what to expect, but it didn't seem real to Babe because she just knew God could fix anything, but finally, Babe had to accept it. She found herself in her prayer closet, hoping that God would save her family, but when reality set in, Babe knew that it would be better if they went their own separate ways for them to be happy. By now, Babe was not a child anymore; she had grown up fast enough to accept what was going on in her life.

With the separation going on, Mother moved the children with her at her mother's place, where she would stay until the divorce was final. Grandmother was glad to receive Mother and all the children, even if the house was too small. Granny made a way for them all to be fed, clothed, and taken care of. Granny wasn't fond of Papa, and she resented the fact that she had to make him marry Mother when she got pregnant with James, to hear about a shotgun wedding. This shocked Babe because she knew nothing of it until they moved in with Granny. Now that Papa and Mother were divorcing, Granny didn't hold back telling him how she felt about him, and all this time, Babe thought they had the best family.

Now to find out that Papa and Mother stayed in the relationship over ten years even though they were forced to get married just proved to Babe that even forcing them to marry didn't assure them it would work, but they had five more children after that.

Mother was the second of two daughters that Granny had. Her sister lived in Texas now, but she had a house in Tulsa that she was trying to sell, and since it wasn't sold yet, Granny agreed that Mother should move into it after the divorce was final. Mother thought it was a good idea, but Aunt Etta's house was small as well. Candi liked staying with Granny because she was named after Granny, and Babe was named after her mother's sister, Juanetta.

They just called her Babe because her papa started with that nickname, and she never outgrew it. James was named after one of Granny's boyfriends, and Joseph was named after Papa. Martin just ended up with his name, and Josie was also named after Papa.

That summer, the family moved into Aunt Etta's empty house—another adjustment to make. The neighborhood was settled, with a few children around the corner. It didn't seem very social, especially after finding out that one of the neighbors did hair in her home and one of her frequent customers was Papa's new girlfriend, much to Mother's surprise.

One day when Papa's new girlfriend was getting her hair done, the brothers found out and told their mother. She had one of the boys tell the lady that she wanted to talk with her after she finished with her hair. Mrs. Bird was Papa's new girlfriend, and it wasn't until later that Papa started bringing her over to see the kids, but whatever Mrs. Bird and Mother talked about that day wasn't kids' business. Babe didn't know if her mom didn't want her to date her father or what; Mrs. Bird didn't carry on as she was upset, but Mom did. Sometimes, it just seemed like adults can be stupid. Babe didn't know how to tell her mother to leave the nice lady alone without getting scorned herself. Babe questioned that if Mother was mad at Papa, she should take it out on him instead of the lady. Nevertheless, it seemed like after that, the neighborhood wasn't going to be a big hit.

With school about to start, they were preparing for the best even if it did seem like the worst. Josie and James, the two eldest weren't around much. James stayed with Granny to help her out, and Josie stayed with Paula, a dear friend of Mother's. Candi and Babe always found things to separate them, but when Papa came by, they would always find a way to be together. Papa started a tradition: right before school started, he would take them out to buy school supplies—notebooks, papers, pens, etc.

Papa started living with his girlfriend right after they all met her, and since they lived in some newly built projects that were much larger than Aunt Etta's home.

Joseph and Martin stayed with Papa most of the time. Mrs. Bird had two sons of her own and a daughter. At times, Candi and Babe would stay the weekend and hang out with Ester, her daughter. Ester was younger than both, but they didn't notice the difference. Since Ester was the only girl in her family, she was glad to know Candi and Babe.

Papa worked on cars on the side, and Joseph and Martin took an interest in cars as well; however, the auto-mechanic course they took turned out to be more than they could handle—neither one of them were doing very well, and this gave Mother a chance to meet the teacher, Mr. Black, who turned out to be more than just a teacher. Before long, it seemed like Mother and Mr. Black had some kind of love connection going on, and whatever was going wrong with Joseph's and Martin's grades, Mr. Black made it better for them.

About that time, Josie was going to the same high school and had met the auto-mechanic teacher's nephew from a nearby town. Josie liked him, and Malcolm liked her; they planned to attend the same college.

One night, Malcolm was over; Mother had borrowed Mr. Black's car, and Malcolm recognized his uncle's car. Babe was silly and young and didn't know what discreteness was. She joked about his uncle's car, but Malcolm didn't know that his uncle was having an affair since he knew that his uncle was married. Mr. Black lived in a rural town, and his wife didn't know anything either.

Mr. Black spent weekends at home with his wife, and sometimes, since he lived around the corner from the school,

Mother would spend evenings with him. Malcolm didn't live in town; he didn't know what was going on, and because Josie was blindly in love with Malcolm, she didn't think it mattered. It was the last year of high school for Josie, and she had made up her mind that she would join Malcolm in Miami, OK. It was the second year for Malcolm, and it would be the first year for Josie. Babe and Candi were glad to see Josie go to college and move away, and it wasn't long before JJ and Martin were on their own. JJ met a girl in the same apartment complex where Papa lived, and when she became pregnant, Mrs. Bird made him marry her, and then he had him a family. At least he graduated from school, both him and Martin. Martin ended up in Texas, away from everybody, but he had a good job, and he did well.

Staying in Aunt Etta's home was getting old because they never did any repairs, and after a while, the house began falling apart, but some new apartments in the neighborhood gave them hope that they would soon be moving into a bigger home, much bigger than the house they lived in, and it soon happened. By now, Babe and Candi were in high school, and they finally had their own bedroom, where Babe could talk and cry out to God whenever she wanted to. They had stopped going to church long ago since Mother didn't have a car, but nothing stopped Babe from going to her private space and talking to God.

One evening, when Babe was trying to understand the Bible, she kept reading about slaves and masters. Babe knew that her people had been slaves at one time, and she had heard some pretty bad things about it. She wondered if this was the way it should be since the Bible spoke of slaves as well. That evening, she cried out to God. "Please, God," she cried, "I know where Jesus came from and I believe in him but, God where, did you come from?" Babe cried with all her heart, and that evening, when she fell asleep, she awakened to a vision, a smoky cloud hanging over a big rock, and when she remembered it, she smiled; Babe knew that God was answering her, but she didn't know what it meant. From that point on, Babe decided to keep her spirituality within her heart to guard her innocence, yet she didn't want to deny her belief, so she just decided to wear a holy cross around her neck. Babe still enjoyed attending church, but with Mother not working, it seemed like they couldn't support anything in the church because she didn't have any money, and now Mother had turned to welfare completely. But they were all glad to have a bigger place with their own bedroom—nothing else mattered.

Now that Babe was in junior high school, all she could think of was getting a job. At thirteen years old, she would walk the neighborhood, going door-to-door at any business that was open, looking for a job. Her efforts finally paid off, but it was at school. One of the school counselors took Babe seriously and found her a job during lunchtime. However, after Babe left the kitchen, she would be soaking wet from washing dishes, making it difficult for her to return to class, but this problem was soon resolved after they switched her to a job after school, cleaning the teachers' lounge. Babe was paid every two weeks, and that check for $27 left her happy to be working. After giving her mom $9, it left her some money for school activities.

Babe was glad to be in school. She found her biology class to be one of the better classes, maybe because her teacher was so fond of her. Mrs. Alexander just loved Babe; she would let Babe help her after Babe finished cleaning out the teachers' lounge. Babe would help her take care of the pets in the classroom. At one point, Mrs. Alexander wanted Babe to take some papers home after school and grade them for her. Babe was looking forward to doing this, but after Mrs. Alexander talked it over with the school counselors, they didn't go along with it because it would make it too easy for Babe to know the answers without studying. But Babe did get to keep the hamsters one summer, along with a neighborhood friend. Glenda and Babe both got to keep a hamster one summer. This kept Mrs. Alexander from taking them home. Neither Babe nor Glenda had to buy a thing; she gave them the cage and all the food. All they had to do was feed the hamsters and clean the cage. Babe named her hamster Casper.

Babe's mom didn't care about having a hamster around; she said it looked like a rat or mice and boy, did she scream loud when she found Casper running through the house. Babe knew what that meant. Casper had figured out how to get out of his cage, and every now and then, he would. Babe knew Casper got bored sometimes, so she started keeping Casper in her room where she could watch him better. Summer was about over, and it was time to return the hamsters back to school. Babe was glad that she took good care of her hamster, but Glenda's hamster didn't live through the summer, and they were sad about that. Mrs. Alexander knew she could count on Babe.

Babe had managed to find a job every summer through the government programs, and when she wasn't working on a summer job, she would find a few odd jobs in the neighborhood, babysitting and selling caramel apples and popcorn balls she had made. While selling caramel apples one day, she met a couple recruiting young kids for Bible school activities. The couple's name was Barb and Earnest, and they told Babe they were ambassadors for Christ through the Campus Crusade for Christ. They recruited kids from most north-side communities for fellowship. Campus Crusade for Christ visited the neighborhoods. Babe thought this was nice because some evenings were so boring, without enough to keep some of the kids out of trouble. Campus Crusade for Christ was a ministry for youths run by young adults. They would go to neighborhoods and witness to kids and offer them fun activities. They were planning a convention at the Camelot Hotel, and Barb and Earnest wanted to invite as many kids as they could. They even had boxes of peanuts to sell to pay for the registration.

Babe was excited about it; they even gave Babe a case of peanuts to sell for the convention. Babe, Glenda, and Candi went to the local shopping mall and stood outside selling the peanuts. Glenda happened to be a neighbor that lived a couple of doors down from the apartments.

It seemed like Babe and Glenda hit it off just fine. She was the only girl in her family also, but Glenda's brothers were nerve-racking. Clyde and Clark were smart when Babe first met them, but over the years, it seemed like the street drugs must have sizzled their brains because they became the geeks on the streets, and that wasn't in a smart way.

Finally, they had sold all the peanuts and were planning to attend the convention. The exciting thing about it was they were going to stay at the Camelot Hotel for an entire day and night—that was the best thing about it. Babe can't remember ever staying overnight anywhere and a hotel was the best place she could think of. Mother didn't mind, and they were off for the convention. It wasn't like they had to do much during summer, and this helped to fill the void in their poverty-stricken lives.

At the convention, it was all about finding yourself in the Lord. They made altar calls, and many young people committed to living for the Lord. Babe knew in her heart that she had made a commitment long ago, but she knew that she couldn't afford to take off and do the kind of work Barb and Earnest did because she needed a job. They were from a wealthy background, but Babe didn't care; she just knew that she had grown to love and respect them for all the love they had for God's people. After the convention, Barb and Ernest had lots of the kids from the projects over at their apartment where they had a pizza party. Barb said they did so well selling the peanuts they wanted to spend the money in a good way by treating the ones that helped sell them.

That summer was beautiful. Barb and Earnest went back to Carolina. Barb kept in touch with Babe. They eventually got married and had a child, but Babe lost contact with them. Babe knew it was God who put them in her life because as she grew in God and even though she realized she couldn't afford to attend college the way they did, she would still try to further her education while working until she was independent enough to help the way Earnest and Barb did.

Papa and Ms. Bird finally got married and officially became a couple. They didn't consider it a honeymoon, but Papa had a brother in Dayton, Ohio, who had been in the military, and Papa wanted to go visit his brother. He invited Candi and Babe to join them, along with Ester and the two of them.

Babe thought since Papa had a large-size car that could hit the road, in no time, they would be there. But the ride was long and weary, so Babe started taking her camera everywhere she went, and she was sure to make fun out of it.

Summer was upon them, and this ended up being a short vacation because after visiting Uncle Eddy, they had planned to visit the amusement park in Dallas, Texas. On the way back. However, Dayton, Ohio. Was a very long way from Tulsa, Oklahoma. They were in for a very long drive, and they had to stop every couple of hours at a rest stop.

When they got to Ohio, they met Uncle Eddy, who lived in a small home with his wife on the east side of town. Uncle Eddy was in bad health; he used an oxygen tank from time to time, and he walked with a cane. He didn't seem to be that old, about sixty-two, but the war had aged him faster.

Uncle Eddy had been married before, and he had two sons, Lonnie and Donnie, in Tulsa, but one moved to Chicago, Illinois, and the other one moved to Las Vegas, Nevada. Babe remembered Donnie being a smarty-pants. As a matter of fact, their mother used to live down the street from them in the new apartments that had just been built.

It was interesting to meet Papa's brother. There was only one still living in Tulsa, and then this one in Dayton, Ohio. Papa also had a sister living in Kansas City. The visit to Dayton was short but memorable. Uncle Eddy passed away several years after they visited him, but they were glad to have met him.

On the way back from Dayton, Ohio, it seemed faster until they stopped at the amusement park in Dallas, Texas. They had to walk so much it was tiring. They didn't have much money to spend, but it was the thought of Papa making an effort for everybody to be together that made Babe think of how nice it was.

After being divorced for five years, you'd think adults could get along better by now. Still Papa would stop by, and the senseless arguing would start. Mother didn't mind waking up the neighborhood.

As Babe grew up, Granny saw how ambitious Babe was, and she began to tell Babe to put her money away and try to save some of it every chance she got. Every summer, if she wasn't taking any summer-school classes, Babe would try to work. Babe had bought herself an old car by now, and she was going to do the right thing in life. Granny always thought Babe was a lot like her namesake; it seemed like Aunt Etta was outgoing, but since she didn't have as many children as Mother did, there was nothing to hold her back.

Living on government assistance allowed caseworkers to stop by periodically to make sure there wasn't a man living there, especially since Mother hadn't worked in years. But teenage pregnancy on the rise, there were also concerns of young girls becoming mothers before their time. Their visits were short and brief, but Mother would be well-informed of what they expected. After one of their meetings, Mother met with Candi and Babe and told them they would be going to see the doctor soon to get birth control pills.

Babe and Candi didn't know what to think because they had never been with a boy; they were still virgins. Mother never asked them anything; she just sent them to the doctor. The doctor prescribed them birth control pills to take. Now at fourteen and fifteen, the two young girls who did not even know about the birds and the bees were taking birth control pills, not even understanding how to take them. Before long, the pills messed up their cycle, and they're back at the doctor's office. The doctor couldn't believe their mother would put them on pills before she discussed it with them. He scorned their mother and told her that these girls didn't need any birth control pills.

While still at the doctor's office, Babe asked the doctor if she could have some diet pills. She had been plump all her life, and she didn't have a problem with boys because she figured she was too fat. The doctor smiled at her and told her to come back in a couple of more years if the diet plan, he gave her didn't work. Candi and Babe both were overweight, and because of that, they felt that the boys weren't interested in them.

Now that sex and birth control pills were behind her, Babe could concentrate on school and a job. Every summer, Babe and Candi would sign up for a summer job, and through the system, they usually ended up with one. They were glad to be able to make their own money. Candi got a job one summer at a different nursery, but it didn't last long. Candi didn't like school, and somehow, she and Babe were separated during senior high school. Candi had to go to school across town. Her grades were bad, and it was difficult for her to get along with people.

With the anticipation of senior year coming up, Babe wanted to look better; she wanted to drop those extra pounds she had been carrying for so long and, hopefully, start thinking about a boyfriend. Most of her classmates had boyfriends and were well on their way to going to college—at least, some of them. None of Babe's friends were mothers; they all graduated without the thought of changing diapers at the same time. A few talked about college, whereas others had to stay at home and work. It seemed like working was just as well, especially when it just wasn't financially possible to move away at the time.

Babe was sure about trying to lose weight, and after visiting the doctor again, it seemed like the pounds began to shed. She was fit for her graduation, and she tried to keep the weight off. However, after losing the pounds she had, Babe looked at her body and wondered what happened to her breast; it was baby fat like Papa said or it was the prayer she prayed. Nevertheless, Babe was glad to lose weight.

Now with all the festivities going on for high school seniors, Babe and a few friends were going to celebrate. Mary, one of Babe's friends who was Catholic, had gotten hold of some weed, and they were going to party in the town. Another friend had just broken up with her boyfriend, and she wanted to celebrate and find another boyfriend. But Babe thought, *Why don't they find a good church and go to a revival?*

Mary was surprised that Babe was thinking about God at a time when they wanted to share their last year in school. Babe just wanted to play it safe, but she knew her friends were about as square as a box and nothing too bad could happen. Babe decided to let her guard down, and they all went out and partied and had such a good time. Mary passed the marijuana around, and they giggled, laughed, and had such a good time. Then they ate and grew tired and slept it off. Babe hadn't experienced marijuana, but it was fun for the occasion. Afterward, Babe was ready to regroup and put these things behind her and focus on the future.

Josie had been gone an entire year. She would write home from time to time. Babe liked having an older sister in college, trying to make a better life for herself, but it was a struggle for Josie; she didn't get any help financially from anybody, and when she would come home to visit, she would tell Babe how she had to shoplift sometimes. She had a job while in school, but it wasn't enough. The thought of going to college sounded great until she realized how hard it was for Josie. Josie resented Granny and how she helped Aunt Etta's children, Ammie and Don, while they went to college, but she couldn't help Josie as much. During Josie's first summer at home, it was discovered that she was pregnant, and they wanted to get married. At least Malcolm was a good man, and it seemed like he didn't mind doing the right thing.

Josie and Malcolm had a small reception in the apartments they lived at. Malcolm and Josie moved to Tulsa and made a home for their family, and soon little Markie was born, and Babe had a nephew to babysit. All was well—Malcolm got a good job with a grocery-store chain, and Josie tended to being a stay-at-home parent, and every now and then, she would pick up a job.

Babe and Candi were getting ready to graduate themselves. Babe had been working at an oil company since her last year in school, and she would continue to work there after school. Babe had planned on enrolling at the local junior college in Tulsa while working full time. Candi had an agenda of her own; she was busy looking for love. She didn't like school well enough to continue with it after graduation. She found a job at a hospital in housekeeping, and she liked it.

Both Babe and Candi graduated in the same year since Candi was held back when they were younger. It wasn't Candi's fault; they both struggled with school and getting good grades. Babe prayed and lucked out and charmed most of the people in her life; she didn't like to study. But to know that both looked forward to graduating and moving on, all Babe could think about was moving out on her own.

Now that all the children were grown, Mother had to think about doing something since government assistance would run out when all the children became eighteen years of age, and if they were not in college, she would be cut off from the program. Babe and Candi still gave Mom rent, but Babe knew she would eventually want her independence; she was an adult, and she wanted to live like an adult in her own place with her own rules, and not answering to anyone anymore.

Babe had worked most of her life already and she couldn't say anything about her mother's lifestyle, but she had hoped she could live a life according to the Bible and try to live the right way. James had been staying in California several years now, since Granny had brothers up there. James decided he would make his life with them, and every now and then, Granny would tell us that James wasn't doing so well; he would stay with other people and never had a place of his own.

Summer after graduation was just enough time to get involved with the crowds at the neighborhood park; it was always fun hanging out at the park, watching girls become ladies and boys become men. After graduating from school, Babe had bought herself a Chevy Vega, and it was fun to drive through the park, checking out the guys. The last guy she had eyes for was Erin, her softball coach. She met him while playing softball one year at the park. Erin was a couple of years older when they met, and Babe, being extremely shy when it came to boys, didn't know how to let him know how much she cared. She was reluctant because of her weight, and that's when Babe got serious about her diet, but now she didn't feel as self-conscious about being overweight. Babe and Glenda would circle the park; most of their friends wouldn't recognize Babe because she had lost about thirty pounds. She was glad to have all that weight off her.

That summer was hot, and the cars had filled up the parking lot. As Babe and Glenda waited for the traffic to move, Glenda noticed a brand-new Good Time van; it still had the new tag in the window. Glenda jumped for joy.

"Did you see him checking you out?" Glenda shouted.

"No, he wasn't," Babe responded. Babe kept on waiting for the traffic to move. As Babe looked up, it looked as if she caught a glance behind the smoke-tinted windows, but she couldn't be for sure. "Yes, probably," Babe said. *And How Many Other Women?* she thought.

Finally, they got a break and were able to leave the traffic behind. All Glenda could talk about was that red Good Times van. It was indeed nice, and any girl would enjoy a ride in it.

Babe decided the next time they saw it at the park, she would approach the driver and see if they could look inside just to strike up a conversation. After a couple of days, they were at the park again when the Good Time van parked right next to Babe. Glenda was with her, and she reminded Babe of what she said. Babe took a deep breath and stepped out of the car. As she approached the driver's side, he saw her coming and rolled his window down. Babe asked him if she and her friend could look at the inside of his van. He was nice to let them see. It was laidback, with a mini bar, a table, and a bed near the back window. They both complimented him for having nice taste. He asked Babe if she wanted to take a ride in it, and she said sure—of course, Glenda was right there with her.

After going several miles and back, they had an opportunity to learn about each other. By now he knew Babe's real name and she knew his. Howard lived in a neighborhood where Babe had grown up, and she knew of his family. He was about six years older than her. *But age was only a number after you reached legal age,* she thought. He asked her if he could call her sometime, and Babe was glad to give him her number. When he didn't call, she could only imagine that he must've thought she was too young.

Since Babe was in the process of looking for an apartment, she thought maybe when she would be on her own, she would not have a problem meeting a real man. Just as she was thinking that the phone rang. She answered, and it was Howard. He caught her off guard, but she was glad to hear from him. He invited her over to see his place later that evening, and he would pick her up. Babe wasn't going to pass up the chance to see him and know more about him.

Later that evening, Howard pulled up in the parking lot, and Babe didn't hesitate to dash out. The evening was early, so Howard suggested a movie since they still had the Motor Movie Drive-In, where they could stay in the van and watch the movie. The movie was an old Western one that neither one of them was into. They talked just so they had something to do while the movie played.

Howard told Babe that he had been in the Marines and that he had a daughter. He claimed the mother had taken him to court over the paternity of the child. Babe listened intently as she thought he didn't need any more children, at least anytime soon.

They went to Howard's apartment and talked over a glass of wine and eventually found themselves wrapped in each other's arms. Howard began to move his hand over Babe's body, and before she knew anything, his hands were removing her clothes, and she had to pull back.

"I'm not ready," she said.

He was upset, but Babe insisted she was ready to go home. As she prepared to leave, she thanked him for the night out.

On the way home, everything was quiet, and Babe could tell that he was giving her the silent treatment. Babe was proud that she didn't get pregnant during school, but she still didn't want to risk that chance now either. When Howard pulled up to Babe's apartment complex, he asked her if they could see each other later, and she agreed. Babe was a little baffled that he didn't seem concerned about protection, yet she began to think about what kind of protection she could get since she wanted to be with him. It seemed like the normal thing to do; everyone was doing it, so that gave her the seal of approval. Babe wondered if the birth control pills were still at work for her. Foolishly, Babe thought that it would be great, but being unsure, she decided to check with others. They also had foam that she could buy over the counter.

Howard did call again to see if Babe wanted to go fishing with him. He drove up this time with a boat on the back of his van. Babe was all set to go fishing, and it was a nice weekend for fishing. The fish were biting, and as the evening approached, they decided to get back before the sun went down. Back at Howard's apartment, he cleaned the fish and cooked some for dinner. After they ate, he asked Babe if she wanted to spend the night.

"Only if I don't have to sleep with you."

"Not again," he said. "I thought you're going to get protection."

She told him she's still looking for the best kind. Then she asked him what he had. He pulled out a pack of condoms and said that they worked all the time.

"Hum!" Babe sighed. "I would rather wait."

After cleaning the kitchen together, they relaxed in front of the television and cuddled against each other. The warmth of their bodies only led to more touching and kissing, and before she could say anything, he was inside of her. She couldn't resist him any longer; she knew that she wanted him as well. Morning was near, and they were still at it, and Babe wondered how it happened so fast.

Howard smiled at her and said, "Sometimes you can't fight nature."

Babe couldn't deny it was wonderful, but she had a concern and a worry as well; she couldn't remember Howard slipping on the condom. Babe ended up spending the entire weekend with Howard, and it was carefree until she got home and started feeling guilty and thinking how irresponsible she was. She prayed to God that nothing would go wrong. Howard dropped her off Sunday night because she had to work that Monday.

At work on Monday, Babe couldn't stop thinking about what a good time she had with Howard, but she feared it would cost her the unimaginable. She tried to stay busy to keep from thinking about him, but when she didn't hear from him that week, Babe began to think he had dumped her. It wasn't like they had known each other that long. Something just happened. Babe left a message on his phone, but he hadn't returned her calls. Babe had still been looking for an apartment, and the one she had left a deposit on called her and told her the apartment was ready. Since the apartment was ready, Babe figured she would just move; he'd come around.

The apartments on Seventh Street weren't far from her mom's place, and since she didn't have much to move in, she figured she would buy things later after she got settled in. Babe hadn't heard from Howard yet, and after work, she would rush over to Mother's just in case he called. Babe didn't have a phone in her new apartment yet, so she would drag out staying over at Mother's place until it was late before going to her apartment. Every now and then, Babe would pass by the park to see if she would see Howard. Babe's hurt turned into upset when she realized that she had missed her period. She double-checked the dates and thought she could be pregnant. *Dear God,* she prayed, *don't let this be.*

The next morning, she woke to nausea and vomiting, and the thought upset her more. Babe let another week go by before getting checked. She didn't want to deal with the problem yet, but as soon as the test proved that she was pregnant, she had already reasoned with herself that the relationship wasn't right; they both had been driven by their lustful desires, and now she had a bigger problem on her hands.

Babe knew Howard was under no obligation to marry her. Alone in her apartment, she cried, "God, I've made a terrible mistake, but does that mean I have to live with it?"

Babe knew that she eventually wanted a child but not any kind of way; she wanted a husband, and she didn't want one without the other. As the sorrow deepened, the gut feeling of being another welfare recipient wouldn't leave. Babe realized how their home wasn't much of a home after her father left and how it would be unfair to bring a child into a world without a responsible father, especially after coming from a broken family herself. Babe just didn't want that kind of struggle. First and foremost, Babe realized that she had sinned, and she alone would need to repent of that. Babe admitting to error in sin was the key to solving the problem and moving on would open her eyes to growing up.

There was no way Babe could afford to raise a child, and she couldn't imagine depending on government assistance and staying with her mother to raise the child. Abortion was the best way out as she thought about something Howard said about his daughter. That's when Babe realized that he was not ready for any more children. Babe knew she didn't want to go through that without a man.

Babe made an appointment to talk with a counselor at an abortion clinic, but she cried so much they had to reschedule her. Again, she tried to contact Howard without any success. *This is senseless,* Babe thought. She knew what to do and informing him shouldn't make any difference. It would make it more difficult; she thought. Her second appointment was a charm; the fetus was terminated, and Babe wanted to know if they had a procedure to use to keep this from ever happening again. The doctor told her to go with the instructions they gave her and return in a month. They had a device that would be a permanent fixture to use as birth control. After the doctor's visit, Babe was thankful that she hadn't told Howard so she could move on.

At work, a friend knew Howard and told Babe that her sister-in-law was also pregnant by Howard, and another lady as well. When Babe found this out, she felt relieved that she didn't go through with the pregnancy. The decision to have the abortion created a financial setback since Babe had moved into an apartment. She decided to move back home with Mother until it was the right time to move again.

Babe knew never to say a word to her mother about the abortion because she didn't want her to know. But somehow Candi knew about it because she had been dating the love of her life, and he wanted Candi to have his children, and Candi wanted to have his children because she loved Stefan.

Candi and Stefan had been dating for over two years, and when Candi knew that she was pregnant, she was so happy because she knew this was what Stefan wanted. When Babe told Candi what she had done, Candi was upset with Babe because if Babe had carried her fetus to term, they would have both had children around the same age, but Babe didn't care about any of that.

Babe knew that Howard was too unpredictable to be another father, but Candi and Stefan had a stable relationship. At least it seemed like it, but the closer the time for Candi to have her baby, the more Candi couldn't count on him. Babe was glad that Candi was happy to be having a baby, but when she was in labor for over thirty hours, Babe thought, *And to think I would be doing the same for a father that wouldn't even be there.*

Babe had bought all kinds of gifts for Candi's baby, and somehow, they knew it was going to be a girl. Babe even had to take Candi to the hospital because they couldn't find Stefan at the time, but the last and final time Candi went to the hospital, Stefan never did show up, even when the baby was born. Babe couldn't believe it. She thought, *They had planned this child together, and now, Stefan didn't even show up to put his name on the birth certificate.* Babe tried to understand since Stefan came from a big family and his father never did marry his mother because he was already married. His father's first wife just wanted one child, but his father wanted as many as he could have—that's how Stefan ended up with so many half-brothers and sisters.

But within his immediate family, there were at least eight siblings. It still seemed hard to grasp because this was his first child. Candi and Stefan weren't married, but Babe understood that's the way life was. Eventually Stefan and Candi married and Stefan proved he could be a responsible father.

When Stefan didn't show up at the hospital even to sign the birth certificate, Babe thought, *So Much for Stability.* Babe had moved back home with her mother for now; however, she didn't want to stay too long.

Josie and Malcolm had settled in and were glad to be in Tulsa. Josie knew that Malcolm missed his family; they were close, and after Malcolm managed to get a house, it wasn't long before Malcolm was moving his family to Tulsa as they had all lived in Shawnee, Oklahoma. Josie was fine with that.

After the entire family got settled in, Josie joined them in their religion, Jehovah's Witnesses. Mother's dear friend Paula—whom Josie stayed with after their parents' divorce since the house was too small for six children—used to be a Jehovah's Witness. Babe had attended church with Paula at times, and she thought it was different, but then, most are. They didn't make a big deal about giving either. Now here, Josie was going door-to-door witnessing. Josie started trying to witness to people. Babe didn't want to be rude, but she lifted her cross from around her neck and told Josie, "Jesus is the only one for me."

There was something about the witnesses that made Babe think that they didn't believe in Jesus—she really didn't know. Before long, Josie was trying to match Babe with Malcolm's brother. Babe thought that it was just too close for comfort. They're both nice-looking men, but Babe couldn't believe that Josie could date him after knowing that their mother and their married uncle were kicking it, or however you would say it.

Babe never told Josie about the abortion; she figured she might not be able to stomach it, but Josie knew that Babe had moved back home with Candi and Mother, and Candi told her.

Josie suggested to Babe that she apply for a HUD home, like the one they lived in. She knew Babe had pretty good credit since she had been working before high school and had established a long line of credit. Babe thought about what Josie had said and thought she would investigate it. When Babe found out that she could own a three-bedroom house with a yard and a fence, she decided that it would be great. She found a house out north, and she applied for it with no problems; her exceptional credit approved her application. Babe prepared to move again, but this time, she hoped that it was for good.

Chapter 2

Moving On

Moving into a three-bedroom house at 4120 N. Franklin Avenue was a blessing. The house was government-owned and had to meet inspections, which granted its good condition since it had no appliance or air-conditioning. It looked as though Babe would be holding down a second job for quite some time.

Glenda helped Babe move in, and with the few items she owned, it didn't take long. After a couple of loads, everything was unpacked and neatly put in its proper place. When they came back with the last load, Glenda noticed a friend of hers living at the corner house. When she invited him over, Babe felt apprehensive since they both began to smoke marijuana. Marijuana usually made Babe cough; luckily, she never acquired a habit for it. Glenda and Babe had planned to spend the evening at the shopping mall where a musical festival was scheduled, so they cut the conversation short. Glenda's friend refused their invitation to go along.

Babe returning home alone was a bad discovery—she had been burglarized. The backroom window was still open, indicating a way of entrance. Alone, Babe paced through the house, trying to fight the fear building within her. The few valuables she owned were stolen. Babe pictured Glenda's friend in her mind. She called the police, and soon officers were on the scene, investigating the backyard and the house. One officer wrote the report as they talked. Babe mentioned to him that she suspected Glenda's friend. Both officers were sympathetic when they learned she had just moved in that very day. Reporting the loss to the insurance company first thing Monday morning was the biggest disappointment because, unfortunately, the deductible was more than her loss, and for consequential reason, they advised her not to submit a claim.

Babe's grief over the loss was accepted after reasoning with herself that it could have been worse. She began to thank God that she didn't have much that could have been stolen. After that incident, Babe made sure she checked all the windows and tried to secure them down better with a nail through the middle of the window to prevent it from opening too easily.

Glenda and Babe kept in touch, and when Glenda found out Babe had been burglarized that same night they went to the festival, Glenda agreed with Babe that the burglar was the guy she had invited over. Glenda apologized to Babe since she was the one who invited him over. Babe figured she didn't know that he would come back to rob her. Glenda told Babe that they ought to go out and put the whole thing behind them. Babe thought that would do her fine.

That evening, they headed out to the Full-Moon Nightclub. At the club, Glenda and Babe partied awhile, but when Babe looked up, to her surprise, she saw Howard. Babe didn't know what to do. She knew if they talked, she would end up telling him about the abortion, so she tried to avoid him. It was all too obvious after he saw her that they would talk.

Howard asked Babe for a dance, and after dancing to a few songs, they sat down and talked. She told Howard how she tried to reach him after they had spent that romantic weekend together, but she failed to contact him.

Now Babe had moved to another place altogether. Howard wanted to keep in touch with Babe; she thought that, at least, it would give her a chance to tell him what she did. Babe hadn't told Glenda about the abortion, so upon leaving the club, when Glenda joked with Babe about lighting the flame with Howard, Babe said that she doubted that very seriously; it was then that Babe decided to tell Glenda about the abortion. Babe told Glenda about the other women that Howard had impregnated and how she would've been the third one if she hadn't gotten an abortion.

Glenda's expression froze when Babe told her. "You didn't," Glenda said, but Babe assured her.

Babe went on to tell Glenda about a paternity suit Howard was already going through. Then Glenda told Babe that the baby was a part of her.

"A part of me that made a mistake," Babe said.

Glenda was the only girl in her family; Babe couldn't help but wonder if that's why she felt the way she did. Glenda expressed her disappointment in Babe, but Babe couldn't let Glenda get the best of her. Glenda couldn't figure out why Babe would still be interested in talking with Howard since the flames had burned out for him. Babe just told her that she wanted to put some closure on the matter.

Later that week, Howard did call Babe, and they got together. When they had time to talk together, Babe told Howard about the pregnancy and the abortion. He seemed upset and told her that she had no right to do that. Babe argued that she tried to contact him, but to no avail. Babe couldn't cry about it because she was strong now, and when he realized how well she was dealing with it, he promised her he would give her another baby. Babe just listened to him, thinking that he must be crazy. She didn't feel that she was no better off than when it first happened. Now you would think that he would realize how he would take care of all the children he already had, but Babe never told him that she knew about the others.

Babe wondered after that if that's all some men wanted to do. Babe avoided Howard after that; she knew it was some sort of game to him. He would call her all the time, wanting to get together, but Babe knew it would never happen again. Babe was anxious to look for an extra job after that. She knew if she were busy, she wouldn't think about him or having a boyfriend. She thought she could take one course at the junior college and work an extra job to get the things she needed.

After applying for a job at the department store, it didn't take long to see that part of her salary was going to purchases, but she decided to stay there anyway for a couple of months. The department-store job was nice, but Babe found too many things to buy with her check.

A local hospital was hiring evening janitorial work. It wasn't far from her home, so Babe decided to switch jobs; that way, she wouldn't be tempted to buy things in the store. After switching the part-time job, it looked like the class at the junior college had to take a backseat. Switching over to the other job gave Babe the weekends off.

Josie only stayed about six miles from Babe. She would visit regularly, and Josie would transport and run errands for Mother since Mother didn't have a car. Mother depended on her kids to help her when they could. Since Josie didn't have to work, she transported Mother to the store and doctor and wherever else she needed to go. One evening, Josie stopped by; she told Babe to expect a phone call from James, their brother in California.

Phone Call from James, Babe wondered, whatever for?

Later that evening, while Babe was trying to clean, the phone rang. "Hello, Babe," the voice on the other end spoke; Babe recognized James' voice right off.

"What a surprise—then again, not exactly. Josie told me you would be calling."

James congratulated Babe on her new home, and then he proceeded to tell her about a friend of his that wanted to attend Spartan School of Aeronautics and would need a place to stay. Remembering the burglary, Babe thought that it would be a good idea. She had completely furnished her home with used furniture, and she was roommate ready.

Hank arrived at the airport within a week; he stood about five feet nine, a lightweight man who looked to be about thirty. He recognized Babe right off. James must've described her or showed him a picture of her.

It was mid-January, and Hank was shivering in a thin sports jacket.

"What's the temperature?" he wanted to know.

"About twenty degrees," Babe answered.

"Back in California, people were wearing shorts," he explained.

The two suitcases he carried didn't seem like an awful lot since his stay was to be a couple of years before his studies were completed. As soon as they got home, he unpacked and lit up a stick of marijuana. His weed-smoking left Babe concerned. Hank had $500 in cash to help him with necessities. He offered Babe some money for his stay, but she refused. She explained to him that she would allow him to stay three months, all expenses paid, then after that, she would charge him $90 a month to cover bills and food if he decided to stay on. He said that it seemed fair enough, and he agreed.

Hank noticed Babe's crucifix, which hung about her neck, and he quickly proclaimed that he was Buddhist and didn't believe in God.

"To each his own," Babe said and turned away.

Hank wanted a response from Babe, so he continued exalting his beliefs. Babe didn't like to get into conversations about religion; she felt it was a personal matter, especially since she didn't attend church or follow the traditional Christian way—meaning, she was still a sinner saved by grace.

Babe felt she wasn't qualified to explain. Hank was determined to know why she believed in God. Finally, Babe told him, "I know that I believe that God is real. He's almighty over any other god. And it's really not important to know anymore."

Afterward, Babe felt like an idiot and began to think of how silly she must be to wear a cross and not be able to explain her belief to others. Then she remembered reading in the Bible, "The secret things belong to the Lord." Besides, she felt there were enough preachers in the world without her help; furthermore, everyone was always talking about how complicated it seems to understand the Bible, so Babe grew content in just believing.

When friends came to visit Babe, she would introduce them to her new roommate, and he would quickly leave to go to his room to chant. They all thought he was strange, and Babe became embarrassed by his actions. As they would talk in the living room, Hank would start his chanting, which would get louder and louder. Babe had to turn the stereo up sometimes. This would drown out the chanting, but it never worked. Behind his back, they joked about him.

The weather remained cold, and Hank was forced to purchase a coat, boots, and thermal wear. Soon he found a job, and they carpooled to work. Babe noticed how irresponsible he acted. Rather than writing to his family, he made long-distance phone calls instead. Babe and Hank began to argue. They argued about the smallest things. One of the biggest problems was shunning off his flirtatious remarks.

Three months had passed, and Hank met new friends at school, some of whom came to the house to visit. Two of these friends, John and Tony, became very fond of Babe, which, in turn, brought out a side of Hank Babe hadn't seen before. She began to show interest in Tony because Hank was beginning to grate her nerves. She decided to date Tony because she thought he was nice looking, and she wanted Hank to know she wasn't interested in him.

Eventually, Babe could see that their platonic friendship wasn't getting any better. They disagreed on too many things. His chanting to his Buddha was driving away the peace Babe once enjoyed in her home. The phone bill continued to mount because of his out-of-town phone calls. Babe felt it was best that he moved out, and because he didn't know anyone in Tulsa, Babe was relieved when he decided to move in with his friends. Tony and Babe didn't date long since Hank got the message, and Babe realized she really wasn't interested in Tony. It took Hank six months to pay back the phone bills and rent, and they did become better friends after he left. Now Babe's friends came to visit more often.

One evening Pam, a friend stopped by to tell Babe about her part-time job at a club, and she asked if Babe would be interested in working with her. Babe didn't see how she could fit it in with her two other jobs; Pam explained the hours were 10:00 P.M.

until 2:00 A.M. Since her other part-time job ended at 9:00 P.M, Babe began to seriously consider her offer.

Babe asked, "When can I start?"

Pam answered, "This weekend."

The first weekend at the club was more like a party than a job. Serving drinks and meeting the customers seemed to put zeal back into Babe's social life. After working at the club for about a month, the tips and paycheck allowed her to quit her second job at the hospital. The club was more interesting than the hospital, and the hours allowed Babe her evenings back. Working at the club was more like entertainment than work. Babe met many new people and received tips on the best after-parties.

A girl named Brenda came to work at the club. When she found out Babe had a three-bedroom house, she asked if she could be her roommate. After thinking it over, Babe agreed, especially since Brenda would be leaving for college at the end of summer.

With Brenda living with Babe, there were always plenty of guests stopping by. One evening, a host of friends came by, and they all gathered in the den, watching television and talking. After the movie ended, they showed the guests out, then they both prepared for bed in their separate rooms. When she was in her bedroom, a strange feeling came over Babe. She looked around to try to figure out what it was. Then she noticed her bedroom window, which she kept open for fresh air. The screen had been unlocked.

Her suspicions were confirmed when Babe couldn't find her purse the next morning, before leaving for work. Babe had reached for her purse, but it wasn't there. Frantically, she searched her mind for the last place she had put it, and she knew it had been in her bedroom. Had someone entered her bedroom while they entertained in the opposite room? Although Babe still wasn't sure the purse had been stolen, she called the police and gave them full details for their files. They said they would let her know if they found anything. After they left, Babe went to work, wondering all the while who would be brash enough to enter her house while they entertained guests.

A week passed before the police contacted Babe. They had located the purse. It was found in a creek about a mile from her home. Babe was surprised to get the purse back although everything inside was missing. Babe was glad that all she had in it was $10. After that experience, Babe hated to see Brenda leave. Brenda was planning to leave in two weeks if she could manage to get fifty dollars for her registration. The deadline date was close to her enrollment. She came to Babe in need of a loan, and realizing how important it was to her, Babe rearranged her budget and loaned it to her. Brenda would be leaving, but the incident of the stolen purse had Babe thinking about installing bars on her windows. The salesman also sold her a door-attachment alarm. The bars were installed not long after Brenda moved. Babe hoped it would prevent any more thefts. The alarm system turned out to be a contraption that was quite time consuming.

Soon Babe had another roommate who needed a place to stay until she could afford her own apartment. An old classmate introduced Babe to Sandi. She loved to party occasionally. Sandi met one of JJ's friends even though he was married, and she took up with him. Sandi and Gary had planned on joining Babe at the club one night where she worked. Gary left early, and after the club closed, Babe and Sandi went home, laughing about the good time Gary and Sandi had while Babe worked the night away. At the house, Babe attempted to unlock the front door, but it alarmed her to see the door was already unlocked.

"Something's wrong," Babe said.

They stepped inside to see a ramshackle mess. Babe held her purse in front of her as though it was a stick to use.

"Let's get out of here while we can," Sandi insisted.

As Babe called the police, she tried to calm Sandi down by telling her. "Whoever did this is long gone."

The police arrived and discovered the bar on the back of the window had been pried off and left on the ground. The burglar had entered the window and left out the front door.

Some Security System, Babe thought.

Sandi was pretty upset because some of her things were damaged as well, and she didn't have insurance. Babe agreed to give her a portion of the claim she received. The claim was smaller than she expected after the depreciation was figured, which didn't allow much for either one of them. She agreed to adjust Sandi's rent to make up the difference, but Sandi wasn't satisfied with her portion, so she moved out. Later, Babe felt bad about the disagreement, but she began to think something suspicious about Gary and suspected her roommate, since she was dating a married man, and it could've been a setup.

It was nice having her privacy again. Those pleasant moments had been missed. Babe had a weekend off at the club and was excited about the free time. As she mowed and picked up the yard, a neighborhood boy stopped by. They visited for about an hour before Babe realized how late it was. She told him that she was going out that night because this was her first weekend off in a long time. He left, and Babe went inside and fixed herself a cocktail to help her unwind. An attempt to call a friend to join her was made, but no one was home; a second friend was called, a college classmate who had recently made a conversion in faith. When Mary began to witness to Babe, Babe told her she knew all about that; Babe said she wasn't ready to make a commitment that she couldn't live up to.

Mary reminded Babe that during senior high school, all Babe talked about was going to a revival, and now she's blending in with the world. Babe reminded Mary, "We are in the world then, are we not?"

Mary thought for a minute and agreed; she then told Babe to be careful and that she would pray for her.

Babe told Mary, "I still talk to God, but I like to party, and I don't see anything wrong with it. I thank God even when I'm dancing."

After hanging up, Babe thought about what Mary said, and she considered her lifestyle. Babe was afraid if she went to church, she would lose her joy, with nothing to look forward to. Babe was glad when Mary said she would pray for her.

Babe changed into a party dress, but the cocktail she had fixed herself was beginning to take its toll. She relaxed her head because it felt heavy. A good night's sleep was what she needed instead. At that moment, the doorbell rang.

There stood Troy, a friend whom she didn't want to be bothered with. She told him she was on her way to Disco World nightclub just to get rid of him for that moment. Troy suggested that he meet her there. After he left, Babe lay across her bed fully dressed, and the doorbell rang one more time.

Curious, she looked out the window, and this time, it was a friend named Bob, a guy from her day job. Babe didn't go to the door. Men friends were never rare but being able to trust them proved difficult.

By now, Babe had changed her mind about going out, and her neighbor's dog was the only thing that was preventing her sleep. This dog seemed to bark at everything. When the fence began to rattle, Babe simply turned over in bed, thanking God for his love before she fell asleep.

Subconsciously, Babe thought she had heard a loud thump. Totally stiffed out, she figured it was a picture frame from the wall, so she ignored the commotion.

The next day, Babe woke up early. She thought to check out the noise she heard the night before, which she assumed was a picture that had fallen. After using the bathroom, Babe went to the living room to see what had fallen. She didn't see anything in the living room or on the floor; she decided to see if the kitchen was intact. When Babe stepped in the kitchen, to her dismay, the door had been kicked in. She held herself tight and thought, *Someone had come in the house last night while I was fast asleep.* She thanked God and knew his angels were watching over her. All that noise she heard, she was glad she didn't get up to check it out, or she would have faced the person head-on, and that might not have been too good.

The next day was Sunday, and if there was any reason to go to church, it would have been that day, but Babe had praised God at home while she was working on getting the door fixed. She couldn't imagine who, for the life of her, could have done this. She thought about the two visitors she had before she fell deep into sleep, but she didn't think it could've been Troy. She knew he was bold, but he didn't have any reason to be, then she thought of Bob, whom she didn't even answer the door for, but neither one was that way at all.

While she was in the garage, she opened the garage door, and a car drove by slowly. It was the young neighbor she had talked with yesterday, who was a good kid, but the way he slowed down as he drove by made Babe think of that kid; and all along Babe thought he was nice. A few of the neighbors' houses had been broken in, and they would tell Babe a thing about the neighborhood.

Across the street were good neighbors and next door as well, but this kid lived at the end of the block, and Babe really didn't know him. She didn't mind being nice to people, but she didn't realize that she should not tell people her business. Then she recalled how she told the kid she was going out that night, and he thought she had gone out. Babe thought how stupid it was for her to hold a conversation with strangers and tell them anything. *When will I learn?* she thought. One of her neighbors told her that not only was the neighborhood full of thugs and thieves, but also a mile away, there were bad kids that looked for houses to target.

Babe started thinking she liked living in her house, and she didn't want to move, but she didn't want to entice anyone or make herself a target, and she didn't want to be rude to people either.

Babe had been working at the nightclub for a while now; she enjoyed meeting different people. One night at work, she was busy trying to take orders when, suddenly, a young man at a table all by himself stopped her and asked her to take his order. He wanted a Coke. She brought back his Coke, and he introduced himself to her.

"The name is Patrick Dell," he said in a deep voice. "Have you ever done modeling?"

Babe thought about her high-school pictures and said, "'Sure," hoping he would never ask to see them. She had lost some weight now, and she wasn't as fat. "Mr. Dell—," Babe said.

He interrupted, "Call me Patrick."

Jokingly Babe said, "Of course, you don't look any older than me."

Patrick reached out and gave her a card. He told her to call him; he would like for her to join a group that would be modeling at the Performing Arts Theater. Babe thought, *Why not? That Would Make Life Interesting. Who knows? A better job than waiting tables could be in the making.*

Later, when things slowed down a bit, Babe pulled the card out and looked at it. "Devonte Modeling Agency Patrick Dell".

Babe figured he didn't look like a big businessman, but no one should despise small beginnings. She figured she would call him later and see what's up with it.

That week, Babe had enrolled in a real-estate class and was looking forward to doing something in real estate on the side. Monday night was class night, and it wasn't until late when she got out of class. After Babe got home, she reached over to hang her keys up and saw Patrick's card. She wondered if it was too late to call him. At 9:00 P.M., she figured she would dial his number and see what happened.

As the phone rang, Babe wondered what to expect.

"Hello," a voice answered.

"Is Patrick there?" Babe asked.

The voice responded, "One moment."

"Patty!" someone shouted in the background.

"Hello," another voice answered.

Babe asked, "Is this Patrick?"

He responded, "Yes, it is, who is asking?"

"Hi, we met in the club the other night. They call me Babe, but my real name is Valleta Juanetta Johnson."

"I'm glad you called. Babe, can we meet at the park tomorrow for a photo shoot?"

Babe thought, *That's Sudden.* " But when she realized her next, class would be the day after she said, "Better now than Wednesday."

"What's happening on Wednesday?" he asked.

"I'm taking classes three nights a week, which are Mondays, Wednesdays, and Fridays."

"Well, tomorrow it is."

"Which Park?" Babe asked.

"O'Brien Community Park, out north."

After getting all the details, it was agreed that they would meet there at 5:00 pm the next day.

At work the next day, Babe daydreamed about the photo shoot. He had told her to wear something comfortable. She didn't think much about Patrick. For some reason, modeling sounds more fun than getting to know him. After work that evening, she went home and changed first and then met Patrick at the park. Babe could tell Patrick wasn't a big-time photographer because he had a little instant camera, but when they began to share about each other, they both found out they were first cousins.

They were a hit as they talked about their families and Babe found out that Uncle Will, Babe's papa's brother, had a kid out of wedlock, and it was still a secret. Babe felt badly for Patrick since Uncle Will was still in denial. Uncle Will was married at the time, and his first wife left him and moved to Michigan. Babe wondered if she knew about Patrick. After finding out that they were related, Babe and Patrick became good friends. They rehearsed up until the fashion show.

Sometimes they would meet at the other park with the other girls that would be modeling, and they would all rehearse together. Babe's schedule became too busy to work at the club on the weekends, so she decided, with the classes she was taking and preparing for the modeling show, she had to drop the nightclub job. She didn't mind because she had paid off enough bills, and she thought the show would be fun.

When Babe found out it was for charity, she forgot about getting paid. Meeting Patrick's family was interesting; he had older brothers Babe had already met while working in the club. His brothers were all nice looking, and Patrick wasn't bad looking himself. Patrick's mother had died, but he stayed with his auntie. Patrick's brothers were the kind that was always in trouble. Babe remembered meeting Troy and Gary before she had met Patrick; they didn't have the same father, so they weren't related to Babe like Patrick.

Babe and her papa kept in touch. One weekend, she decided to pay him a visit and inform him about the upcoming fashion show. Babe knew that Papa worked out of his cousin's garage. When Babe got there, there were still a few people getting their cars serviced. Babe mentioned to Papa that she met Uncle Will's son Patrick, but Papa didn't remember him.

Anyway, Babe proceeded to tell Papa about the fashion show she would be modeling in, and she told him she would find out about the tickets since Patrick was taking care of all of that. Babe left thinking he acted as if he didn't know Patrick. Babe could tell it seemed like Patrick despised his father for not accepting him.

Babe knew Uncle Will's first wife and daughter; Josie and his daughter were about the same age, and they played together when they were younger. Jonni was her name, and she was the only child Uncle Will had, and now to hear about Patrick. Babe had heard that Uncle Will had remarried after his first wife left him and went to Michigan, but he didn't have any children by his second wife.

As Babe was unlocking the front door, she heard the phone ringing. She reached it just in time.

"Hello?" Patrick was on the other end.

"I was just thinking about you," Babe said.

"You were?"

"Yes, I was wondering about the tickets, who's selling them, and where a person can buy them if they want to attend."

Babe mentioned to Patrick that she saw her father and told him about Patrick. Patrick told her he didn't remember him.

Patrick said he was quite young when he saw her papa, and his mother was still living at the time. That's how he met his daddy; his mom took him over to see his father's family. Patrick did look like Uncle Will—he had his height and facial features. If they had DNA testing during that time, it would probably be a match, and now that time has passed, most people just let bygones be bygones.

As they switched the conversation back to the show, Patrick told Babe that if she wanted to give a few tickets to the family, he would get some for her. Everything happened so fast Babe didn't know if she had told anyone else in the family. Everyone was scattered, and she didn't actually think it was going to happen. Candi was on her own now; she had a family and a husband, and it was seldom that they ever saw each other. It was then that Babe thought they were probably not interested in attending anyway.

During the last rehearsal at the park, Patrick told Babe to be ready to be fitted. That night, Babe was fitted for two really cute outfits: One was a two-piece—a beige after-five strapless jumpsuit with knickerbockers made from sheer, soft chiffon fabric. It included a throw around for her shoulders. The other was a casual two-piece—a red, black, and white plaid skirt and white blouse, which was fitting for a day at the office.

After trying them both on and strutting around the room as they practiced, Babe felt like a million dollars. She knew that they were much too expensive for her to own, but she was glad to have a chance at modeling them. They had to label the outfits for the fashion show after taking them off. Her name was pinned on the top, so now she knew what she would be wearing. She would have to match up her own shoes.

Babe knew just the pair—her two-inch heels would be perfect, with their thin straps and open toes. She wore them every now and then at the club. Patrick seemed to know all the other girls as well. Babe didn't know any of them; she didn't have time when they were at rehearsal. She figured, with her classes and all, she did well to squeeze the fashion show in.

Plans were being made for the fashion show that weekend, and Babe had asked Papa if he could come, but he had other things planned. Patrick informed Babe they would be taking pictures, so she thought maybe she could buy the pictures and prove that she was actually in a fashion show.

Everyone participating in the show had gathered in the back, behind the stage. With all the chattering going on, no one was aware of the audience waiting behind the curtain. The director gave his pep talk and encouraged everyone to do their best, and Babe modeled her first outfit: the casual plaid—a red, black, and plaid skirt. While she waited for her cue, she began to be somewhat nervous. Babe had rehearsed quite a bit, and she didn't think she would freeze, but when she saw the crowd behind the curtains, she was glad that all she had to do was walk down the runway, turn, and come back.

But not so fast, she thought.

She calmed herself as she heard her number, which meant it was her turn. Gallantly, she walked to the beat of the music as she held her head high, looking to see if she recognized anyone, but she didn't.

Babe thought: "If only family could see me now"

The flashing of camera lights startled her for a minute, but she gained her composure, turned, and returned behind the curtains. Others cheered her as they all prepared to exit on schedule.

Quickly Babe headed for the dressing room to change into the other outfit, the one that she felt was erotically dashing. Babe thought this one was the best. She wished she could use it on a night out, for she knew she would turn heads with it.

As she rushed to model her second outfit, the program was almost over, and she was glad she had saved the best for last. Patiently she waited until her number sounded again.

Confidently she strutted like a peacock, holding her head back as she tossed the wrap around her shoulder to reveal her bare shoulders, then she positioned the wrap around her waistline and then around her neck. As she approached the end of the runway, Babe turned and headed back toward the curtain. She almost lost her footing when the heel of her shoe bent over. Babe hoped it wasn't noticeable when she skipped a beat, but then got right back on track.

Wow! That Was Close, she thought.

After the show, Patrick invited Babe to join him and some friends for drinks at the club in the hotel next to the Performing Arts Theater. They had live entertainment as they socialized, and they ate peanuts and popcorn. It was getting late, and Babe knew she still had more studying to do—a couple more chapters and she would be finished with the real estate course and preparing for the exam would be next.

Chapter 3

Bewildered Yet Beloved

The modeling days were behind Babe, and there wasn't going to be anymore that she knew of. Patrick had made himself an agent for the occasion. Babe and Patrick agreed to keep in touch; they were like family now. And the thought of how Babe met Patrick opened her eyes to a whole new world. Babe realized that she was blessed to have met him even if it was in a club.

The pictures were ready, and Babe needed to go pick out the ones she wanted. When Babe saw the pictures, she thought, *Look at me! Wow!* She looked like a real model. Who would have known she was just doing it for the fun of it? Babe had another week, and she was going to go to Oklahoma City for the real estate exam. She found herself studying all night long, and sometimes, she would close herself in and just study.

After work one evening, Babe closed herself in her bedroom and didn't come out. She studied all night long. She had forgotten to turn the porch light on, and suddenly, Babe woke to some noise, and as she turned to check on it, a dark shadowy figure ran toward her. Before she knew anything, he was upon her with a knife at her throat.

Babe shocked at what was happening just followed the man's demands. He ordered her to the hallway where he stripped her of her clothing and assaulted her. He covered her face with a pillowcase and ordered her to stay there until he left. As Babe listened for him to leave, she thought, *Dear God, what should I do?* Babe just stayed there, thinking of how filthy she felt and how ashamed she felt. She felt too ashamed to call or tell anyone. She finally got up and ran some bathwater and washed herself off. She then lay in bed, crying and thinking how she was going to be ready for the exam and what she would do. Babe realized that if she didn't call the police and report to them, this man may continue to do this and get away. She then called the police and reported the incident.

It wasn't long before a couple of officers were there taking a report. Babe told the officers what had happened. As the officers investigated the home, they saw that he had cut the phone wires in the living room, but he didn't know about the one in Babe's bedroom. The living room had a lower window that had been taken out, and because the man wasn't that big, he must have crawled through the window after pushing the stereo out of the way. Babe had forgotten to turn the porch light on.

After she finished giving them the report, one officer told her she needed to go to the hospital for a specimen exam.

"What's that?" Babe wanted to know. She said OKAY, but when the officer found out she had taken a bath, he told her it was too late. Babe didn't know she had washed the evidence away.

The officers told Babe she needed to come down and identify some mugshots. Maybe she would recognize this person, so they left Babe the information for her to come later.

Babe was exhausted after the officers left, but she decided to call Patrick. Patrick came over and comforted her. He knew she was planning to go to Oklahoma City within two days. She didn't know if she should, but she had already paid her money for the test, and it was too late for a refund, so she decided to go anyway. Patrick could see that Babe was troubled over the rape.

After the rape, Babe really began to think about protection. She had lived through too many burglaries, and she was too old to go back to living in the projects with her mother. Babe had made up her mind that she would buy herself a gun. Patrick decided to stay with Babe until she took the exam, and they would go to Oklahoma City together. He wanted to visit some friends while he was there.

On Saturday, Babe decided to visit the pawnshop and see what they had for protection. She picked out an automatic .22-

caliber revolver. She purchased ammo to go with it, and at home, she loaded it and tucked it under her mattress.

On Monday, Babe and Patrick left for Oklahoma City early. She felt that ever since the man invaded her, she hadn't been able to study or concentrate. Patrick told her to try not to think about what happened. When they arrived at the testing site. Babe left the car with Patrick while she went in for the test; the exam would be anywhere from two to four hours. Babe figured she would need the entire four hours since she didn't test well, especially since she felt blank anyway.

After four hours, Patrick picked up Babe, and she told him she didn't think she did well, but they would let her know in about a week.

On the way home, Babe was still sad over what had happened. All the burglaries never scared Babe like the rape. She still liked living there since she had done so many improvements; she had even looked into building a pool. Babe was determined to stand strong. She didn't know anybody else to tell, and she didn't really need the therapy or the gossip. She managed to get by as she had, for Babe didn't want her immediate family to worry about her.

When they got back to Tulsa, Babe decided she wouldn't worry about it anymore. She wasn't working at the club, and she was about to switch to another day job. She decided before she went back to work at the nightclub, she would spend time looking for another day job since the one she was on left no room for advancement. Babe had been in the same department for five years since after high school.

Since Babe had worked for an oil company, she figured it would be nice to have a job with another oil company. Babe had a few applications out there; she was just hoping to hear from someone. Babe always found something to be thankful for. When she thought about the rape, she thought about how some don't live through them or some that were killed or beaten so bad they need medical and mental help. Babe felt fine, just a little shaken and ashamed, but not enough to let it get her down anymore. Patrick left Babe knowing she would be all right. He had made plans to catch a flight to Dallas, so he fixed Babe's bottom window and made sure everything was secure. Babe, determined not to let it get her down, put on a renewed strength, which energized her. She began to look forward to the start of a lot of good things going on.

Pam made her appearance every now and then since she didn't see Babe at the club anymore. She would stop by or call. Pam always had good gossip about the club, but when she stopped by this time, she could see Babe's mind was on something else. Finally, Babe opened up and told Pam what happened the week before. Pam could see Babe was trying to put it behind her. Babe told her she had to go to the police headquarters and look through some mugshots. Pam asked her when she had planned on doing it. As Babe thought about it, she figured as soon as she could; she needed to put some closure on the matter. Pam insisted that Babe hurry and get it out the way.

The next day, a female officer from the police department called Babe. Her voice was abrupt and loud, and her tactless manner upset Babe. The officer began to question her about the rape before she even identified herself. Babe asked her about the mug shots she was told about. The officer told her she needed to come down and review some pictures. Babe told the officer she would be right down.

Babe took the instructions the officer gave her, taking the elevator to the second floor. Turn right toward the bulletproof window. When she arrived, she met Detective Jones personally. Detective Jones asked her to have a seat as she pulled out the albums.

While Babe looked through the mug shots, the detective asked Babe if she knew the guy, and Babe told her that she didn't know him. Page after page, Babe was getting concerned because it seemed like so many of them. As Babe looked through the pictures, she glanced at least a hundred times. She didn't know if she could be sure.

About the time she finished, she noticed a picture that she thought had some resemblance. Babe went over the picture again, and she thought for sure, this one guy stood out. It was just a week ago, and Babe didn't know for sure, but she had identified someone that fit his description. When she pointed the picture out to the detective, she grunted as if she were annoyed. She didn't tell Babe what the guy had been accused of before; she didn't seem like she cared at all. She had asked Babe again if she knew the guy, and for the third time, Babe told her no. After it was over, Babe felt as though she was the criminal.

When the details behind the mug shots were over, Babe thought about the advice the officer gave her about going to a clinic. Since it would take a few days before she could see a doctor, she decided to drive over to the clinic. When Babe explained the problem, they ushered her in. She was told the doctor would call her back in a couple of days with the results, but the doctor assured her everything looked normal. They gave her a number for rape victims if she needed it. Babe figured she wouldn't pursue the case since she didn't know for sure that the picture, she identified was him. And since the help from headquarters wasn't solid enough to go on, she had to move on with other things.

A couple of weeks after the exam, Babe received a letter in the mail telling her that she didn't pass the exam. Babe wasn't surprised; she had felt blank when she was taking it. *Although Two Points Off Wasn't Too Bad,* Babe thought. Included in the letter was a list of dates for rescheduling, but Babe was too discouraged to think about going back.

Babe wasn't finished with the mail when she noticed a letter from an oil company where she had applied for a job in the accounting department. They were interested in her application and wanted an interview. Babe immediately called and scheduled the interview. The next day, she went to the interview, and during the interview, Babe shared her past experience and education. The supervisor was polite and listened intently, asking questions as they talked. The supervisor especially wanted the details about her working while in school through COE (Cooperative Office Education). Babe thanked him for the interview and left thinking no more about it. In fact, she applied for another job on the way home that evening.

At home, Babe felt depressed and decided to pull her Bible out. She opened it to Proverbs 3:5, one of her favorite verses. "Trust in the Lord with all your heart lean not to thy own understanding." Surely that was one on the top 10 list of scriptures. It seemed like there were many hurts and pains in the world, and no one understood but God.

Babe had heard that scripture as a child, but now it really meant something to her. To her, it was saying that if she trusted

God now, he would bring her through this trial. As she put the Bible away, the phone rang; it was the personnel office of the oil company, offering her the job for which she had interviewed. She was told the salary, and she immediately accepted. After she passed the physical, she would be ready for work. Her attitude had changed, and she had God to thank. Babe's first day at work renewed her totally. She didn't give up on the real estate; she just didn't want to tackle it again too soon.

At her new job, a few of the employees gathered around a bulletin board where they had posted photos from their childhood. They were laughing and joking about the photos. One girl asked Babe to bring her baby pictures. Babe was too embarrassed to explain that she had none. After work, Babe remembered the days in church when the pastor and his wife took pictures of her in the Easter pageant. Surely, they would have a picture of her somewhere.

Taking pictures was a great pastime for Babe, but she had mostly pictures of people and scenes—none from her younger days. Visiting this pastor took some courage since it had been before Babe became a teenager when Babe last saw him, then she drifted out of church. Babe knew they stayed in a house behind the new church. She convinced herself there was no harm in visiting them to see if they still had pictures. Pastor Morgan and his wife had retired now. But they still had that gentle spirit. Babe remembered how sweet both were. Their age had brought about senility, and they didn't remember Babe until she told them she was Barbara Johnson's daughter. Then they remembered Babe from church and other events.

Pastor Morgan wasted no time in asking Babe where she went to church. When she told him she was too busy working, he invited her to come back to Shiloh Baptist. Babe told him that since her mother attended there, she would like to find a church of her own someday. Babe didn't think she would feel independent enough if she were going to her mother's church. Not to mention she didn't want to go to church until she was ready. Babe grew up in a home where they had double standards, and she just didn't want to live the same way as when she went to church. Pastor Morgan just smiled and spoke. "A child shall lead them."

Together they searched their old photo albums, but there were no pictures of Babe. On Babe's way home, she stopped by Aunt Josephine's. Babe remembered Aunt Josephine keeping photo albums, so perhaps she would find some pictures there. Aunt Josephine had several picture albums, but not one held Babe's photo. It was disturbing to think no one kept one photograph of her.

"They Must Have Lost Them, Babe thought."

When she returned back to work, she heard them discussing the pictures. One lady said, "What a fun way to look back in history, at past events captured by a single sheet of paper."

Babe thought about the fashion-show pictures, but she didn't think they're as nice as having childhood-memory pictures. The fashion-show pictures were too glamorous.

Babe decided she would take more pictures of everything and everybody. She had a camera already, but it wasn't that good. So, she had made up her mind to purchase a better camera. She went directly to the pawn store and found a 35mm camera, with a carrying case and several lenses and filters that Babe knew nothing about. It wasn't long before Babe enrolled in a photography class at the junior college. She was thinking of using photography as a part-time job, and she needed to know all she could to make it work. Word got out that Babe was a camera buff. She received a few requests to take pictures in the club and special parties. There was no getting away from the club scene. Babe met a lot of people as she played the photographer. She made a few mistakes, but it was all in the learning and the fun of it.

Larry, the owner of Disco World, bumped into Babe at one of her parties, and he asked her when she was coming back to work. Larry told her that everybody missed her and would like to see her again. Larry pleaded with Babe since the last three waitresses didn't work out, and he knew he could depend on Babe. He offered her more money, and she was glad about that. Larry told Babe to call him or just come by the club. Babe didn't confirm that she would, especially after thinking about the rape. She didn't tell Larry about it, but she pondered on whether it happened because she had worked in the club. She reasoned with herself when she remembered reading about a girl coming home from church and got raped, when it had happened to her. Babe realized it could happen to anyone anywhere.

Babe reasoned with herself, "There are many perverts in the world." Before the week had ended, Babe called Larry and told him he could count on her. He was pleased because he knew Babe was a good waitress. The job gave Babe a positive outlook. Since she didn't have the bills, she had before, she was hopeful to save money now. The first night back at the club was like old times—the bartenders complaining about too many orders at one time, everyone talking, the music pounding as the floor seemed to be vibrating, the employee's agreeing to take turns having breakfast at different homes. The guys would buy the food, and the girls would cook.

At home, Babe's busy schedule resumed. One evening, she narrowly missed being hit by another driver, and they both came to a screeching halt. The gentleman got out of his car. Babe knew she had cut out too soon, and she was sure he would be angry.

"Are you all right?" he asked with genuine concern.

She assured him she was fine and apologized. Babe was in a hurry and wasn't watching where she was going. Their cars were off to the side, and surprisingly, they simply began to talk as the traffic sped by them. In a matter of minutes, the sudden shock had transformed into a friendly acquaintance.

His name was Vince, and he seemed very interested in Babe. Vince wanted to contact her later about a date. After telling him about her schedule, Babe wondered if it seemed possible that he would be able to catch her. But they exchanged phone numbers just in case. Vince caught up with Babe the next day. He understood about her jobs and was tolerant of her busy schedule. Vince had a hectic schedule also. He was a foreign-exchange student in addition to working a full-time job. Babe assured Vince that her job at the club was safe, and the employees were like family, especially since she didn't see much of her own family. Babe and Vince began to spend more time together. They began doing things all the time. Vince knew when to call, and Babe really liked him. Vince lived with his brother and cousin; they're from Venezuela. They were all here to go to school; Babe liked learning about their culture. Babe thought Vince was hot, and she adored his curly black hair. She wasn't crazy about his thick bifocals, and he wasn't that tall, but she thought his intelligence made up for it.

Valentine's Day was approaching, and Babe wanted to do something special for Vince, so she invited him over for dinner and asked him to be her guest at the club. After dinner, he presented Babe with a gift, a book titled *"101 Ways to Make Money in Photography"*. At the club, Babe sat with Vince until his brother and roommate arrived, then she started work. Babe personally tended his table and gave them the red-carpet treatment. Larry noticed the special attention she was giving and asked jokingly what he had to do to be treated that way. All that week, Vince talked about what a good time he had and asked when she would invite him again. Babe told him he could come every weekend if he wanted.

Work at the club again became routine. Everyone was on Babe's case because she had stopped having breakfast afterward with them. Babe wouldn't get home until 6:00 A.M., and that was too late for her. Friday night at the club was as busy as ever. Babe waited patiently until the clock shifted to 2:00 A.M.

Her nights at the club were tiring at times, but nothing she hadn't been through before. It seemed like her job at the club had its highs and lows, especially since she couldn't drink—probably a good thing since it was easier to figure out if the customers had reached their limits. As she paced the dark aisle, clearly shouting, "Last Call," she picked up her pace a bit, seemingly more anxious now that closing time was near. She watched security escort the people out, then she began counting her change, since she started with $20 and anything over that would be her tips. After counting $28, she figured at least she didn't lose any.

"Are you sure about that?" a voice behind her clearly stated.

As Babe looked behind her, she saw Edward, an ex-boyfriend trying to lure her out for breakfast. It was a nice thought, but Babe refused Edward's offer since she was dating Vince, and she didn't want to seem like she was cheating on him. As Edward waved good night to Babe, he blew her a kiss and told her to call him. She signaled okay to him as she finished cleaning the place. She reminisced on how it had been with Edward. He was fun-loving and adventurous, but not the kind to settle down, Babe thought.

Finally, the doors closed. *I can now rush home to a relaxing bed,* she thought. Living a couple of miles from the nightclub gave her a short distance to travel. A light sprinkle still existed from an earlier rainstorm. Babe knew she had to be careful in the wet weather because of the wet streets and the narrowing curves could be an accident waiting. As Babe approached her home, she noticed a dark-blue Cadillac parked on the edge of a neighbor's curb, indicating that the neighbor might have guests. Babe was not aware that the car wasn't there by coincidence—a man was lurking around the corner, waiting for the right time to attack.

At 2:08 A.M., Babe was driving in the driveway. She liked the fact that she didn't live far from her part-time job. Every now and then, she would work the weekends, sometimes an extra day or so. Deep in her thoughts and wondering how she could avoid getting wet, Babe was totally oblivious to the fact that she was being watched.

Since it was still wet, Babe used her light jacket to shield her from the sprinkles still falling. She reached for her jacket to cover her head. Hurriedly she approached the porch to unlock the collection of locks on her door; the three locks made her feel somewhat safer since she had already experienced a few robberies.

Unlocking the last lock, she moved forward against the door, but it seemed to have opened much too easy, as if it were a push. As she looked behind her, the shock of seeing a man behind her was all too unsettling. As Babe tried to scream, his hand went over her mouth, and a struggle ensued. Near the door was a sectional couch, and the struggle caused them both to stumble over it. He then pulled out a long-bladed knife and held it to her throat. Now Babe's heart was racing in her chest; she was so afraid, she could hardly speak as she questioned him with a stuttering speech, "Who are you? What do you want?"

"Shut up and listen," he said in a raspy voice.

Babe felt the knife on her neck as he led her to the hallway and ordered her to take off her clothes. Babe tried to drag time out, but he could tell. He then ordered her down on the floor. The minutes seemed like hours; after he violated her body, he grabbed her from the floor and led her into the bedroom where she slept. He took the ski mask off her face and replaced it with a pillowcase. A ray of hope quickened Babe's thoughts as she remembered her .22-caliber revolver under her mattress.

As he exited the room, all Babe could think about was holding the gun in her hand and detaining him for the police. Her hands felt for the gun, and she firmly embraced it. She yanked the pillowcase off her head, and, half-naked, grabbed a robe that was draped over the door, then she ran to catch this beast of a man.

He was leaving at the front door, but Babe held up the gun and ordered him to stop. Flashbacks of a previous attack on her life made her determined to avenge herself of this hideous experience. The guy was still in the living room, not yet out the door.

"Stop!" she yelled at him, fear in her eyes. Then she braced herself to shoot him. Ignoring her, he turned to leave. Carefully, with trembling hands, she positioned the .22-caliber revolver and ordered him to stop. Again, he turned, and as his hand came out of his pocket, she envisioned him hurling the knife at her, and her fingers reacted by squeezing the trigger. The first bullet hit the window.

"My God!" she cried, then targeting him again, her panic power-emptied the gun.

The man was in a heap on the floor. She ran back to the bedroom for more ammunition, then locked herself in the bathroom to reload the gun.

When she returned, he had crawled to the middle of the room and was crying for help. Finally realizing he could no longer hurt her, Babe then called for an ambulance. As she dialed, she could hear his pathetic cries for help.

"I wasn't going to hurt you," he wailed.

The dispatcher who answered the phone attempted to engage her in conversation until help arrived; she explained the situation to her while they waited. Her voice faded in and out as she mumbled several utterances, something about "Who's this man, why did he do this to me, now what am I going to do?"

"Are you all right?" the voice on the phone asked.

"Sure, I'm just upset, I guess."

The officers arrived and were invited in after hanging up the phone. They questioned Babe as to his identity. Babe told the officer she didn't know him. They pulled his wallet out of his pants to identify him. As the officer flipped through the wallet, he pulled out some money and the officer mentioned that he had several hundred on him.

Babe quickly responded, "He didn't get it from me."

At that moment, the ambulance arrived, and the paramedics got the rapist ready to go. A backup set of officers was to escort the ambulance. One officer told the paramedic, "Let me ride with you, I want to make sure he doesn't get away."

The other officers sat with Babe, and she went over the story. After writing everything in detail, they were ready to go, and they told Babe she would have to have a specimen test at the hospital. They asked Babe if she wanted to drive or if she would rather ride with them. She preferred to ride with them. It was so quiet you could hear a pin drop. Babe was still baffled over everything, and the officers didn't want to say anything to offend her, but they were soon at the hospital. It was better being escorted by the police officers; it seemed like it didn't take as long, and the next trip was downtown to talk to the district attorney. In a large conference room with a large table and some chairs, Babe waited by herself, and it seemed like the minutes turned into hours.

While Babe waited, she thought about her life, and for some reason, she knew that nothing would ever be the same. She thought about the rapist and wondered who he was, if he had family, or what would happen to him, then she silently prayed that he would be all right. As Babe asked for forgiveness from

God, she pleaded earnestly because she knew she acted on instincts. Babe continued waiting and wondering what was taking so long. She wanted to leave but knew not to. *Maybe That's What They Wanted?* she thought. It was disturbing that she couldn't shed a tear and immediately started praising the Lord after asking for forgiveness. Then Babe prayed for the strength of God to deal with this. The night was long, and it seemed like morning would be longer. With her head still on the table, the officer finally knocked on the door and told her the district attorney would see her now.

Officer Green introduced Babe to the district attorney.

"Call me Ted," the DA said softly.

As they sat down, he apologized for the long wait and then asked her to review the story with him again. Following that, more questions were asked. When all was completed, Babe was informed that the rapist had died at the hospital. She was stunned but tried not to show any emotions in front of them. On the DA desk laid a folder that was stamped Justifiable Homicide. Then the case was closed.

"It's all over now," one of the officers told her.

"You can go home."

"Thank God," was all Babe could say.

The officer drove her home and tried to make her feel better by telling her how courageous she was. When they drove up to the house, Babe didn't feel very courageous; she felt like running away from it as fast and as far as she could. Too many horrible nightmares had taken place there. But she didn't run; she lifted her head high and walked in. Everything was clean; there was no blood on the carpet and virtually no sign of a struggle, although Babe noticed a small bullet hole in the glass of the front window that wasn't there before. Again, she thought of the dead man and began to cry. "I didn't want him to die." She sobbed as she realized it wasn't a bad dream; it really happened.

The ringing of the phone startled her. It was Edward. She explained to him what had happened; after Edward knew it was no joke, he commented, "Breakfast would have been better."

Call waiting allowed another call to interrupt the conversation. It was JJ, her brother. When she told him what had happened, he thought she was joking, but he soon realized that she wasn't joking about this. The tone was serious. Immediately, JJ and his wife, Joyce came right over. As soon as they arrived, the phone rang again. Joyce answered it. A local television station wanted to interview Babe. Joyce explained that Babe couldn't come to the phone.

After only a few minutes, another station called. Joseph Jr. suggested they go to their house. As they walked out of the house, the phone rang again, but this time they ignored it.

At JJ's house, Babe knew Vince would be trying to contact her, so she called him and told him what had happened. He was flabbergasted. Vince was the serious type, and he knew she was telling the truth. He told her how sorry he was and asked when he could see her.

"After work tonight," she told him.

Vince was upset, saying, "I can't believe you're going back to work."

"Why not? I've got to tell Larry what happened. I have nothing to be afraid of."

Vince was the reason Babe passed up breakfast with Edward. They had been dating about six months, and she didn't want Vince to think something was going on with her and Edward, so Babe decided not to tell Vince about her offer to have breakfast with an old friend. Babe sensed disappointment in Vince's voice as they hung up the phone. Larry, the owner of the club was especially nice to Babe; they'd worked together at another club when Larry was a security guard. He hired her at his club in a heartbeat, knowing she worked hard and was dependable. Babe grew despondent as she hoped Vince wasn't feeling second best to Larry; he had met him only a month ago when he and his brother visited for Valentine's Day.

Joyce and JJ could tell the heaviness Babe was feeling over the misfortune. JJ had overheard her tell Vince she was going back to work.

"If you didn't work at the club, this might not have happened," he said.

"That's not true," she countered. "Nine months ago, I wasn't working at the club. I was minding my own business, and someone entered my home and assaulted me." The fact that she was single and lived alone seems to make her easy prey for bad people. "But I bet they'll think twice before bothering me again," Babe stated.

JJ continued to talk against the waitress job at the club.

"Jesus went around sinners," Babe stated defensively.

"But you are not Jesus, and if you're not careful, that place will be the death of you."

"Then so be it!" she snapped. But after a few minutes, she recanted. "After tonight, I promise I'll think about quitting."

That evening, they watched the news together, and there was Babe's house on TV. The newscaster was telling all about the justifiable homicide. Thankfully, no name was ever mentioned, but all her friends knew her house. JJ joked about her being a celebrity, but somehow it just wasn't funny. They tried to talk her out of going to work, but when they saw it was useless, they let her go.

Later that evening, Babe left. She wanted to change clothes and meditate before going to work. At the club, she told Larry the whole story. He asked if there was anything he could do. He suggested accompanying her home to check the house, but she told him she wasn't going straight home. He insisted that he at least walk her to her car. Babe agreed to that, thanking him ahead of time.

Babe wanted to leave after letting Larry know, but she decided to wait it out. The disco lights were rotating wildly, or was it just in Babe's mind? As every step grew heavier, she felt the unease of people watching her. Multiple-colored lights revolving around the disco dance floor made the room appear as if it were spinning, causing her head to ache without any sign of relief. The first customer she waited on knew about it. He was a friend of a cousin. He blundered over his words, saying something like, "I heard you were raped last night."

"He didn't live to talk about it," she shot back.

Seeming to be confident in what she said, she didn't skip a beat as she continued serving the customers. Her coworkers were a comfort, but she could feel the tension among the customers.

After work, Larry escorted Babe to her car. There she informed Larry she wouldn't be back. He was sad, but he knew that she had to do what she felt best. Vince would be waiting for her at his apartment; she felt strange and watched closely that no one followed her. She was glad Vince was watching out the window and came out to meet her as she drove up. He greeted her with a hug.

"I heard all about it on the radio and the paper. You're a hero," he said.

His brother and roommate were eager to hear the story. Her voice trembled as she shared the humiliating experience. They were supportive with hugs and joked about getting an autograph. Vince was planning to return to Venezuela within two weeks and asked her if she would go back with him. The thought of leaving Tulsa sounded good, but still upset about the rape, she couldn't bring herself to take that chance. Babe didn't think that leaving would erase what had happened, and she thought maybe Vince felt sorry for her, not really loving her, but the thought of Vince asking her made her think that perhaps Vince really cared and was special. Still, she wouldn't go. She knew she had to deal with the situation herself. With all the commotion going on, Vince and Babe saw little of each other before he left, but he promised he would write.

Babe's entire family became very concerned for her. After she quit the club, she agreed to live with her sister Josie for a time. While gathering clothes to take to Josie's house, her neighbor Nancy stopped by to visit. She said she wanted to have a word of prayer. She had heard about the rape-murder. Nancy had always been a good neighbor, and of all the neighborhood children, hers were the best. Since she lived right next door, Babe considered her a good friend. Nancy had recently made a conversion in her faith and was Pentecostal. As she prayed, it seemed like God was present. Babe listened to her speak to God, and she felt her concern. Nancy's prayer strengthened Babe.

After she finished praying, Babe asked her if her guest had left. Nancy didn't know what she was talking about.

"There was a car in front of your house the night it happened." Babe thought she had a guest staying overnight. It was then that they realized the car belonged to the rapist.

Nancy stood to leave. "It wasn't your fault," she assured Babe. "Stay strong in the Lord." When she learned Babe was going to stay with her sister for a while she said, "May God be with you."

At Josie's house, dinner was being placed on the table. Babe always enjoyed Josie's cooking, but she had no appetite. She put her things away while they ate. Afterward, she helped Josie clean the kitchen, and they talked.

"I only want to stay a few days," Babe said.

Josie patted her shoulder. "Stay as long as you like, Babe."

Later, she was laying her clothes for work the next day, and Josie looked at her. "What's that for?" she wanted to know.

"Clothes for work."

"You're not going to work, I hope."

"Look," she said firmly, "I've quit one job, you don't expect me to quit the other one, do you?"

"Of course not, but you could take a few days off."

"I don't need to take any time off," Babe said.

"Whatever you say." Josie shook her head and walked off.

Afterward, the house was quiet. Babe lay down on the couch and wondered about the commandment in the Bible that says, "Thou shall not kill." She whispered a prayer to God to forgive her then fell fast asleep and slept well.

Waking up early was a practice of Babe's. However, listening to kids fighting and fussing wasn't the best thing to wake up to. Josie had cooked breakfast, but Babe still had no appetite. As she dressed, she wondered if her coworkers had heard the news as yet. She knew she would have to face them sooner or later; it might as well be now.

At work, she arrived about ten minutes early. The place was quiet; a few of the workers were busy preparing for their workday.

Alice, a close friend at work, came in. When she saw Babe working, she exclaimed, "What are you doing at work?"

"I'm a paid employee here, just like you, remember!"

With tears in Alice's eyes, she stated how she'd seen Babe's house on the news and had heard the whole story. Looking into her tear-filled eyes, Babe quipped, "I should be the one crying."

They both laughed, breaking the awkwardness of the moment. It was sort of strange. Before all this happened, Alice jokingly used to call Babe a child prodigy. Babe never figured out why—maybe Alice was reading too many books? Now she was commending her for her courage and told her how proud she was of her.

"Please let me know if there's anything I can do for you," she added with a smile.

When everyone else had arrived, the whispering among the employees was more than obvious. One girl shouted out, "Etta, was that you that killed that guy?"

Without thinking, Babe said, "I could write a book," inwardly thinking that would answer the entire story.

Throughout the day, visitors were browsing the area, and Babe was aware of the different expressions and reactions from both fellow employees and the public. Even her supervisor had a peculiar stare. She began to look forward to the noon hour and the chance to get away. Just as Alice and Babe were leaving for the cafeteria, the phone rang. It was a reporter.

"KTEW, Ms. Johnson. I've tried to catch you at home, I just want to ask you a few questions, and it won't take very long," Babe heard the voice say.

Hoping to keep them off her back, Babe granted her a short interview over the phone. After the series of questions were completed, the reporter asked Babe if she was religious, quickly Babe responded no. Within minutes of hanging up, guilt set in. Babe knew she had been a believer all her life but to say she was religious just didn't fit. Babe felt terrible and asked Alice to excuse her while she went to the restroom; there she had a chance to recant. "Oh, Lord, forgive me if it seemed like I was denying my belief in you, you alone give me strength and hope." Babe held the cross around her neck; she knew it was deeper than she could explain.

Lunch didn't have much appeal, and a small bowl of soup was more than enough. As they ate, Alice asked how long Babe would live with Josie.

"Not long, I hope."

While Alice talked, Babe's mind wandered about things elsewhere. Scenes at the club crossed her mind. During one particular time, a gentleman had asked her where her man was, and she boldly held the crucifix before him and proclaimed, "Here he is." *Could it be that I am supposed to be a nun?* thought Babe.

A little shaken by her thoughts since Babe was baptized in the Baptist Church at a very young age, the fear of being a nun didn't settle well with her. Neither did the idea of being Catholic sound right to her. She didn't go to church, but for some reason, Babe had a habit of wearing a cross around her neck. This was more or less to identify her belief in Christ even though her lifestyle wasn't exactly what you would call holy. Babe believed that God loved her, and with time, she would totally commit to him. She didn't feel ready to go to church; she had hoped to be married first before committing to a church.

The next day, the *Oklahoma Eagle* came out with an article that identified the attacker as having a past history of rape. It revealed information that wiped away all the awful rumors that were being circulated.

In the *Tulsa World*, it said that the rapist had been under police surveillance. Babe found herself wondering where the police were when he was stalking her. It didn't matter since the truth did prevail.

Staying at Josie's turned out to be longer than she had expected. One evening, Babe stopped by her place to pick up a few things. A classmate who worked in a hospital had barely caught Babe in time to give her an orchid that a doctor had sent to Babe. They talked for a while then departed. On her way to Josie's, Babe was overwhelmed by all the people that felt sorry for her and kind of resented it even though she knew they meant well. She kept mulling over it. "Lord, I don't want their pity."

By now Vince was in Venezuela, and Babe was trying to put him out of her mind, thinking maybe that it was his way of walking out on her forever. Even though he said he would write, somehow Babe thought that it was just an alibi, and she was sure she'd never hear from him again. Nevertheless, Babe couldn't worry about Vince; she knew Josie was waiting, and she didn't want to keep her waiting. Just as Babe arrived at Josie's, the phone rang. It was her mother.

"How are you doing?" the voice spoke.

"Fine. Josie is making me feel very welcome here," she told her mother. As a matter of fact, Babe told her mother she was thinking about her on the way over because she used the travel bag they had when they were vacationing awhile back.

Babe's mother wasn't big on talking, and Babe found herself making conversation.

Mother spoke again, "You be careful."

Their conversation came to an end, and now with her luggage unpacked, she could relax and grab a bite to eat.

Malcolm, Josie's husband, traveled a lot with his job as a truck driver for a local food chain. Even when he was in town, he knew Babe like a sister himself. Josie appeared to be blessed with a loving husband as well as a healthy son. She didn't work other than being a housewife and a mother, which seems to be the ideal job. Josie lived only a couple of miles away, which was probably why she and Babe seemed to be the closest in the family. James called from California to see if Babe was okay, and Martin, their brother, called Joseph to see if everything was okay. Candi still lived in Tulsa; they didn't visit much, but she did call to see if Babe needed anything.

When Josie saw Babe's carry-on luggage emptied, Josie thought an overnight bag would have been fine. Josie jokes, looking a little disappointed.

Babe trembled as she responded, "Josie, please let me stay a week. I'm going through something, and I don't want to be alone."

Josie smiled, and her expression seemed to reassure Babe that it was okay. The week passed by fast.

Malcolm and Josie's son was six years old; he enjoyed spending time with Malcolm's family—his uncles and aunts along with a host of cousins. Malcolm's family was close, and Josie liked it. Markie was a little spoiled, being the only child; plans for Markie to spend the weekend with Malcolm's family gave Josie and Babe plenty of time to shop. Babe wasn't big on shopping, but Josie loved to go from store to store, sometimes not buying a thing. For Babe, it was just a pastime.

As Babe prepared herself for work the next day, she listened as Josie responded to a phone call she received from Malcolm. It sounded like Malcolm would be coming in early, probably by Thursday or Friday, and he would be home for the entire weekend.

There go plans for shopping, Babe thought.

Babe knew she didn't want to wear out her welcome knowing that Josie and Malcolm had been trying to have another child. She didn't want to deprive them of their time together.

Josie wanted more children, and the doctors told her she had a few extra fiber tissues in the way, but with time, it could happen. Since Malcolm was due in by the end of the week, Babe prepared to leave that Wednesday.

Chapter 4

A Different Horizon

Time away from Babe's home was appreciated and gave her peace. Spending time with loved ones gave her some comfort as well, but she was ready to return to her home. She moved back into her house, and the memories of what had happened didn't bother her as much, and the idea of regaining her privacy was comforting. The house was dusty and dirty from her absence and in need of a thorough cleaning.

Babe stopped by the supermarket for cleaning supplies, and while there, she was moved to see an old classmate, whom she had a crush on while in high school.

"Clarence is that really you?" she said with disbelief.

They both agreed how they had changed a great deal since their school days.

"Are you seeing anyone?" he wanted to know.

First thinking about Vince and then realizing he was gone, she responded, "Not really." "Let's get together," he suggested.

Babe gave him her home number, hoping Clarence would call her soon.

On the way home, Babe began to look forward to hearing from Clarence. *Perhaps this would be the person to fill the void Vince had left,* she thought. Clarence called that evening, and they talked for hours. She invited him over for a home-cooked meal at her place the next evening, and as they hung up, Babe wondered if he had heard about what had happened. She was afraid to mention it for fear it would scare him off, but then she decided it would be better for him to hear it from her. Babe decided she would tell Clarence herself. The next day, she hurried home from work to prepare dinner. The phone was ringing as she approached the door. She stumbled through her keys, trying to get to the phone before it stopped ringing. It was Clarence, but she couldn't concentrate on what he was saying. Things were rearranged in her living room; items were missing. Babe had been robbed again! She interrupted Clarence to explain that her place had been burglarized. He offered to come right over. Calling the police began to be a redundant practice.

Two officers arrived in separate cars. They instructed her to take account of everything missing for the insurance company. They discovered the bars had been taken off the back window again, and the garage was used as an escape exit. They continued investigating while Babe paced the floor, thinking how she could continue living at her home. Babe told the officers about the rape and justifiable homicide that she had recently lived through. They verified what she said and mentioned moving to her. The thought of moving sounded good, but she had a mortgage on her house and didn't want to lose it. Reporting burglaries were a practice that was getting very old; in fact, she was sick of it.

Preparing dinner was no longer on her mind. After the officers left, Clarence arrived and offered to take her out to eat. He ordered a steak, but all Babe wanted was a glass of tea. She was worried that the matter was getting out of hand. Perhaps now was as good a time as any to tell Clarence, as he finished his dinner. Slowly she explained about the past burglaries, the two incidents of rape, the killing, and now this. Clarence took the toothpick from his mouth and laid it on the plate.

"Would you like me to stay with you for a while?" he asked.

The invitation made her uncomfortable, but fear forced her to give in. "Thanks," she answered. "I would like that." She didn't want to continue imposing on Josie.

Back at the house, Clarence's company made her feel somewhat safer. As they straightened up the mess, they talked of old times. He then told her he had a two-year-old son. He explained about his son's mother and how he discreetly broke up with her. Babe sensed he missed them.

"They're back in Hawaii, where they're from." Clarence reached over and kissed her and assured her that she was beginning to fill the emptiness in his life.

It was obvious that Clarence still cared for his son and his son's mother, and for that reason, Babe secretly vowed not to fall for him too quickly. She didn't exactly fear for her life, but she still sensed trouble, and she didn't want to defend herself again, so his presence was buying her time for now. That evening, they shared about their work. Clarence was a shop worker at the manufacturing plant located about three miles from where he lived. He stayed in a duplex not far from Babe's place, about seven miles from where she lived. He told Babe about his Doberman pinscher named Danger. Danger was still just a pup, but Clarence hoped one day he would be a good guard dog. As the evening grew late, Babe knew that if they didn't get any sleep, they both may not be able to work effectively on their jobs the next day.

Babe didn't want to tell Clarence about the abortion since she didn't think it would matter; she knew she didn't want to be intimate with Clarence and wondered if he would understand. Before showing Clarence to the bedroom, Babe told Clarence. She wanted to wait instead of rushing into sex.

"I'm mentally not ready to engage in a sexual relationship."

Clarence hesitated but then agreed. "It will be better when you are ready."

That night, they cuddled in each other's arms as they slept. Babe felt secure while she silently prayed.

The alarm clock woke them up early. Five was routine with Babe, sometimes earlier. Clarence wasn't into waking so early, but since he had to go home before he could prepare for work, he struggled to stay up. While Babe prepared herself, Clarence made conversation.

"I'll bring Danger over tonight."

"That will be fine." Babe thought that it was a good idea, and from his place, she could go to work.

Babe followed Clarence as he left the driveway. It only took fifteen minutes to reach Clarence's place, and since Babe was still about an hour and a half ahead of her schedule, Clarence offered her coffee to drink while he prepared himself for work. His duplex was a 2-bedroom duplex, which he leased from his grandmother, who raised him.

The smell of Danger was eminent; Danger was big for his age. He playfully jumped on Clarence, and Babe could see he was far from being dangerous as his name claimed. Clarence made a good cup of coffee. Danger licked Babe's hand as she reached out to pet him. With about forty-five minutes before work, Babe decided to leave to be on time. Clarence demanded a hug before she left, and he assured her not to worry, promising her that he would be at her place between six or seven that evening.

At work, the first thing Babe needed to do was to notify the insurance agent. The insurance had only saved Babe once because the deductible wasn't enough to be bothered with, but this time, it seemed like there was much more damage as well as loss. The receptionist put her on hold as she waited to be transferred to an insurance adjuster.

"Kyle Thomas," the voice answered.

"Mr. Thomas, my name is Valleta Juanetta Johnson, and I have insurance with your company. I need to report a burglary yesterday. The police were called out and I have a report."

"Ms. Johnson, we need to appoint an adjuster to estimate the claim."

"That is why I called," Babe said.

"What about Tuesday around 9:00 A.M.? I will meet you personally."

"That will be fine."

Immediately, Babe made plans with her supervisor to be late that Tuesday. She had to explain why Mr. Turner hired her a year ago and had always felt that Babe was reliable and never abused her privileges. Even though Babe felt suspicious of many man made tests that she probably didn't pass, she resented being put on trial by man to test her trustworthiness.

Alice was anxious to hear why Babe was in the supervisor's office. She observed while Babe seriously took care of matters that she didn't know about. Work had been delayed as Babe made sure arrangements were made. Now she silently sorted the tickets to catch up.

Alice, sitting next to Babe, mentioned, "Are you going to tell me, or is it any of my business?"

Babe looked at Alice as she worked. "Let's talk about it during lunch."

It was agreed that they would have lunch together. During lunch, Babe caught Alice up on everything within those two days of changes. Alice was glad to hear about Clarence, but she feared Babe didn't really like him. He seemed convenient for her at the time.

Alice mentioned Vince, and Babe shunned her, saying, "I miss Vince, but I'm not sure if Vince will return. Don't worry. I think Clarence is missing his son and baby momma. And it may be that he's buying time as well."

After work, Babe hurried home, wanting to surprise Clarence with a well-prepared meal, which he missed the other day. As she checked her mail, there was a letter from a lady in Nebraska. Babe didn't recognize her name. In the letter was a check for $100. She was amazed that someone cared enough to offer her money.

On the check was a telephone number, and the name on the check read Rosemary Wells. Babe read the letter. Rosemary seemed concern about Babe; she had been following her life since the rape, and she had read the paper and read about the burglaries as well. In her letter, she expressed a desire to help her. Babe thought it was appropriate to call Rosemary and thank her. She dialed the number and asked for Rosemary. It sounded like a housemaid had answered the phone. Rosemary was summoned to the phone. Babe introduced herself and thanked her for the money. Rosemary asked Babe if she wanted to move to another place, and if so, she would help her move. It was kind for Rosemary to make this generous offer. Babe didn't know how she could explain that she now had a friend living with her and that she would be all right.

When Babe told Rosemary about Clarence staying with her now, there was silence on the line. Babe could tell by the silence that she didn't approve of the situation. Babe broke the silence by suggesting that they have dinner together some time.

"I seldom accept dinner invitations," Rosemary said. "But I'll consider having tea with you at my condominium next time I'm in town. Usually, I'm pretty busy on my two-hundred-acre ranch, but let's keep in touch."

Talking with Rosemary had Babe thinking seriously about a move. This thing with Clarence was a comfort for her now because of what she had just lived through, but she didn't know if it was right to jump into a relationship. Even though she was attracted to Clarence, she thought perhaps she didn't think it through.

While she prepared dinner, she thought of what she would do with her house. The option of leasing her house was an idea. With a mortgage hanging over her head, she couldn't just move out.

Dinner wasn't anything special since Babe hadn't shopped for groceries, but even tuna casserole and vegetables would make a meal, she thought.

Clarence arrived just as the meal was ready. Danger was with him. Babe was glad that Clarence let Danger stay outside while they ate. Babe told Clarence about Rosemary's letter and her wanting to help Baby move. Clarence told her how he couldn't believe a total stranger would help and how he would hate for her to give up her home.

"The house is almost haunted now. I've lived through countless nightmares, and I don't think it's worth giving up my peace of mind," Babe said.

"What will you do with your house?" Clarence asked.

"The possibility of leasing it out sounds okay."

After dinner, Clarence let Danger in to protect them—at least that is what he said. They continued discussing the idea of Babe moving. Finally, Babe admitted to Clarence.

"How long do you think this might last?"

Clarence looked awkward. "What do you mean?"

"I know that you still miss your family, and I know they will always be first in your life."

Clarence looked away, not knowing what to say. "If this is your way of saying you don't want me, don't blame it on my family. They're gone, and I'm here all alone. It's not a crime to want someone for me now."

Babe confessed to Clarence, "I truly don't know what I want, Clarence. I don't want to use you for my safety. The thought of having someone here seemed like a good idea, but I don't know where we're going with it. I was involved in a relationship before I met you. Vince wanted me to follow him back to Venezuela. I don't think I'll hear from him again, and I don't know if I'm ready for another relationship."

Clarence approached Babe, embracing her in his arms. "I'll be whatever you want for now, if you need protection, I'm here, as well as a friend."

It seemed right having Clarence there even though Babe felt the situation was unpredictable. The more he held her, the more she desired him.

At bedtime Clarence's warm body comforted her, and his advances grew more inviting.

Babe halted his move as she explained, "I cannot."

As he shifted his body to see her speak, he asked, "Why? Does it bother you because of the rape now?"

Babe stated softly, "I don't want to rush."

At night, it seemed longer than ever, knowing that Clarence was anxiously waiting. However, the thought of being with Clarence sexually was becoming harder to avoid. *Things are happening too fast,* Babe thought. *Maybe That's why the relationship is going too fast. We're living together like husband and wife.*

As she realized what she had got into, she began to see her mistake. Clarence gave her space, not wanting to rush Babe; he could see she was going through something. He became supportive of whatever she wanted. As she talked about moving, he could see that she was serious.

On Sunday, Clarence awoke thinking about church, hoping Babe would attend church with him. Clarence's and Babe's grandmothers attended the same church. But Babe wasn't interested. Clarence attended alone. After Clarence left, Babe silently thought about God. She didn't know why she didn't want to attend church; she believed in God and always prayed. She reminisced about her childhood experience with God and her baptismal at a very young age. "How dare you condemn the sinner, Jesus's blood paid for her sins"—her words at the first Easter pageant that marked her as an elect of God. At the tender age of seven years old, Babe seemed to know how to please the Lord.

Her personal commitment to wear a cross always identified her belief in Christ, but now she wondered if it had caused part of her problems in life.

Before dating Vince, Babe remembered a short relationship she had with a very wealthy guy that lived in Chicago. He was an atheist. And they argued about things that seem irrelevant, but Babe believed that he picked things to argue about because he didn't like it when she wore her cross.

Al blamed God for retarded children, but Babe denied that God was responsible, and not knowing the Bible that well, Babe didn't know how to defend God; but she didn't let it keep her from collecting her hearts and crosses. Babe and Al eventually broke up; the nice gifts weren't worth the risk of denying God.

Babe knew that her lifestyle wasn't perfect, but she knew that she didn't harbor hatred in her heart for anyone, and she never met anyone she didn't like. At least that's the way she tried to be, but the way the churches needed money, it would probably be another bill for her at that time, and she was trying to pay off some bills. Babe knew that it was scripture to give to the church and she didn't want to be a freeloader, but in time, Babe felt that she would commit to a good church. Her old classmate and friend Mary had been praying for her.

Mary used to be a Catholic, but she switched to Pentecostal. Babe wanted to have a relationship with God and didn't want to be in bondage to what appeared to be in some churches. Then she started thinking about the abortion, wondering whether God had forgiven her. She had prayed about it and felt his peace, but the churches called it murder.

Killing a rapist is one thing but having an abortion—some people would want to condemn her to hell for both, she thought. Suddenly, an urge to read the Bible appeared to be a good idea. Babe reached for the Bible and prayed for God's understanding. As she began to read Psalm 23, she knew that the Lord was her shepherd and that he would lead her through the still waters. Babe felt so thankful, thinking about all that God had allowed her to live through. Shortly after the first rape incident, she read about a young lady walking to church and was raped. That proved to Babe that working at a nightclub wasn't the reason for the rape. After reading the Bible, she felt that it was a good sermon directly from God. Clarence was returning from Church with his Bible in his hand. When he entered the door, it looked like gloom had hit him instead of a spiritual uplift.

Babe questioned Clarence, "What's wrong? You didn't like the sermon?"

Clarence responded, "It's okay, I guess, it just seems like they preach money all the time. I don't remember the sermon."

Babe shared with Clarence how her Sunday sermon went at home.

"Sometimes I feel distant from the church. They have many dogmatic beliefs."

"What's dogmatic?" Clarence wanted to know.

"Sort of like twisting the law to say what they want it to say, like preaching mostly on giving instead of the love of God or condemning others for their sin."

Clarence suggested they go out to eat; he saw a friend and made plans to join him with his date after he picked Babe up. Clarence insisted that Babe get ready.

"You remember Willet, our classmate?"

"How could I forget Willet?"

Clarence had spoken of him all the time. They had grown up together and attended the same church. They all graduated in the same class. Willet was a little in the fast lane. Babe remembered a hot romance he shared in high school with a neighborhood friend; she became pregnant and was now raising Willet's son.

"Who's the date for Willet?"

"His longtime girlfriend, now his fiancée. Willet is getting married. They haven't planned the date, but they're serious."

At the restaurant, Willet and his date were waiting. The waitress ushered Babe and Clarence to the table. Willet recognized Babe and was glad to see her. Babe remembered the last time she saw Willet and his fiancée; they're at a nightclub where Babe was taking pictures of a fashion show. They immediately struck up a conversation about the fashion show and the pictures Babe took of Willet and Sharon. Babe remembered them both.

Before dinner, they talked about high school and old friends. Willet was a music teacher at a local high school, and Sharon's father taught Babe in a woodcraft class. Babe told them about the tables she was still using that she had made in her summer class. After dinner, Clarence wanted to visit his family. On the way home, he stopped by and introduced Babe to his cousins, uncle, and aunt. They didn't live far from Babe's place.

They were all glad to see Clarence and entertained him with a game of dominoes. Babe played as Clarence's partner. She admitted that she hadn't played lately and was rusty. Clarence bragged that he would cover her. Tony, Clarence's cousin partnered with his father, Clarence's uncle. The game was going smooth until Tony asked Clarence if he had heard from Christine, Clarence's son's mother.

Clarence admitted that he received a letter from her last week. With all ears opened, Babe heard and began to wonder why he hadn't said anything to her about it.

Tony insisted, "How is she doing?"

"Wanting money, as usual," Clarence responded.

Babe wondered if Clarence had told his family anything about what Babe had just lived through. A lot of the talk was just general, other than talking about Clarence's family in Hawaii.

Clarence and his uncle stood. As Clarence grabbed his wrap, Babe could see they would be leaving. Tony and his uncle both welcomed Babe to come back anytime, boasting that the next game would be theirs.

As Clarence drove, he asked Babe, "Did you have a good time today?"

"You made my weekend," Babe assured him. She mentioned that she and Josie would have been hanging out doing nothing, but her outing with Clarence was refreshing, especially after seeing Willet, their old friend.

Clarence reached over to hold Babe's hand. Babe proceeded to tell Clarence what her agenda would be like that week—her appointment with the insurance adjuster and how she feared they wouldn't give her what her valuables were worth. She told Clarence she only collected once, when she had a roommate, and how the roommate wanted her to pay for her things with the insurance money. Babe told her that she was going to adjust the rent for her roommate, but she became upset about it and moved. The insurance company didn't give her much to start with, and her roommate wanted her stereo and jewelry replaced. Babe grew upset about losing a roommate and a friend but was leery about the situation since she was having an affair with Babe's sister-in-law's husband. The insurance didn't kick through for all the other burglaries Babe experienced because the deductible was too high.

Tuesday wasn't long in coming, and Babe was seeing Clarence off to work. It was sort of good to have Danger there; he appeared to be good company as Babe waited for the insurance adjuster to arrive.

Babe went over the list of items that was taken, trying to remember if there was anything else. Serial numbers and receipts were located to be attached with the police report, which the police left with her.

About 8:45 A.M., the door knocked. Babe hoped it was the adjuster; she didn't want to wait too long. At the peephole, she noticed a tall white man holding a briefcase. She figured that he had to be the adjuster.

As the door opened, she asked him to identify himself.

"Kyle Thomas, insurance adjuster."

Babe welcomed him in. First, they went over the details of the burglaries, and she gave him a list of all the missing items along with the police report.

Kyle glanced around the house with admiration for her decorating style, and as he complimented her, he asked, "Do you live alone?"

Catching Babe off guard, she didn't know how to identify Clarence since he had just moved in, and she wasn't sure about it all. With a feeling of faith, she responded, "My boyfriend moved in after the burglary."

As he wrote his notes, he confirmed her address. "4120 N. Franklin Avenue," and suddenly, it dawned on him the event that must have happened over a month ago. "Did you hear about the woman on the north side that killed a rapist? Wasn't that somewhere around here?" he asked.

Shocked that he would ask about that, Babe couldn't hold back, "That was me, and now another burglary."

"Wow, you killed the guy." Babe tried to defend herself; she mentioned that she was tired of all the burglaries and that was the second rape she had experienced. "I was forced to buy a gun."

Kyle marveled at her as she talked. "I don't blame you," he said. With all the details recorded, Kyle asked her if he could look around. He toured outside the house and through the garage, making a note of all the dead bolts.

When he returned, he told Babe his assignment was over, and he would contact her within two or three weeks for her claim. As he turned to leave, he mentioned the weather being nice, suggesting a nice day to move. Babe smiled to let him know she got the point.

Babe let Danger out before locking up; she didn't want to come home and see everything torn apart. The adjuster was prompt, and she appreciated that since she knew she had to be at work. Babe was conscientious of being late, and she was glad she could still make it to work by 11:00 A.M.

At work, everyone was busy preparing for lunch, and since she arrived late, she decided not to take lunch. While working, Babe thought about what the adjuster said regarding moving. It seemed like everyone had the same idea. Even Clarence began to accept it. Maybe moving would make the difference. As she thought about it, a plan to make a move started rolling. Anxiously, Babe planned to pick up application forms along with a newspaper to seek what the market was for renting. Not only would she be renting her house out, but she would also be looking for a place to rent.

After lunch, everyone returned except Alice. Babe hadn't noticed before if Alice was at work. She figured that she would be all ears, wanting to know what had happened.

Curiously, Babe asked Sandy, "Is Alice in today?"

"No, Alice called in sick today."

Babe couldn't remember Alice saying anything about being sick. Babe wondered if something was wrong. Alice didn't call in sick much, leaving Babe to worry about her. Not wanting to take away her time from work, she planned to call Alice after work.

Leasing her house would be a new experience. At home, Babe reached for her real estate book—basically a book from the last class she took—thinking she could pick up some pointers. A section about landlords caught her attention, but nothing about how to lease; it seemed like practical knowledge would have to teach her.

Babe purchased application forms and lease agreements at the office supply store. The forms were sold separately and didn't cost much, one of each, and then she could duplicate them and save money.

At home, Clarence was looking through the paper when Babe walked in. She mentioned, "Save the Classified ads, I'm looking for an apartment."

The newspaper had listed several apartments, and it pleased Babe to learn that rent for an apartment would be much less than what she was paying on her mortgage note, which meant she could lease her house for a higher price.

Clarence and Babe looked through the Classified ads together. The nicer apartments were on the south side, which didn't bother Babe because she worked out south. Even Clarence began to sound excited about it. Clarence suggested he assist her in moving, which pleased Babe.

Move or lease—Babe didn't know what order it should happen. She knew she had to lease her home first. Since she couldn't place an ad to lease until the weekday, Babe thought it would be nicer for her and Clarence to go sightseeing.

None of the apartments in the paper seemed to interest Babe; instead, they decided to look around to see what the neighborhoods were like. They came upon one neighborhood that seemed secluded. The entire area was a cluster of apartments; they were all clean and well-kept. Deep in the seclusion was a group of condominiums. Royal Palace, the billboard identified. For some reason, they appealed to Babe. It looked as if the clubhouse was open, so they parked the car to check it out.

The clubhouse was nice and cozy, with an upstairs loft. Babe hadn't lived in apartments much, so she didn't know what to look for, and the atmosphere was nice. Inside the clubhouse, a lady appeared to be leaving. She looked like the receptionist. Babe asked her about a one-bedroom vacancy.

"Upstairs or down?" she wanted to know.

"Is there a difference in price?" Babe asked.

"No."

"Then I'll look at an upstairs one first."

They followed the lady past the swimming pool and parking lot to a condo facing the clubhouse.

The receptionist unlocked the door, appearing to be for downstairs, but as they entered, they could see it was a stairway leading upstairs. They followed her up the stairs where the living quarters started. The rooms were spacious. The fireplace caught Babe attention. She had never lived in a place where there was a fireplace. The closet was big and roomy.

Dishwasher, how nice, Babe thought.

Babe had completely made up her mind that she would enjoy living there. She asked the receptionist if she had any more available in case someone rented it before she could put a deposit on it. After assuring her that there was another one available, Babe and Clarence both left with a made-up mind. The thought of moving had Babe excited, and now she was ready to take the necessary steps to lease out her house.

With the weekend behind her, Babe was anxious to report to work, with plans to lease her house during her lunch hour. She completely forgot to call Alice over the weekend until she saw her at work that Monday.

"How are you?" Babe questioned.

"I'm okay, with the exception of being pregnant."

Pregnant! Babe looked at Alice to see her expression. She looked serious, and Babe asked her if congratulations were in order. Alice wasn't excited about it, but she feared another abortion. Her and Herb weren't married, but she decided to have the baby this time.

Alice's situation seemed a lot more serious than Babe's. They put off talking about it until lunchtime, and since Babe had planned to make a phone call at lunchtime, she explained to Alice they could meet later.

Placing an ad was of utmost importance. The ad agency told her the ad would appear as soon as the next day. Knowing if she got that behind her, everything else would fall in place. She brought the application and lease form to work to make several copies. While Alice waited, she ran the copies without anyone noticing.

In the cafeteria, with only fifteen minutes before lunch would be over, Babe joined Alice at her table.

Babe knew she didn't have time to eat.

"Well, fill me in," Babe said.

Alice seemed calm as she told Babe that she found out she was pregnant. She and Herb discussed having the baby because Alice didn't want to go through with another abortion. Alice looked upset because Herb wasn't ready to marry her. But she loved him, and nothing else mattered. As they prepared to return to work, Babe mentioned to Alice that she was making plans to move into some apartments not far from where she lived.

"First I have to lease out my house." Babe placed an ad during her lunch hour. "Just think, we're going to be neighbors, and if you need me, I can babysit for you."

The weeks following, Babe had accepted a young couple to lease her house. They had lived out of town prior to their move. With them planning to move in, Babe was preparing fast to move out. The condo that she liked was still available, and she was scheduled to move the same weekend the couple would be moving in. It didn't seem that it would be enough time, so Babe decided to schedule a day off. They had boxed up mostly everything, and Clarence had planned to use his company truck, along with his supervisor, Robert.

On Friday, Babe took over as many boxes as she could by car, along with her phone; she also arranged her telephone service and address to be switched. That evening, Clarence and Robert assisted with the heavier items. Babe gave a bedroom suite to Clarence. She had too much furniture. Candi, one of her sisters, had already taken some of the furniture. A girl at work bought her washer and dryer. The couple of loads were lighter since Babe had already gotten rid of the items, she wouldn't have room for.

After all the loads were emptied out of the house, Babe went through the house and cleaned as thoroughly as she could since the couple would be moving in that weekend.

Robert took the company truck back with him, and Clarence need a ride.

Instead of leaving, he suggested he stay the night with Babe in her new apartment, and knowing she still needed her bed set up, Babe agreed that it would be a good idea.

Moving a bit of clutter, Babe and Clarence made their way to the bedroom, where he started putting her bed together. They both were tired and wanted to sleep, but the bed had to be assembled. He finished with the bed, and Babe didn't feel like putting any linen on it, but Clarence insisted on at least a sheet and spread. Clarence helped, and they were soon ready for sleep. Babe reached for a short housecoat, just taking off shoes and their street clothing, then they both lay close to each other. Babe held Clarence's hand as she thanked him; Clarence tried to say something but was soon asleep.

Sleeping late came easy for the both of them; Clarence awoke first. As he stared at Babe while she snuggled a pillow, he couldn't resist the desire to touch her, and as he wondered if she could be his, his body started caressing hers.

Before he knew anything, he was kissing her all over her body while she, half alert, responded. Clarence had aroused himself, and the feeling was mutual. Babe thought that she might miss him when he left. Clarence could tell he would have to be gentle with her; Clarence felt good that Babe was relaxing a bit more with him, and he felt that things would get better eventually.

Even for a quickie, he was comforted, thinking maybe the apartment was making a better change already.

That morning, he helped Babe unload boxes until everything was put in its proper place. He had to go back to his place and insisted that Babe join him. Babe pretended she had made plans with Josie, knowing she needed some time alone.

As she drove him home, he complained that she just didn't want to spend time with him.

"We've been together all week."

"What are you talking about?" Babe snapped.

"Okay, I'll see you later on."

After dropping Clarence off at his place, Babe decided it was a good time to visit Josie since they only talked on the phone briefly because Clarence was always over. Josie and Clarence both lived on the north side, and it would save on the gas for now. Now late in the afternoon, Babe figured everyone would be up, if not at home. Malcolm answered the door, seemingly somewhat surprised.

"Long time no see, stranger."

"You said it, and for how long."

"Where's Josie?"

Just as Babe mentioned Josie's name, she came with her apron on, insisting that Babe join her in the kitchen, where they all sat and caught up on new times. Malcolm questioned Babe and her relationship with Clarence and her new condo.

"Clarence is nice, but I think we're going too fast, and I can't stop it."

"You can't or you don't want to?"

"Something like that, I guess," Babe agreed.

"When do we meet him?" Josie suggested.

"Is tomorrow, okay?"

It was settled that Babe would bring Clarence over to meet Josie and Malcolm the next evening for dinner. After briefing them on her new home and giving Josie the address and her new phone number, Babe decided to leave; she didn't want to stay long since she didn't feel comfortable telling Malcolm about everything, and she didn't want him to excuse himself.

Babe thought, with all the extra time on her hands, she could browse the local pawnshop, where she would sometimes purchase things.

The downtown pawn shop was known to offer bargains from time to time and even had a layaway plan. Not a big crowd to overwhelm her like at the stores, Babe slowly went through, looking for a good deal. And as she scanned the Tv's there, to her amazement, was the television set she had owned herself. Not only was it the same style and model, but there was also the same cigarette burn on the top. The same as it was when Babe purchased it from an auction. She kept quiet and continued looking. In the music department was her stereo, which she had kept in her spare room. The stereo sat in a corner with a sold sign already attached to the big speakers. Further down was a camera and its accessories, with the unmistakable brand that was known as an antique because it was no longer being sold. Knowing it belonged to her, she continued to look in hopes of finding her other items. Around the corner was her microwave. Babe was convinced that all her things were at this pawn store.

Carefully, she pondered on what she would do and then decided not to look anymore because what she saw was enough. Immediately, she went to the salesman behind the counter and explained what she had found. When he checked his records, it was verified her items were brought in the day her house had been burglarized.

"Ever heard of Phillip Underwood?" the salesman asked.

She shook her head as if to say no.

But Phillip had already been paid, and there was nothing the salesman knew to do.

Babe left upset and surprised at the same time, thinking she should call the police station and notify them as soon as she could. At home, she dialed the police station and left a message for the detective to call her at her new number. Due to the weekend, she thought it better to wait to call the insurance adjuster.

Later that evening, Clarence called, and Babe told him what had happened at the pawnshop. Clarence could tell she was still upset over it and asked if tonight would be okay to see her. Since she was waiting for the detective to return her call, she didn't think so. Babe suggested he join her at Josie and Malcolm's the following day for dinner. Clarence had heard Babe speak of Josie and her husband, and he looked forward to meeting them. She promised she would pick him up the next day.

Even though Babe didn't think she would hear from the detective until next week, it was a good excuse, knowing she still wanted some time to herself. With the apartment half clean, she reached for a book to read while she relaxed near the fireplace. The built-in bookshelf was already being put to good use. The first book that caught her attention was the book Vince had bought her; *"101 Ways to Make Money in Photography"*.

Vince was a pleasant memory, and Babe had decided he's probably involved with someone else by now. Babe had been busy with other matters in her life and never thought to visit Vince's brother and cousin, who still lived in Tulsa, and since they had only been seeing each other short of six months, it didn't seem like the relationship was strong enough to believe for more.

As she read the book, she thought of her hobby of photography. Babe really hadn't made much money in it, but she once thought it would replace the nightclub scene or add to it. Thoughts of what happened made her feel like she would probably be marked for life now, after killing that rapist. Wondering if she would ever enter a nightclub again, it all seemed so crazy, especially since she still liked to dance and party. She reflected on her life. *If anyone is to blame, it's the rapist, he was asking for trouble,* Babe thought.

Browsing through the book gave Babe ideas on how to work on the side and establish a part-time photography job; maybe a new location was perfect for a new start, she thought.

After flipping through several pages, she set the book down and allowed herself the privilege of a luxurious hot soak in the bath, and the aroma of baby-powder mist scented the condo as she absorbed the private moment for her peace and tranquility. Babe couldn't remember the last time she was able to relax without the interruption of anyone disturbing her or the fear that someone would intrude upon her. A song of thanks and praise to God was uttered from her lips as she enjoyed her newfound environment. Before she realized what she was doing, she began to feel crazy, thinking it was strange to praise God that way.

At dinner the next day, the highlight of the conversation was about Josie being pregnant. Josie and Malcolm had been trying to have another child, and it finally happened. Just the thought of a baby prompted Clarence to talk about his son, Clarence Jr. He would be two years old now, and Clarence cheered up as he bragged about how his son was holding a bottle when he was only three months old, and it had been nearly a year now since he last saw him. Josie mentioned that Markie, her firstborn, didn't seem excited about being a big brother. He had just started Head Start and didn't seem to be adjusting well with all the other children.

Clarence expressed how he missed seeing his son. Hawaii was a long way from Tulsa, and his ex-girlfriend wouldn't send him a picture.

Afterward, on the way home, Babe suggested that he call to see how Clarence Jr. was doing. Clarence thought that it would be a good idea since it was obvious how much he missed him. After settling in from the move, Babe looked forward to a productive day at work. Chaos had completely consumed her personal life during the last couple of months; her personal matters kept her too busy.

At work, Babe thought to call the detective, but decided to wait at least until noon. She moved fast to sort through the tickets and tray them up, knowing that her day would appear to be a complete waste if she didn't make up for the time on the phone. On a normal day, her speed was fifteen trays a day, but due to the fact that the mail hadn't arrived, sometimes she would complete about twelve. Babe knew her speed was up to performance, and she always tried to help out others when she could. But when her schedule was interrupted, she would do good to get about ten trays out. Some in her group were slower than that. The older ladies were doing well to get seven trays out on a busy day; she didn't worry too much about her personal time. She felt that her speed was good enough to carry her on the bad days.

Alice was off work again; she had been having a lot of morning sickness. Most of the people in the department knew by now that Alice was expecting. Small talk about Alice was the center of attraction in the department. When Alice wasn't at work, they would pile the questions on Babe.

"Is Alice going to marry Herb?"

"Why is he doing this to her?"

Babe didn't like discussing Alice's personal business with the other employees. She considered Alice to be a friend even though they were as different as night and day. Alice enjoyed reading and waiting on Herb to be her main man; she was like a homebody. Alice looked forward to Babe telling her about the action at the nightclubs, but she would never be seen in a club, probably because she came from a small country town two hours from Tulsa. The only reason she moved to Tulsa was because the jobs were more plentiful. Herb was the first man she met and the only man she loved. Her old-fashioned ways kept her preserved, but naive. Babe didn't think Herb was faithful to Alice, but she would never tell her that.

While the group continued talking among themselves about Alice, Babe secretly prayed that Alice was doing the right thing. She lived in an efficient apartment that had the bedroom and living room together. She knew Alice didn't make a lot of money on the job, and when the baby came, it would need much more than Alice could afford on her salary.

Just as Babe looked up at the clock, the phone rang. It was for her.

"Detective Johnson," the voice said. "Did you call last weekend needing a detective?"

"Yes, sir, I called you because I had a burglary several weeks ago. Last weekend, I discovered my stolen goods at the pawn store."

As the detective listened to Babe, he recorded the information and repeated what she had said. He questioned Babe if she knew the individual that sold the items to the pawn store. Babe assured him that she didn't know the person. He told her he would get back with her after he checked into the matter.

Detective Johnson didn't call her back immediately; it was about a week after that. It was an unpleasant surprise for Babe when he told her that she would be called to testify in court at a hearing. The hearing was scheduled for Friday at nine, and today was only Monday. The guy who sold the items to the pawnshop had been apprehended, and Babe was needed to testify in court. Anxiously, she panicked as she thought of the long wait until Friday.

When she asked Detective Johnson if she had to be there, he informed her that he would subpoena her if necessary, leaving her no other choice. She agreed to cooperate.

"What's to be expected?" she wanted to know.

"They'll question your association with the assailant and whatever else they need to know pertaining to the case. Don't worry, you called me because you want to see justice done, right!"

"Of course, but I've been through hell already! What if this guy is related to the rapist?"

"We'll protect you."

Another change caused Babe to take vacation again; the entire year had been a chaos. All her vacation had been used for emergencies such as this. At work, she informed her supervisor that she needed to schedule a vacation day for Friday. When she returned to her desk, her co-worker determined by the look on her face that the news was not good. Babe explained about the upcoming trial, but her co-workers told her not to sweat it.

"Just tell it like it is," they said.

Jokingly, one supervisor called her Tiger. Yet Babe still worried if this man was related to the rapist and what would happen after she testified. Mixed emotions flooded her mind. Thoughts of defending herself flashed through her mind. Keeping the gun seemed like the logical thing to do. With the rate of crime like it was, Babe figured it was the only way to survive.

Even now she felt she would pull the trigger again if someone forcefully invaded her rights like before.

At home, just as Babe walked in and settled down, Clarence called with a tone of excitement in his voice. He told Babe that he had a chance to talk with Clarence Jr and his ex-girlfriend wanted him to come to Hawaii and spend some time with them. Babe's heart dropped as she listened to Clarence. She feared that if Clarence left for Hawaii, he would probably never return. Knowing that somehow this day would come, she knew that his heart was yearning to see his son, and if he got back with the mother, so be it, Babe thought. Anyway, it seemed like things were going from bad to worse with all the changes occurring in Babe's life. Clarence continued telling Babe that he was making plans to travel to Hawaii. As she listened to his overjoyed reaction, she decided not to tell him about the upcoming hearing.

Since he would be leaving Saturday, the day after the hearing, Babe didn't want it to keep Clarence around; she knew how excited he was about returning to Hawaii.

Babe wanted to know if Clarence was okay with a ride to the airport. It had already been planned that his cousin would take him. When Babe found out Clarence's ticket was only one way, she demanded that he tell her what was really going on. Clarence gave in and told Babe that his son's mother wanted to try again at their relationship, and he felt the same way. Silence covered the airwaves, but Babe broke the silence and expressed her best wishes with them mending their relationship. It was as if Babe knew Clarence and she were going separate ways. At first, Babe wanted to make Clarence feel guilty about their breaking up, but she knew it wouldn't be fair since Clarence was secondary to all her problems and still Babe wasn't totally convinced that Clarence was the right one for her. He just came in handy for the time.

Clarence suggested they see each other before he leaves, but Babe didn't want to, knowing she had to deal with the mixed emotions of the hearing, and she didn't want to bother him with her problems, thinking somehow that might have ran him off.

"You've been a good friend that I will not forget," Babe said.

"I'm going to miss you, but I know you will be alright," Clarence said.

They hung up the phone and Babe was there thinking that she should be crying, but instead, she felt some peace in knowing that

Clarence had finally realized to follow his dream, and it would be better for the both of them.

Another call interrupted Babe. It was Josie. Babe told Josie about the hearing, and Josie wanted to attend because it sounded exciting. At least that was her excuse, but Babe thought Josie was worried about her, and it was a way for her to lend some support. Babe was glad since she knew she didn't want to go alone.

It was planned that Babe would pick up Josie that morning, and they would eat lunch afterward.

Friday came faster than Babe wanted and as she prepared for the big day, she paused to pray on her knees in her bedroom. Babe considered herself a believer and talked to God in her normal way, but sometimes she didn't commit time to a strong prayer life or make sacrifices like the people in church did. She felt that if she prayed while working or walking or while preparing for sleep, it was just like any other prayer. That morning, she left early to pick up Josie; she was radiant like a light, zealous and looking forward to the day in court. Her positive attitude was the encouragement that Babe needed. Josie's enthusiasm beamed as she bragged about how courageous her little sister was, calling her a better detective than the police themselves.

Downtown Central Courthouse opened at 8:00 A.M. It was already full of people hanging outside of the door. Squeezing through the crowd took some tenacity that Josie displayed best, but Babe thought it would be easier just to leave and forget the whole thing, especially when she confronted the crowded room. Boldly, Josie grabbed Babe's hand and led her through the crowded section where surprisingly, they found a bench not quite full. They pressed their way through the crammed area and found a seat.

Jokingly, Babe mentioned to Josie that she was already on edge. "I'm getting used to it, sitting on the edge of this bench."

Tension stirred as the people waited; you could hear talking and murmuring about the delayed wait. Finally, a short, stout man entered from the juror's box section. He approached the front for all to see and announced.

"All stand."

Simultaneously, everyone stood, and all were silent.

From behind the closed doors, the judge, a tall distinguished-looking man in a black robe, walked in and sat in the presiding judge's chair. The bailiff announced for everyone to stand before the judge came out, and after the judge sat, the Bailiff announced everyone to sit. Silence penetrated the room as the judge began to announce the cases before him.

It was near 8:30 A.M., and Babe was beginning to wonder who was first since they started late, or did they? The first case was a woman who had been caught shoplifting. The public defender pleaded with the judge for leniency, but the judge gave her five years because of her past records. Teary eyed, the woman was escorted out by a guard.

Different cases were reviewed before Babe's; Josie was in awe just looking at how the judicial system worked. Babe didn't know what to expect; she thought back to the last time she had been in court for a speeding ticket, and that was about two years ago, a memory that she didn't like after being fined $90 by the city for speeding at a rate of 90 mph.

Suddenly, a piercing voice summoned: "Valetta Juanetta Johnson," which alerted Babe that her case was up.

Josie hunched Babe from her moment of daydreaming.

Nervously, she took the stand, and after being sworn in, she answered the questions as well as she knew how. The public defender asked her of her association with Philip Underwood. She denied any connection or relationship with this person. She glanced around the courtroom, trying to identify a face but recognized only Josie's. The sheriff escorted a guarded young man in prison clothing, handcuffs on his wrists, and shackles on his ankles. Babe looked him over from head to toe. Again, she was asked if she knew the person standing before her accused of the burglary, and again, she said no. As she stepped down from the stand, she looked at the frail undernourished young man, feeling sorry for him.

The worst was over, and they were allowed to leave. Josie suggested finding a McDonald's to eat at before going home. They were both hungry and looked forward to eating. As they sat at the restaurant, they struck up conversation.

"I'll bet you'll never work in a club again," Josie said while they ate.

"What's wrong with working in a club?" Babe demanded to know.

"I just thought maybe more people recognized you in a place like that," Josie said.

"As far as I'm concerned, working in a club has nothing to do with the things that have happened to me. So why should I sit around worrying about whether people are recognizing me? If anybody messes with me, they're going to get what's coming to them."

Their eyes met, and they both started laughing.

After Babe dropped Josie off at her house, she went back to the quietness of her apartment. The remote surroundings enveloped her with a sense of peace. From her bookshelf, she pulled out the book on photography, which Vince had given her, and began to read. She had the entire afternoon to herself since she didn't have to return to work.

Babe's 35mm camera was stolen during the last burglary, and a notion to replace it sounded like a good reason to go shopping.

Shopping would make the day seem like it was the vacation it was supposed to be. She had money from the insurance settlement, which was enough to buy a brand-new camera at the store. Babe tried to save money by purchasing secondhand items, trying to be conservative, but they usually didn't work right. Now she felt she would finally get to own a new camera from the box, with instructions and a warranty.

At the local camera store, Babe looked at the wide choices of cameras with excitement. She purchased one with several interchangeable lenses along with some special-feature filters. It looked professional and durable, one that would last a long time. A spark of energy challenged Babe to switch to her photography hobby more.

Chapter 5

Welcomed Addition

Alice was futher along in her pregnancy, and everyone was looking forward to her expectancy. A baby shower was being planned at work. Hush-hush and whispers kept the secret in suspense while everyone bought gifts and stored them in the conference room, normally used for business meetings. Alice was somewhat petite in size, and the weight of the baby made her very pregnant as she leaned backward to walk, carrying the delicate load with ease. All the talk about Alice not being married was water under the bridge; everyone put on a good face to assure Alice that it's what made her happy that counted. She anticipated the baby more now than ever. Her ultrasound test revealed that the baby girl showed no visible signs of birth defects.

It was already planned that, for lunch, a few of the employees would take Alice on a trip to the cafeteria and return her to the conference room while everyone else prepared for the surprise. Since Alice had planned on working until she had the baby, it seemed like a good idea to have the shower during the last month the doctor predicted the arrival.

The conference room was decorated with yellow and pink bunnies; Alice knew it was a little girl, so she had already picked out a name closely related to Herb's middle name: Christine. Herb's middle name was Chris. As the door sprung open, Alice's facial expression showed that she was surprised. A seat was reserved for her near the gifts, where Babe handed her each gift to be passed around for others to see while another employee recorded who bought what. The punch and cake were desert since others had already eaten; some were eating while the shower was in progress.

After the shower, Alice called Herb to tell him about the shower and how she would need him to come prepared to help her with all the gifts. Alice was staying at Herb's apartment more now that she was almost ready to deliver, and the doctor had told Alice not to drive during the last months of her pregnancy. Herb was pleased to know they had a shower for Alice; he hadn't bought much of anything other than a baby bed. All the excitement at work left Alice feeling a little tired, so she arranged for Herb to pick her up early. Babe helped Alice gather all the gifts in a mail cart. It was near freezing outside, and Babe expressed the danger of walking on the slick pavement. Alice was well prepared with her snow boots on. The month was February, and the weather forecast predicted freezing temperatures for another week.

About the time Herb arrived, Babe had everything already loaded. All he needed to do was load the car. Herb thanked Babe and told her she didn't have to be a stranger since Alice was staying with him, extending an invitation to visit them both.

Within that week, Alice delivered a healthy eight-pound, three-ounce girl; at work, everyone feared that she would have the baby in the office. Now Alice would be off at least a month or more. It seemed like having babies was in the making.

Josie soon gave birth to another son, calling him Jerry. Josie was happy about the baby, but she wanted a daughter. Malcolm made her a promise that he would give her a daughter the next time. Josie was really busy with two kids and a husband.

Babe helped out Josie when she could; it was hard for Babe not to think about a family herself. It was Babe's plan to get serious about marriage after she reached the age of twenty-five, but it seemed like the changes that occurred in her life left her putting it off more so, and whether by chance or not, it seemed like the dates weren't serious enough for her anymore, as she could not know if she could trust a man after what had happened. Would they like her for herself, or would they only be using her or feeling sorry for her?

Babe was glad to know that she could rejoice in the families around her. She hadn't heard from Clarence since he moved to Hawaii to be closer to his son, so chances were that Clarence, and his baby momma were doing fine. It was kind of expected, Babe thought.

Nearly three months had passed before Babe heard from Vince, with the change of address and all, but the letter and souvenir she received in the mail. Puzzled her trying to figure out the small wooden vase with floral print and a stick was? It seemed like some type of depression took over her mind, and the thought of Vince reminded her of the hell she went through, causing her to forget him altogether. As she attempted to write him back it seem like Clarence impression on her left her blank and unable to write him back.

Boredom left Babe longing for involvement until a friend called; Pam called and invited her to go out with her. Babe didn't hesitate to say yes. About 10:00 P.M., they headed for one of the neighborhood clubs where many older adults hung out.

Judie's Club was a more mature setting on the north side. It was busy as usual, and the security guards were on the outside checking for loafers. They entered the smoke-filled room, and the music rocked the place. The desire to party rose up within Babe. Before they could find a seat, a young man asked her to dance, and it was all the therapy she needed. Dance after dance, she seemed to make up for lost time. Later, she made her way to the seats Pam had found. And now Pam was up dancing. As Babe sat there alone, she observed two men checking her out.

She tried not to appear as if she noticed them. She picked up Pam's cigarettes, pulled one out, and lit it.

The men were whispering and staring at Babe. An alarm signal cautioned Babe. Soon one of the men approached her; he was the nicer looking one. He asked for a dance, but she kindly refused. He seemed persistent as he invited her to an after-party. When Babe told him, she wasn't able to go, he was still determined to know more about her. He asked if there was any way he could keep in touch. Their conversation seemed safe, but Babe was unsure about his motives, so she gave him a fake phone number.

He walked back to the corner where his friend stood. Babe watched him show the fake number. *Won' they be in for a surprise when they discover it's the wrong number,* she thought to herself. The other guy reminded Babe of the rapist who lay on her living room floor, and she wondered if they could be related.

When Pam returned from the dance floor, Babe started to tell her about the guy but changed her mind, thinking it might scare her and she would want to leave immediately.

Babe's suspicions began to affect her spirit as she worried inwardly how safe she was. Her expression was blank until a gentleman stepped forward, as if he knew her.

"May I have a seat?"

Babe looked up; she did recognize the young man—an associate by the name of Ronald. Babe once worked with Ronald's ex-wife, Patty. Patty's parents lived down the street from Babe, and Babe briefly dated Patty's brother, Harry. She knew Ronald had run for an office as senator of the Northeast District and was politically active as an entrepreneur of sorts.

"Considering any more political roles lately?" she asked.

"Too busy with my weekly publication. I don't have time for it anymore."

Ronald began to explain about the publication, of which he was the owner. Then he mentioned a need for a photographer. Babe listened a bit then asked him questions before suggesting herself. She explained how she loved taking pictures and had done a little freelancing, but she hadn't had the opportunity to work with a business. She offered to show Ronald her folio album, and his attitude began to radiate. She expressed hopes to supplement her income with photography. Ronald suggested that he might need her for a few daytime jobs.

Babe told him that she held a day job. "But we'll worry about that when the time comes," she said.

They exchanged numbers, and Ronald anxiously mentioned that he had a couple of assignments coming up with which he would need help.

Their mutual interest in photography had consumed the time; a waitress walked up to the table and asked if there would be any more drinks for this was the last call.

"No, thank you," Babe responded.

As they prepared to leave the club, the two men were still watching. Babe asked Ronald to walk them to the car where they talked long enough for the men to lose patience. Ronald couldn't tell Babe was just making conversation. She observed in her side-view mirror the two men get into a medium-sized beige and dark-blue 1987 Chevy Impala.

On the way home, Babe told Pam about the two men and the phony number.

Pam laughed and said, "I'm glad you didn't tell me about it earlier."

The next morning, Babe was up early to do laundry. Josie called before she could get out the door. When Babe told her about the incident at the club the night before, Josie got upset, as if a big crime had been committed.

Then she apologized, saying, "I wouldn't worry about you so much if I hadn't heard that the family of the rapist wants you dead."

Unalarmed, Babe interrupted her and said, "I don't want to hear about it. If his family wants a fight, I will be forced to give them a fight, then so be it. Life is too short to live in fear. I refuse to live in fear. My gun will stay loaded, and if anyone violates my life, in all fairness, I'll have to defend myself. I don't want to hurt anyone, but in this world, if you live by the sword, you will die by the sword, and if I die then, I die, so don't worry about me."

Josie was a cosmetologist and did hair at her home. She had heard from a customer that Babe's life was in danger. Before hanging up the phone, Babe asked Josie what she would suggest.

Josie could only say, "Be careful."

After hanging up the phone, the laundry still went unattended as another phone call delayed her chores—it was Ronald this time.

"I hope I didn't wake you," he said.

"Hardly, I've been up for a while."

Ronald wanted to know what Babe had planned that evening. He was scheduled to work a house party for a political party he was to cover, and Ronald wanted to know if Babe had any black-and-white films and slides, suggesting Babe accompanied him. Babe didn't expect him to call so soon, but she was ready.

That evening, Ronald picked her up at seven, and they discussed the plans and procedures. He gave her a list of instructions in order to remember whose picture she was to take. Babe didn't know the people on the list personally, but she recognized that most of them were of influential background, and she looked forward to meeting them.

The setting that evening was of formal attire, and in attendance were prominent businessmen and their wives. As they entered the two-story brick-framed Spanish Conquistador-style home, exquisitely decorated with marble and brass trinkets, Babe felt an ease of comfort when she recognized an old high school teacher displaying her artwork. Her old teacher recognized her, and they struck up conversation immediately.

After asking the teacher if it was okay to take pictures of the artwork, Babe captured the artwork on camera and marveled at how beautiful the oil paintings were and how unique the style of African heritage was. The teacher was proud of her work, you could tell by her willingness to tell Babe what each picture meant and the history. It must've been the icebreaker because, from there, the teacher introduced Babe to some of the ladies. They all identified their husbands and their businesses as well.

Ronald could see that Babe didn't need any assistance in getting to know the people. Her forward personality drew the people to her charisma. With a camera around her neck, Babe's purpose was easily identified. Babe sensed these people knew this was a way to promote their business since no one showed signs of being camera shy, and Ronald would be showing the pictures in his weekly publication.

Around her neck, she carried her camera while her shoulder-strap bag contained an assortment of interchangeable lenses.

Try to change lenses, Babe sat down by a gentleman whom she knew operated a local funeral home. She introduced herself, and they began to make small talk. They discussed burials since that was his line of business; Babe mentioned that she thought cremation would be less costly. He looked at her as though she'd said something wrong. Then he quoted a Bible scripture: "From dust we're formed and to dust we will return."

"What's the difference? I believe that God will bring us back in any form or fashion," she said. "Anyway, it seems to me that cremation would be less costly."

She could tell by his puffed-up attitude that it was time to change the subject. *Naturally He Would Disagree,* she thought, *especially since he didn't offer that service.*

"Is it okay if I take a photo of you and your wife for the *Downtowner* publication before I leave?" she asked.

He consented and called his wife to join him; Babe quickly took the photo and thanked them both before leaving to meet the rest of the lively group.

Everyone mingled with one another as an introduction and speech was being expressed by the host. He reminded them why they were all there, encouraging them to vote and let their voices be heard, making a difference in the community. Briefly he introduced some of the key people, along with acknowledging Ronald and his assistant. With a smile on his face, he looked at Babe.

He sure knows how to make a person feel as if they belong, Babe thought.

The two-story house was full of people on both levels. The refreshments were downstairs level. An urge to quench her thirst led Babe to the refreshments table before making her way upstairs. Timing was well enough to meet the homeowner and the host of the party, an attorney with an established law firm. Babe commended him on the collection of certificates and degrees that decorated his wall.

He is a humble man, Babe thought when he took no less credit than to give God the Glory. Maybe he thought Babe was religious since she had her cross around her neck; he didn't know it was Babe's custom by now.

Before long, Babe had met everyone downstairs; she followed the spiral staircase upstairs. There she found Ronald with several men, watching a football game on TV.

"How did it go downstairs?" he asked.

"No one's discussing the election," she mentioned. "I got plenty of pictures and made notes of all the names as well."

Ronald explained that this meeting was simply a get-acquainted party; he suggested that she photograph a few of the men in the corner, who should be acknowledged.

They were finished after taking about two rolls of film. As the people gathered their belongings, the crowd began to diminish. It was late when Ronald and Babe left. They both talked about what a good group of people it was, not like the nightclubs Babe mentioned. She told Ronald about a fashion show she photographed at the Celebrity Nightclub; the same night the club had sponsored a group that had performed at the local pavilion center and had a sellout crowd—a wall-to-wall of people with the commotion of chaos. Ronald assured Babe his assignments were low-key with low risks involved. Just as he said that Babe thought he was trying to say something about the justifiable homicide.

Thinking to herself, Babe thought it wouldn't be fair to withhold it from Ronald, especially if her working with him would put him at risk of endangering his life since Josie had already warned Babe what people were saying. Just when conversation was at a highpoint, Babe knew that she would have to tell Ronald. She waited until he expressed his last sentence about the party. Then she asked him if he heard about the rapist that was killed by his victim. Ronald tried to appear as if he didn't know what she was talking about. Babe admitted to what happened and asked Ronald if it would make a difference in what they were doing. He then acknowledged hearing about it and applauded her for her bravery, expressing that it would be an honor to work with her instead of a risk.

Relief overwhelmed Babe as she thought, how many people have to talk about the justifiable homicide? Why can't they bury it like the rapist?

It was late when they finally drove up to Babe's condo. Ronald expressed that it was considerate of her to tell him, even though Babe didn't seem to worry about her life. She knew that she didn't want to endanger anyone on her behalf. Babe didn't invite Ronald in; she told him to call her, and she would let him know when the pictures would be ready. The film developer wasn't open that Sunday, and it would be over the weekend before dropping them off. Babe thought it would be at least next week.

Ronald called earlier instead of the following week. He had other things on his mind. The next day being Sunday was a mission for Ronald to invite Babe to attend church with him. He called Babe early with an open invitation for church with him. Babe vaguely remembered he had mentioned that he was Catholic the night before.

"I'm not interested," Babe said.

Ronald didn't want to take no for an answer as he tried to bring a stronger conviction on her about not attending church. Babe didn't know how to respond without reverencing God. For some reason, Babe knew that she wasn't interested in the Catholic faith, but yet it seemed like she didn't follow any faith other than her own. Ronald preached a sermon about assembling oneself with other believers, and Babe didn't argue with him; she only agreed to think about it.

Within minutes of talking to Ronald, Babe felt a surge of anger as she thought that Ronald would be a normal friend whom she could learn from. She didn't feel attracted to Ronald and didn't want to hurt his feelings. Another puzzling fact was that she began to realize that she didn't feel drawn into the Catholic Church, regardless of whether she liked Ronald as a special friend or not.

Before ending the conversation with Ronald, Babe decided to level with him and be honest about her feelings. She told Ronald that she would seek out her own soul's salvation, and she wasn't particularly interested in attending a Catholic church; furthermore, she looked at Ronald as a friend and business associate and didn't want him to be misled.

He seemed to understand her refusal, but her decision weighed heavily on her heart. She thought about the different denominations. How can they all be the same with different traditions and rituals? Then she convinced herself that she had Jesus in her heart, and as soon as she was settled in her ways, she would find a church that suited her.

That week, Babe picked up the pictures. She was pleased with how well they turned out. She couldn't wait to tell Ronald. His anticipation was high as well because the phone was ringing when she arrived at her apartment door.

When she told him how well they looked, he said, "Say no more. I'll be right over."

They looked over the pictures, and both marveled over the clarity and distinctive focus they showed. Ronald paid her for the work and the pictures and thanked her, reaching to embrace her in a sensual way, but she stepped back, trying to block his move.

"Does this mean you don't want to see me anymore?" he asked.

"If there's a photography job, I'd love to help, but I don't want the relationship to become too personal."

When he left, Babe could tell he was hurt. She was sorry he was hurt, but she knew he would be misled if she didn't make things clear to him. When he failed to contact her for further assignments, she realized he had taken it personally.

Babe decided not to worry about things like Ronald, knowing that friends come and go.

Chapter 6

Moving Didn't Matter

It was just a matter of time before the IUD Babe had inserted right after her abortion began to cause her a few medical problems. Babe had to have it surgically removed because it should have been removed after years; however, ten years had already passed, and it created some problems. After it was surgically removed, the doctor told Babe that she wouldn't be able to have any children. Babe was upset at first, but after she thought about it, she realized that she didn't have to worry about birth control anymore. After the doctor removed it surgically, she was able to return to work and felt no side-effects afterward. Babe was glad that she had insurance to take care of everything.

Several years had passed, and Babe had gone through two different sets of tenants, and she was getting tired of living in apartments. Babe almost missed her home, but she thought about the problems, and she began to think of how she could afford a better home closer to family.

Babe had equity in the rented home, and she thought she would consult with a real estate agent about refinancing the house which would allow Babe a chance to move back into a house. She was beginning to think apartments were a waste of money—no room to grow in.

When Babe called up an old church member that sold homes, he told Babe that it would be a good idea since she had the mortgage on the home for several years now. Mr. Langford was instrumental in helping Babe go through the refinancing, and when it was done, he knew that she would use him to purchase another home.

The refinancing went off perfect on a second mortgage. When the loan officer presented Babe with a check for $12,000, she wanted to sign the papers and kiss everyone there, but she calmed herself so she could go over the details of the new mortgage note. The rental house payment wasn't as much as the monthly rent coming in, so she would have no problem meeting that obligation.

Babe left quickly to notify Mr. Langford. He was pleased and said she would be more qualified for a better house now. They agreed and began looking as soon as possible. Mr. Langford's persistence wore Babe out; she could tell Mr. Langford wanted her to hurry with a decision, but Babe didn't see any homes she liked.

Eventually, when she did find one that she liked, it had an "As is" sign on it. The appearance of the house attracted Babe, and she was willing to take a chance, so she put $1,500 down as a security deposit. Mr. Langford warned her that since it was "As is," if the loan company didn't approve the loan, the agency could keep her deposit. But Babe felt sure she would be approved since one mortgage company had already approved a second mortgage.

Finding a source to finance the house was the next project. She checked with the bank located in the same office building where she worked. When she was informed that she had been rejected because of the state of the house, she panicked. Quickly, Babe left work early to apply with another bank.

After a couple of days, the second bank notified her that she was again denied financing for the house. Her hopes began to diminish; she didn't understand. The house had everything she wanted: three bedrooms, two-car garage, large combo living room with built-in appliances, a sliding patio door, central heating and air-conditioning, and bars already on the windows. It was the perfect house, priced at $13,000 below the appraised value. It was a good deal. Babe was disappointed when she didn't get the loan, and now she was concerned about the deposit as well.

Babe called Mr. Langford and explained that the house couldn't be financed. He was disappointed because he knew she might not get her money back. The clause in the contract clearly stated it. Mr. Langford did taxes at the end of the year and suggested Babe to claim it as a loss on her income tax. When he saw that advice wasn't comforting, he suggested talking to the director of government housing development. That sounded like a better idea.

"Tomorrow, I'll let you know when he'll see you," Mr. Langford told her.

The next day, Mr. Langford had bad news. "Mr. Jones, the director, is a firm man who honors only what's in the contract."

But Babe wasn't ready to give up so soon; she wanted to speak to Mr. Jones herself. So, she called and made an appointment with Mr. Jones herself. Babe didn't know what she was going to say, but she knew she had to talk to him. She pictured him as a big guy who never smiled, but to her surprise, he was a short, stocky man who wasn't that difficult to talk with.

Babe explained how she really wanted the house, but that the financing sources just didn't come through. She explained that the first house she bought was a government home. She is just trying to make small talk, hoping Mr. Jones would restore her faith in the system. She asked Mr. Jones if he would suggest a way to get the house financed. He informed her it was too late for that particular house because a couple had already gotten it financed and was preparing to move in.

"However," Mr. Jones went on, "we do have a special selection of houses at a special interest rate. They haven't been advertised on the new list yet. You can have the first choice."

He showed her the special payment plan and then showed her his personal list of homes for sale and advised her to have a real estate broker notify him when she came to a decision.

Babe walked out of his office; she felt she had a ray of hope and immediately called Mr. Langford. There were only twelve houses on the list, and she had a week to make up her mind.

They went through the list fast because none of the houses were as nice as the one Babe really wanted. Mr. Langford was getting annoyed with her response; she was in a quandary. Everyone had been so nice to help her, but she was getting weary. Mr. Langford told her they would let her select new carpeting, and they would winterize the house before she moved in, which was encouraging to know.

It wasn't long before Babe selected a house just a couple of miles from Josie's home.

Within a month, Babe had moved in. Her first visitor was Josie. She brought a housewarming present and toured the house.

"Don't bother me now," she teased, "just because we live a few miles apart."

"Don't worry," Babe responded. "Knowing you and those kids, I'll have to pretend like I'm not home half the time."

Josie praised her accomplishments, but Babe gave all the glory to God. Since Josie was of the Jehovah's Witnesses belief, she didn't comment. Babe sensed she must have said something wrong because Josie left soon after.

Employment at work was flourishing. Babe had a new position that allowed overtime, which kept her from seeking part-time work. The people in the department seemed nice. On a few occasions, Babe would find herself joining another department on the same floor for lunch. One girl had been an acquaintance with Babe since her teen years; they lived in the same neighborhood. While sharing with a couple of ladies during lunch, Babe discussed with them that she had worked for another oil company. One employee asked if she knew her sister when she worked at the other oil company. When she mentioned her name, Babe did remember. Her sister had been a devout Christian, whom Babe remembered was always praising the Lord. Babe had thought she was different, and then she learned of her tragic death. She was found dead, locked in the trunk of her car. That's when Babe's old neighborhood friend turned the conversation to Babe and asked about the time, she killed that man.

Caught a little off guard, Babe told Cherry, "I don't want to talk about it, you can read the paper."

Silence covered the air as Babe gathered her things to leave and politely told the group it was time for her to return to work. Cherry didn't seem to be upset with Babe's response as she expressed to Babe to join them another time.

When Babe started back to work, she felt bad about the cold response she had given her. But she really didn't want to talk about it, especially not in front of a group. So many people had falsely accused her of wrongdoing—people didn't know the whole story. She didn't want any more rumors to start.

She hated that the killing ever happened. She wanted to forget the whole thing, but everywhere she went, someone identified her with the incident. Through her tears, she told herself that she did what she had to do. Even in the Bible there were men of God who had to fight for their rights.

Free from working the extra jobs left Babe seeking something else to do. Time was beginning to mature Babe, and she didn't want to party as much, not to mention that most of her friends had started drifting off. Pam moved to Texas, and Alice returned to her hometown to go back to school after she had her second child.

On the way home from work one day, Babe went the long way, and as she crossed the lights a mile away from home, the little church on the corner suddenly caught Babe's attention. Then she remembered Mary, a high school classmate who had invited her to the church long ago, when Babe still enjoyed partying.

It seemed like Babe could remember it as if it were yesterday when she called Mary, seeking someone to party with her that night. All her other friends and associates were out of pocket. Mary was quick to remember that night after graduation, when Babe and a few of her friends were together for the last time, and now they're either all married or divorced.

Everyone wanted to do something exciting, like find a party, but Babe wanted to find a church and go to a revival. Mary had since settled down and became a mother and wife and was trying to recruit souls for the kingdom of God. As Babe listened, Mary had been praying for Babe ever since she switched lifestyle because she knew Babe sounded like she had known God and would always know him. But as time passed on, the church didn't make any lasting impact on Babe. Babe realized the several brushes with death were interventions from God that saved her life.

Suddenly, Babe realized as she passed that little church on that corner that maybe God was trying to save her for his will after all. By the time Babe turned in her driveway, she thought perhaps she could call up Mary and find out more about that little church on the corner. Of course, Mary was glad to hear from Babe since she was still in the business of recruiting souls.

She told Babe that they had a new believers' group Babe should attend on Wednesday. It was Friday, and after hanging up, Babe thought she would try to attend next week and possibly Sunday.

That weekend, things took a turn when Pam came in from Dallas and called Babe up to party. It wasn't every day that Babe heard from Pam, and she was glad to hear from her.

Pam's sister, Andrea, joined them at the nightclub that night along with an ex-neighbor. With everyone together, it seemed like old times. Babe thought about the days when they all lived in the same neighborhood. Pam stayed across the street from Babe with a neighbor that she almost married. Diane stayed a couple of doors down, and Andrea lived around the corner. The gathering was like a reunion.

At the nightclub that evening, Babe's half-brother, Sonny, was there. It had been a long time since she had seen him. Sonny drove a semi-truck and traveled a lot. After filling him in on the family business, he shared with Babe some of the adventures in long-distance driving. Sonny loved to party when he was in town, and he knew a number of people. At the table, a gentleman came up and asked if he could sit with them. Babe was curious about him.

Sonny introduced his friend as Curt. Curt, offered to buy everyone a drink; he seemed like a flirt. He was quick to let her know he was like family.

The body heat from the dancing began to warm up the club. Sonny and Curt went out for a breath of fresh air. This gave Babe an opportunity to ask Pam about Curt since they're both from the same rural town.

Pam said simply, "He hung out with my older brother. I'm not sure what he's like."

When they returned, Curt's suave personality was more charming than before. He had Babe's curiosity aroused. While Curt danced, Babe questioned Sonny about him.

Sonny's response was, "He was just a good ole homeboy back when we were growing up, I haven't seen him in a while, and I don't guess he changed."

Curt was persistent in showing an interest in Babe, and she wondered if there could be anything to him. In a conversation, he told her he was a licensed welder. *At Least The Potentials Are There,* Babe thought, since it made a difference to her whether a guy had a job or not. Before Curt left, he must've passed the test, for Babe gave him her number.

Babe decided that before the girls left, she would invite them over for dinner since they hadn't seen Babe's new place. At dinner, Pam warned Babe that Curt and her brother were in the fast life.

Babe told her not to worry. "I've reached the conclusion that I'm not falling for anyone until Mr. Right comes along."

It wasn't long before Curt did call, and Babe found herself putting him off. She didn't feel like being bothered with anyone, and he was no exception. When he finally caught her in a good mood, they talked on the phone. Curt invited Babe to the movies, and she accepted, thinking there can be no harm in it. The movie was great, and the fact that Curt was a jack-of-all-trades left Babe thinking of greater potentials. Babe didn't want to take things too fast because she didn't know if he was serious or just wanted to play games.

Babe had successfully leased her house out for three years. It didn't surprise her to run into complications. The tenant leased through a government agency, which inspected periodically. Babe was notified that she needed to make some repairs before it would pass inspection. Replacing the kitchen and bathroom tiles wasn't an easy job, but she figured she could save money if she did it herself. Babe called Josie and asked her to help; Babe had helped her do her kitchen, so she was ready for the challenge. Josie was preoccupied, so she purchased all the supplies and began the job herself.

Curt would call from time to time, but since she couldn't get Josie to help her out with the floors, Curt came to the rescue. When Babe discussed her plans to lay tiles in the rented house, he asked if he could help. Babe was more than grateful to accept his help.

Thanks to Curt, the tiles were properly installed. Looking at the size of the job, she couldn't have done it alone. While observing the outside of the house, she could tell it was time for a paint job, when Curt called again. Babe offered to pay him if he would help paint. He wasn't excited about the paint job, but after Babe offered to cook dinner for a week, he had a change of heart.

They started immediately since there was a deadline to meet or the government would delay the rent or terminate the lease. The house needed to be sanded in most of the areas before they got started. After they got started, they had a pretty good time since they started early that morning. By evening, it was all over.

Curt's help was really appreciated. Babe paid him what she agreed to pay him. Since they both painted the house together, he didn't complain about the arrangement. He liked her company more than anything.

Time brought out a different side to Curt, and Babe grew to like him more. They began to spend more time together; she never needed to call him, but one day, when she did, a lady answered. Babe thought she had the wrong number until she verified that Curt did live there but wasn't home. The lady took Babe's name and said she would have Curt call her.

Somewhat surprised that a woman would be occupying Curt's home since he had not told Babe about her, Babe couldn't help but wonder if something was going on between them. But she decided not to judge too fast. After all, she had a male roommate once, and the situation was strictly platonic.

That evening, Curt phoned, and Babe asked him about the woman. He said she had been put out of her apartment and needed a place to stay. Babe believed him and was glad that he offered to help someone in need. But when Babe continued to call him, the woman's voice changed from pleasant to not-so-pleasant. Thinking it was only her imagination, Babe tried to overlook the situation.

Curt eventually had to move his lady friend out since she wasn't very friendly to Babe when she called. That gave them more private time to talk about the future. Curt began to talk about having children, and Babe's hopes turned to gloom when she remembered complications from the contraceptive device that damaged her female organs and what the doctor told her. She didn't want to mislead Curt, so she told him what the doctor had told her when he took the device out. Curt's humor was always uplifting as he joked about what fun it would be in trying, but when she suggested adoption to him, he hunched his shoulders. Babe could tell he wasn't thrilled with the idea.

When Babe wasn't with Curt, she watched Josie's children. Now Josie has three children. Malcolm made good on his promise to give Josie a daughter, but all of a sudden, Josie had a busy schedule, and Babe didn't understand why. Josie had no job, so Babe couldn't understand what was keeping her busy. Babe didn't mind keeping her two smallest children because they kept her motivated. Jerry and Sharon were mischievous and always had something going on. They were friends with other kids in the neighborhood, and when they got on Babe's nerves, she would send them next door to play.

Slowing down from her busy schedule gave her time to consider going to that church Mary attended. Babe called Mary and told her to look for her; she would finally be attending the new believers' class.

The first night of Bible study, Babe understood how blessed she was to have lived through the things she did, and she hoped that someday she would be able to pay God back for his kindness to her. She was enlightened to see some familiar faces stand to share their testimony. An old neighbor gave his testimony about how he came to Christ and had made a change for the good.

Anxiously, Babe waited to tell Curt about church that evening. When he called, Babe told him about the Bible study;

he wanted to know what she had learned. Babe told him about the testimonies that went forth, and since it was the first night, they discussed the curriculum that had to be ordered, but several testimonies she heard were uplifting as they gave all the glory to God.

Curt changed the subject and asked Babe to go to a party with him over the weekend. That weekend, they went to the party, and the party lasted so long that Babe overslept and wasn't able to make it to church that Sunday. She recalled waking up in time but dreaded getting up for that purpose.

Finally, a visit from Josie woke Babe up. To her surprise, she had a few things for her—a bottle of cologne and a few brass trinkets that someone had given her. When Babe asked why she was giving them to her, she claimed that she owned the same things. Babe went on to explain about the church she had attended and her plans to attend church that morning but slept too late.

After a pause, Babe couldn't resist asking Josie about Kingdom Hall, a church she once attended. She told Babe they stopped going because her brother-in-law was asked to remove his membership after he and his wife divorced.

"It seems something else might have been done instead of such harsh punishment," Babe stated.

Josie had married into that denomination and just went along with her husband most of the time. Babe could remember the zeal she first had when her marriage was new. She was full of energy, going door-to-door witnessing for Jehovah's Witnesses. It was like you couldn't help but see the good in the people. Babe really did admire them, and she knew it took more than a notion to go door-to-door. Having the door slammed in your face had to be insulting, but they continued to work for the Lord.

It really hit a sore spot when Josie switched her faith to Jehovah's Witnesses since the family was raised Baptist, but it seemed like they weren't much Baptist anyway. For some reason, Babe didn't know enough about the Jehovah's Witnesses faith, but because they were trying to lift up the name of the Lord in some way or another, Babe just thought they should be respected and dealt with in a more diplomatic way.

Chapter 7

One Thing Led to Another

Something was going awry, and it wasn't clear what it was. Babe's attendance at the little church didn't seem to make a difference with Curt or Josie since they were her most regular visitors.

One evening, Josie stopped by and convinced Babe to go with her over to a friend's house. At her friend's house, Josie introduced Babe to Joyce, who looked as if she had just crawled out of bed. Joyce showed them to her bedroom, where she opened her closet. This closet was like nothing she'd ever seen. It was a shopper's paradise. New garments hung on the rack with the tags still attached, boxes of shoes galore, and in another corner were a selection of brass trinkets and bottles of cologne and perfume.

Josie insisted that Babe select a dress and a bottle of perfume. When Babe asked how much it would cost her, Josie said, "It's on me. I wanted to pay you for all the times you kept my kids."

Babe didn't think twice when she said that. The selection was vast; it took her a few minutes to choose the dress she wanted. Finally, she found a silk dress—which was a lavender floral-print fully lined dress. The original price tag said $115. Babe asked Josie if this one was okay. Josie nodded then reminded her to choose a bottle of perfume as well. Perfume was always a hit with Babe, and she knew them well, it only took a minute to select Channel 21, a fragrance that she hadn't owned, but she knew Chanel anything was a good fragrance.

Joyce sacked up everything as if they were in a store. When they left, Babe asked Josie what that was all about.

"Joyce is a booster," Josie said. "She does that for a living."

"What's a booster?" Babe asked.

"A shoplifter."

"You mean these things are stolen?"

Sure enough, that was exactly what she meant.

Josie was slow in responding, but then explained that her husband, Malcolm, did business with her. Malcolm was always in some kind of a business deal, but she couldn't imagine what she meant. Malcolm had a horse he had bought and was involved in gambling at the horse races, but Malcolm had gotten so bad about gambling that he couldn't hold a conversation without betting you something.

That evening, when Curt visited, Babe showed him the new dress and told him about Joyce. When Curt confessed that he knew Joyce, Babe was dumbfounded.

"When I used to sell drugs, Joyce would exchange stolen goods for the drugs," Curt explained.

Curt had never elaborated on that part of his past, but since Babe accepted Curt for who he was and not for what he had done in the past, she decided not to investigate the situation.

Josie and Curt soon met and found out they knew most of the same people. Babe couldn't help but wonder what really was going on. It wasn't long before Curt and Malcolm met, and since they hit it off so well, plans were made to attend the horse race together.

The four of them coupled off and decided to take a trip to the horse races. Malcolm owned a horse and had him in training. That was another one of his ideas for making money.

Afterward, Malcolm and Curt began to run together, and it seemed like more than a coincidence that they hit it off so fast. It seemed like Babe and Josie were the closest in the family now since they lived so close, and for some reason, Josie was slowly building a wall against Malcolm's family. Babe remembered how close Josie used to be with Malcolm's family, and she couldn't figure it out, maybe because they were all Jehovah's Witnesses and the disappointment of Malcolm's brother being banned from the church.

Josie and Malcolm's fifteenth-year anniversary were coming up, and Babe thought perhaps she would want her to keep the children, but instead, Josie asked Babe to hold a small reception.

A few appetizers and drinks drew the people that Josie had casually invited—nothing big since Babe was caught off guard with the very request. Her small house wasn't quite the site for a nice formal gathering, but then since your home is your palace, Babe thought the people that came would be comfortable. And all of a sudden, Babe was the ear that Josie confided in.

Josie stopped by for regular visits. Babe sensed that something was on her mind, but she wouldn't open up.

One evening, Josie picked up her children from Babe's house and sat down to talk. While Jerry and Sharon were still at the neighbor's, she asked if Babe had used cocaine. Out of the blue, the question was asked. Babe started to say never but thought about the party she went to long ago with Pam, where cocaine was used in a pipe and was smoked.

"Did you like it?" she asked.

"I don't remember any special effects at that time and didn't see any need in fighting over it, that's how the party ends."

Josie brought out a little white paper that looked like a gum wrapper. Gently she opened the paper, displaying the sparkling white powder.

"What's that?" Babe asked.

"Top-of-the-line cocaine," Josie said. With a small straw in one hand, she leaned forward to sniff a line in her nose. "Try it," she urged.

Babe reached over to do the same and blew cocaine all over the table.

Josie panicked. "Don't you know how to sniff?" she demanded.

"Let me try again." This time it wasn't so bad.

Babe sniffed it up her nose, and within minutes, she began to feel a tingling sensation inside her body, and her mind shifted into a faster gear.

They sat there talking about cocaine and how it was supposed to be a recreational drug. She said it increased a person's thinking ability. "Lots of people use it to study with." she explained.

Babe wasn't sure about all of that, but she figured it was expensive. Babe tried to get Josie to tell her where she had gotten the stuff, but she told her she'd rather not say.

After the paper containing the white crystal powder was empty. Josie pulled out another one, but she still wouldn't reveal her secret.

That thin line of cocaine gave Babe such a lift, she cleaned house, constantly looking out the window, making sure the children didn't walk in to see this while Josie sat there talking. "Does this stuff always affect people this way?"

"Usually it does," Josie said, "but it affects people differently, and some use it differently."

Eventually, Josie went across the street to pick up the kids. Sharon and Jerry would get so involved in playing that they would forget they had to go home. After Josie left, Babe found herself wanting more of the white powder until she realized that's how people get hooked on the stuff. *Maybe it wouldn't be so questionable if it was used in moderation,* she thought.

Josie had no restrictions on visiting after that, and she always had some white powder with her. This wasn't like Josie. She didn't smoke cigarettes, and now she was smoking secretly behind Malcolm's back.

One evening after work, Babe wanted to go home and rest, but the moment she lay down, Josie stopped by. She had some errands to run and was hoping Babe would go with her. Babe could tell Josie wasn't going to leave, so she grabbed her things to go.

It must have taken about forty-five minutes before they reached the destination. They passed several road signs indicating that they were no longer in town. While Josie was driving, she noticed Babe nodding, so she passed over a package of her stash. After taking a sniff, Babe told her they should call this stuff eye-opener. She stayed alert after that.

Outside of Tulsa City limits and into Glen Arrow, a new housing edition, Josie pulled into the driveway of a nice two-story house. When the car came to a stop, Babe quickly asked, "Who lives here?"

"You don't know them," was all she said.

Excitedly, a man answered the door and showed them in. It was obvious he was expecting them. The house was in disarray. At the dining room table, Josie brought out a small, clear plastic package with white powder, and he brought out a sack for exchange. His sack was full of all types of medicine. He also gave Josie some money to even things out. After the exchange was made, they left.

It was apparent that Josie was much deeper than Babe knew. At last, she told her that Malcolm had been getting drugs from a dealer who fronts it to him after it's sold, and Malcolm gets more drugs.

Josie was surprised that Babe didn't know since Malcolm and Curt had been working together, and then she realized why their association was so close.

Back at the house, they talked about it some more as they both snorted from her personal package.

"How much longer do you and Malcolm plan to be involved in this mess?" Babe asked.

Josie simply hunched her shoulders as if to say, "I don't know."

Malcolm had dreamed of opening his own feed store and becoming self-employed.

After seeing Josie off that night, Babe lay in bed, wondering if it was a sin to use cocaine. She tried to reason with herself that it was probably all right if used in moderation. Then she realized it was a sin to use money for that when there were many needy and hurting people in the world who could use a meal or a place to lay their head. Babe's conclusions left her justifying that only the elite, who were rolling in money, could afford to use cocaine.

Babe knew that Curt used cocaine because Malcolm and Josie made it so available, but she didn't know Malcolm was running Curt. When she questioned Curt about his involvement, he admitted that he helped Malcolm at times. He always seemed to keep drugs after that. Babe began to enjoy it more and never gave a thought to what it could lead to. However, she had her limits. Using cocaine was for pleasure until they began to question her about going in on a deal; that's when she said no. Josie had exposed her to freebies, and it was nothing for her to bring a package of cocaine. But that was no reason for Babe to make a career out of it.

As time went by, Babe saw the drastic change the white powder was making in everyone's lives. She began to look forward to running errands with Josie, knowing there was a bonus to appreciate afterward. Curt wanted to lease out his house in order to change locations, and they agreed that if he moved in with Babe, they could split the bills. Since Josie and Malcolm had been in and out of the house, Babe began to feel uncomfortable being alone.

Curt's presence didn't matter much after he moved in. He stayed out half the night, or all night, working with Malcolm. When he did come home, he would start on drugs himself, turning Babe on and starting a desire that only left after consuming valium, which would put her to sleep. The habit and craving for drugs grew worse. Babe was beginning to check herself; she knew she didn't like what she was seeing, and truly she was regretting it. A notice was made that it wasn't the rich buying cocaine; a big percent of their customers were oppressed welfare recipients.

At times, Babe would cry herself to sleep, praying to God that he would stop her from using drugs, yet she still did not want to admit that it was a real problem to Josie since it was their career.

While at home one evening, Babe answered the door, and it was Josie. She was trying to catch her breath and calm down.

"What's the matter with you?" Babe asked her.

She paused to drink her beer then told her story. She had attempted to make a delivery when the people said they needed to go to the store to get change. Instead of getting change, they were going to rob the store. They were frightened away when the police pulled up. Josie was in the car with them.

"I didn't even know they had a gun until we drove away," she said.

"That ought to be enough to make you want to leave the stuff alone," Babe told her.

Josie began to confide in Babe since she was her only friend; she told her that she loved her, but Babe had to interrupt Josie and tell her that she's going to need to face reality about the drug scene. She also told her it would be better if she and Malcolm would leave the drugs alone.

Josie insisted, however, that Malcolm was determined to make money in this and was now considering quitting his job. Babe shuddered as she thought of the new car they had recently purchased.

"Josie, why don't you get a full-time job and let him do drugs if he has to?" Babe suggested. Since Josie had never been anything but a housewife, with the exception of a few part-time jobs, she wasn't sure anyone would even hire her.

But the suggestion was taken. Together they scanned the classified ads each day, and Babe would call her from work to get her motivated. Sometimes the phone would ring twenty times before she finally answered it.

Josie's search for a job was difficult because she was looking for good pay. She had been deluded by the vast opportunities the drugs afforded her. She was able to exchange drugs for food, clothes and all sorts of miscellaneous items, which left her feeling secure.

Joyce supplied her with clothes for her children regularly. Joyce became so familiar with Babe she didn't think twice to stop by the place if she was looking for Josie. Josie was at the house so much her customers would stop by as well.

Curt stayed gone half the time and Babe found herself turning to drugs more. Pleasure was found in doing cocaine without him; it seemed more economical, and she didn't have friends, nor did she want any because when people found out she was related to a drug dealer, it became the focal point for the friendship—to have a better connection.

Babe discovered there weren't too many people you could trust. Josie warned her that people came to her because they were sisters, and she gave her discounts. She was right! Her customers were exceptionally nice and did everything they could to be friendly. But Babe had to keep a wall up, or they would try to use her.

As long as Babe continued to make it to work, she felt she didn't have a habit to worry about. But soon she wanted more than Josie could give. Withdrawals from her accounts left concerned that she was more deeply involved than she realized.

Curt was paying for half the expenses, which left her ahead in that area, but then Babe used that money toward drugs. Curt was upset when he learned what she was doing. He insisted that she invest that money instead of blowing it off so she could make a profit and still spend on her habit. Babe did try Curt's suggestion, but soon found she was losing money with him because he controlled everything, and she couldn't trust him. Josie then told Babe how Curt had worked with Malcolm on a deal and wasted the drugs he should have made money with. Strife developed in their relationship, and Josie began to warn Babe against Curt.

One morning, Babe was awakened by the phone. It was Josie. They talked about how the drug dealing was becoming even more frightening.

"If anything happens to me, Babe, would you keep the children?"

Babe was frightened, but she didn't hesitate to say yes. Josie was bitter and broke; she was doing good to keep the bills paid, and she was fed up with all the problems she was having with Malcolm and his family.

After their conversation on the phone, Babe fell to her knees and prayed that nothing would happen to her beloved sister.

Returning to that little church was the last thing on Babe's mind since she became involved with drugs and Curt. She just couldn't feel right about going to church.

Upon visiting another sister, Candi, whose husband smoked marijuana and purchased it from Malcolm, Candi noticed the change in Josie also and questioned Babe. She knew they were involved in drugs. Candi and her family didn't go to church; Babe thought their prayers would get through faster than hers. She asked her to pray for them.

One Saturday morning, Babe had slept late but was soon awakened to the phone ringing. It was Markie, Josie's oldest son, asking if she knew where his parents were. They hadn't come home last night, and he thought perhaps they were at Babe's house. Markie said they had no breakfast. Concerned and worried, Babe hurried over to see what she could do.

On the way, she couldn't help but remember what Josie said about keeping the kids if anything happened to her. Even though she had told her she would, she wondered if she could actually afford to do it. When Babe got there, Josie and Malcolm had just walked in. They were tired; they went right to bed while the kids and Babe went out for breakfast.

Keeping the kids all day and that night gave Josie and Malcolm some time to rest. When Josie picked them up, Babe could tell she was upset, but she wouldn't tell Babe why.

Somehow Babe could tell they'd been fighting. From the different things Josie had told Babe, she knew Malcolm had begun to act like his dope-dealer friend who felt he had to hit a woman to prove he's a man.

Josie had a way of hiding most of the problems about her marriage. She knew Babe would be honest and tell her how she felt, and Josie wouldn't be able to take anything said against Malcolm. Once, Babe suggested that Josie separate until their lives were straightened out. Josie didn't want to hear it, and they nearly got into an argument over it.

Trying not to say anything against Malcolm was hard, especially when Josie spoke out against Curt. It didn't bother Babe because she wasn't in love with Curt, and he could be out of her life without a second thought. But it wasn't that easy for Josie.

Christmas was just around the corner. It wasn't planned; something just happened, and the entire family planned a gathering. James from Los Angeles had come to town with some friends and called Josie to pick him up at a nearby town. Two other brothers from Dallas came in unexpectedly. It was only a couple of days before Christmas, and all Babe's shopping was done. She felt she had accomplished a great feat.

Josie's family didn't celebrate Christmas, so Babe wouldn't wrap their gifts. When Josie stopped by and saw all the wrappings for the other gifts, she then requested that Babe wrap her family gifts this time. Babe did just that.

Dinner was at Papa's house and then a small reunion at Josie's afterward. Papa was glad to have them all together. They were not as close as other families, but they tried to make the best of the occasion. At Josie's house, everyone ate more and played games.

The Christmas spirit and other spirits were lively that night as they drank and played card games. The children tore open their gifts and thanked Babe for everything. It was surely a delight to see the children overwhelmed with excitement in their eyes. It was all new to them to be like the other kids and receive wrapped gifts at Christmas time.

While the men were all playing cards with old neighborhood friends, Josie and Babe both observed how thin and frail their older brother James was. He coughed a lot.

Some were concerned that he smoked too much. Babe went out and purchased some cough syrup for him.

While the guys played cards, Josie and Babe talked. Josie mentioned how rare it was for a family to get together as they had.

"I've heard there's usually a death afterward," she said.

After Christmas, things returned to the same lifestyle. The New Year had Babe thinking about resolutions and new beginnings; she knew she had kidded herself about cocaine far too long. Even though she enjoyed it, she knew it was taking a toll on her life as well as others around her. Too many problems had developed because of it, and the only way to a better life would be to leave it behind.

Then Josie called and told Babe Malcolm had quit his job. Babe knew they talked about it, but now that he did, she knew this meant trouble. Now they would have to rely solely on selling cocaine on a regular basis. Before long, their habits were as bad as their customers.

Their condition worsened as everyone else's did, and when they ran out of cocaine, they desperately searched for a fix, calling around to buy drugs for themselves. It got to a point where Babe didn't want to be with Josie. And since Josie knew how paranoid Babe was, she didn't bother Babe as much.

Curt talked about marriage and tried to convince Babe that it would work, but Babe was doubtful, knowing she didn't love him. Babe tried to convince herself that she could learn to love him. He purchased a ring, but they didn't set a date. There were too many things that needed to be resolved first. Babe was tired of his involvement with drugs and told him that their relationship would never work unless he left drugs alone. Curt was famous for staying out all night. One weekend, he didn't make it home at all, so Babe told him to pack up and leave. She had warned him repeatedly, but he ignored her pleas. She knew it wouldn't work, even though she tried to give him the benefit of the doubt.

Keeping Josie's children kept Babe aware of the needs and concerns about them, especially after a neighbor discovered Josie's six-year-old daughter roaming the neighborhood at 5:00 A.M., crying for her mother, who was not at home. Things were on the verge of a catastrophe, and Babe sensed it. But everyone ignored the warnings. Their sinful habits had blinded them. Their marriage was on the rock, and Josie was speaking death wishes.

Crying out to God became a practice of Babe's even though she didn't feel her place was in the church. She had always known from childhood experience that God listened to everyone that called on his name; she knew she could never turn her back on Josie if she ever needed her. Faithfully, Babe watched her children, taking them to their tutor since their grades were failing. They weren't to blame for a family gone wrong, knowing they weren't responsible.

Josie was still good as gold. Whenever she found a good deal, she kept Babe on her mind. In a conversation one day, Josie asked Babe if she wanted to sell her rent house. It hadn't occurred to Babe, but since there was an offer to be considered, Babe told her money talked and nonsense walked; meaning, it would have to be money only. Babe was aware that junkies sold off homes and anything else in exchange for heroin and cocaine to their dealer.

Babe felt she had to be specific. Since she already had it refinanced, it seemed to be a good way to get from under it.

Arrangements were made to meet at Babe's place in order to talk over the deal with people they knew. Malcolm called Babe up and told her she'd be crazy not to take three ounces of cocaine in exchange for her rented house. Babe was sure then that she would have to rely on them to sell it for her. That would leave room for many problems. Malcolm informed her that she could make three times as much profit.

"Forget it," Babe said.

Later, she agreed on a price for the buyer to assume, and they set a date for closing. Mixed feelings surfaced, and Babe regretted selling the house, especially since the buyer was associated with drugs also. But the fact that it was all legal made it hard to rule out. The tenant was notified that the house would be sold.

Josie and Malcolm couldn't wait to hear from Babe, hoping she would consider going in on a deal with them. Constantly, she reminded them that she didn't want that kind of business. Babe couldn't believe they were still denying that drugs were a waste of money, everything goes up in smoke and then your soul. She regretted that they were involved in drugs.

One day she searched the papers and noticed the apartment classified ads. There were so many nice ones near where she worked; she could rent her house easily since the interest rate was low. Babe thought maybe she was glad she hadn't been able to buy the house she really wanted. She placed an ad in the paper in hopes of renting her house.

Later that day, Babe told Josie what she had done. Josie said she felt like she was losing her only friend. Babe assured Josie that she could always count on her, no matter where she lived. But for the sake of her sanity and perseverance, she wanted and needed a change of location.

Prayers went forth every day that her house would rent fast so she could escape the influence she was under. Babe listed several different sources with no results; she became discouraged.

Although she was tired and scared of the involvement, still she found she had an irresistible urge to take advantage of the dope when she could. The fact that Babe had a clean record, and she didn't want to be caught up in anything illegal, made her reluctant to be involved with them.

Josie joked about her customers going to the rehabilitation center for help, but then coming right back to her again. Babe was hurt at how cold Josie had grown.

After dinner one evening, Malcolm began to joke about the crucifix Babe sported around her neck. He told her that she either had to be hot or cold or God would spit her out. Babe knew that was scriptural because she had heard it before. It didn't matter to her at that moment since she had never taken much time to understand half the scriptures in the Bible.

Babe responded to Malcolm, "I can still believe in God."

Josie started in on her, saying she could never go back to that way of living.

"But I don't want to be blind forever," Babe said.

And that started Babe to think just how lost they really were, and she was caught up in the middle of it all.

No one ever answered the classified ad to lease her house, so Baby just dealt with it. Josie still had a key to her place, so it wasn't unusual to find her at the house when Baby came home from work. Babe could tell she wasn't feeling well. This was the second bout with sickness Josie had experienced. The first resulted in a trip to the hospital because of a severe kidney infection.

Josie was famous for pushing herself in order to meet financial obligations. At times, she would work all night selling drugs. Babe felt relieved when she had found others to work with her rather than herself. Babe was more trouble to her than good. The sight of a police officer frightened her, and everything in the air seemed to be following them or, at least, that's what she thought. Josie had a sinus problem that wouldn't clear up because of the intake of cocaine she was using. There were other problems as well. Babe suggested she go to the hospital for a while, and she would keep the children until she was better. One doctor told her she needed surgery, but Josie refused to consider the thought of being hospitalized.

She continued to work around her physical problems.

Chapter 8

Family Ties

It wasn't normal for relatives from out of town to visit since the Johnsons weren't a close-knit family. When the news arrived, that Jonni was in town and staying with Uncle Will, all the girls decided to visit. Jonni had left Tulsa and relocated to Michigan over twenty years ago when her mother divorced Uncle Will. Uncle Will tended to be somewhat of a Casanova; he wasn't faithful in his first marriage, and after both families divorced, it was hard for the family to keep up with family ties. Uncle Will, who was Patrick's father, lived with his girlfriend. He had been married twice and was living together out of wedlock with a lady friend now.

Uncle Will's daughter, Jonni, and her husband had come from Muskegon, Michigan, to visit. Jonni and Josie were the closest cousins when they were growing up and had twin names. Jonni had married a preacher and had two children. When she learned her father was living in sin, she insisted that her husband officiate at his wedding. They arranged the private wedding in her father's home.

The evening of the wedding, Candi, Josie, and Babe loaded all the children and attended the wedding. It was small and private, but nice. Jonni didn't know what Josie's life was like, and it was like no one wanted to volunteer that kind of information.

Jonni was as beautiful as ever, with a certain glow about her. They all chatted about old times, and suddenly, Babe thought about Patrick, Uncle Will's son and Jonni's brother. When Babe mentioned him, Jonni had never heard about him and wanted to know more. Babe told her as much about him as she could; Patrick hadn't met everyone in the family.

Uncle Will walked out of the room while Babe was telling Jonni about Patrick, and Babe couldn't help but wonder if she had put her foot in her mouth. Before leaving, they all exchanged phone numbers and addresses in order to keep in touch.

Babe promised to send pictures of Patrick to Jonni.

Later that evening at home, Babe thought about how Uncle Will left the room when she started talking about Patrick, as if she had said the wrong thing because of how Uncle Will responded. But it seemed unfair for him to deny his fatherhood to Patrick.

A month later, Patrick was in town again. He knew Susan, a friend of Josie; he had her convey a message to Josie. Soon they had planned a get together at Babe's house for dinner. Patrick had not changed. His slim appearance indicated he hadn't slowed down. Patrick showed pictures of his son, who lived out of town with his girlfriend, who was somewhat connected to a celebrity singer. Patrick hadn't been married nor did he speak of getting married. Yet through the conversation, it was like Babe could detect a spirit of deception. She didn't care one way or the other, but she began to wonder what he was trying to hide.

Babe's main concern was that Patrick meets his sister, whom he'd never met. While they sat talking, Babe dialed Jonni's number, and Patrick and Jonni talked for a good thirty minutes. Babe felt such joy in having connected them together. They exchanged addresses and promised to keep in touch.

When Jonni and Patrick finally met over the phone, Babe felt a sense of joy since they had never met. Patrick disappeared afterward; he was too busy to keep in touch, and after Babe saw that Patrick was into cocaine like Josie and Malcolm, she knew it wouldn't be worth it to keep in touch.

Josie's condition worsened. Her sinus ailment never cleared up, and she was hit with the pressure of Malcolm's decision to quit his job. Malcolm's continuous use of drugs was seriously affecting his lifestyle.

With Josie's health failing and Malcolm going off on deep end, danger was in the air.

One Sunday evening, Josie wasn't feeling her best, and she called Babe over to deliver a package to Joyce. When Babe returned, Josie was still suffering from a sinus infection. Malcolm drove up, complaining about everything. Josie was so fed up with the whole mess; she suggested that she consume the whole bottle of valium tablets sitting on the kitchen table.

That Monday Babe grew weary about Josie's condition and was sick of everything she was going through. She called in to report her absence at work, hoping she could somehow convince Josie to check on her health and to leave the drug scene to Malcolm if he insists on doing it. Instead of accepting any of Babe's advice, Josie lured her into running errands again.

Joyce stopped by and left a few goods in exchange for drugs. Joyce's habit was indeed bad. She was using the needle, which was more addictive. Joyce was leaving and Babe was returning, and their conversation ended as though Joyce was coming back later.

Since the kids had missed sessions with the tutor, Josie suggested Babe pick them up from school and take them to the tutor. On the way there, Babe's car was giving her problems. She called Papa at the tutor's home. After failing to reach him, Babe called Josie to come and pick them up. Because of the commotion, they weren't able to make the tutor session. Babe left her car at the tutors, and they went to Josie's house. Again, Babe tried to talk with Josie, but company was present; it was not the right time to talk to Josie. Josie told Babe to take her new car since her car was still stranded at the tutor's. Babe had been off work for two days and would need a car to get there.

At home that evening, Babe located her papa and asked him to check on her car. He said he would later on that week. While stretched out on the couch that night, Babe lay staring at the ceiling, thinking about Josie and all she was going through. Babe knew she was tired of trying to keep her family together. She was breaking laws, getting further from the truth, but she was still holding on.

How Strong She Must Be, Babe thought.

"God, I wish I was that strong," Babe prayed, hoping God would hear her and know her heart because she really felt lost for words. Babe feared the sin she was in had separated her from God.

It was two in the morning, and the ringing of the phone awakened Babe; it was Mother, and Babe could barely understand Mother, for her crying. Josie had been rushed to the hospital by Life Flight. Mother was mumbling through her sobs. Someone had badly beaten Josie. Mother needed Babe to pick her up and take her to the hospital. Quickly, Babe dressed and was thankful to have Josie's car. The roads were empty, without a single car to hold up traffic. As Babe sped across town to the hospital, she thought of Malcolm and how they had been arguing; she prayed he hadn't done anything foolish.

Mother and Babe arrived at the hospital. Papa and Candi were already there. They sat in the private waiting room where the doctor met them and told them Josie's condition was critical. They needed to begin surgery right away. Since Malcolm was at the police station for questioning, Mother signed the release for the surgery.

Before the doctor left, he asked if anyone wanted to see Josie before they took her to surgery.

Babe stepped forward, softly speaking, "I do."

Her head was bandaged, and the nurse explained that a part of her skull was broken, and vital parts of the brain were exposed. They gave her a 20-percent chance to survive, and if she did live, she would be a vegetable. Babe leaned over and gave Josie a kiss before they rolled her off for surgery. Babe could hardly believe that only a few hours earlier, she was talking to Josie.

Many family members were at the hospital; Babe decided to go on to work. She had already been off two days, and the thought of waiting would only frustrate her. Her best remedy was to always stay busy after an upsetting experience.

Babe went directly to work and arrived early. Since she was the first person there, she had plenty of time to cry to God. Her memory flashed back to what Josie had said last Christmas. "There's usually a death soon after a family comes together."

"Dear God," she prayed, "please, not Josie."

Tears ran down Babe's cheeks. No matter how hard she tried to hold them, she had a strange feeling that this was the end for Josie. The only one who could help her was God. Inwardly, Babe pleaded for God's mercy and grace to spare her life, hoping he would turn it around for good.

A coworker came in and asked Babe how she was feeling, somewhat shocked to look into the coworker's face because Babe's face was swollen, and tear stained. Babe knew it would be difficult to share the story.

After she explained what had happened, the coworker patted her shoulder and said she would explain to the supervisor so she wouldn't have to repeat the details. Babe thanked her. Early that morning, they called her from the hospital. The surgery was completed, but Josie's blood pressure had dropped. She started hemorrhaging while in surgery. Suddenly, Babe realized it was better to pray for God to have mercy on her soul more than anything. Babe's mother wanted her there with the rest of the family. Babe told her supervisor how critical the situation was and that she needed to return to the hospital.

All the family was at the hospital; the three brothers out of town were notified and were due to arrive any day now.

At the hospital, everyone was huddled together or was pacing the floor. Josie was placed on a life-support system and wasn't expected to live long. Babe didn't know what kind of support they expected from her; she was barely holding on herself.

Babe's mother told her that the doctors thought they had lost her on the operating table. Mother cried in Babe's arms.

"If she's still unconscious in seventy-two hours, Malcolm has the right to disconnect her from the life-support system and sign the death certificate."

After several hours, they allowed the family to see Josie in intensive care. Her unconscious body lay there, stiff and bandaged. They had cut all her hair off for the surgery, and her body was swollen and covered with dark bruises. She looked nothing like herself.

As Babe left the room, she thought of Josie's three children. Everyone left knowing there was nothing they could do but wait and pray. Babe didn't want to go home; she felt uncomfortable there. It was as if her papa could tell, so he stepped over and asked her to follow them home, and they could check on her car the next day. Her papa invited her to pack a few things and stay with them until the end of the week. Babe had never spent much time with her father and stepmother, but now they spent the evenings talking about Josie. They had not been aware of Josie's involvement with drugs.

Thursday, Babe went to work and had lunch with Cherry, who was a born-again believer. Babe told Cherry about their involvement with drugs. Cherry and Babe had known each other since they were kids. When Babe asked Cherry if she thought maybe, she was reaping what she had sown because she killed the rapist, Cherry explained that her sister was dealing with Satan in the involvement with drugs and that Satan came to kill, steal, and destroy her life.

"Sometimes, if we are not walking with the Lord, he will allow things to happen because we've rejected him," Cherry said.

Cherry told Babe to go to the hospital and speak to Josie as though she were alive and command her to live in the name of Jesus, praying that she would be a living testimony. Babe thought about how Malcolm and Josie chastised her about wearing her cross, as Babe recalled Josie's refusal to seek God's way anymore.

Lunch was a blessing even though Babe couldn't eat. Cherry's counsel was a great help. At work, Babe continued to stay busy and prayed at the same time that God would let Josie live to become a living testimony.

"I'll help her to go the right way, Lord, please have mercy on her soul at least." The thought of going to the hospital and speaking to Josie scared the wits out of Babe. Babe never thought she had a scared streak in her until it came to this.

After work, Babe headed straight to her dad's house, hoping they would see Josie later, then she could pray for Josie the way Cherry instructed her. But she found out her father was checking on her car and didn't come home until late, so they never made it to the hospital.

Finally, two brothers from Dallas made it in, then the other one came from Los Angeles. The seventy-two hours on the life-support system had elapsed, and Malcolm had the legal right to have the system disconnected. They wanted to hold on, but hope was dim.

On Friday, November 22, 1985, at 9:00 P.M., the assisting nurse prayed a prayer of salvation before disconnecting Josie from the life-support system and pronounced Josie legally dead. The immediate family included all of Josie's sisters and brothers and parents and Malcolm; his family preferred not to enter, yet everyone wept frantically when they realized that Josie had been disconnected from the life-support system and there was life no more in her. It was two days before Josie's thirty-fifth birthday.

Malcolm came out of the room, weeping, and reached for Babe, but she couldn't comfort him; she was bitter because he had started all this mess with drugs, which brought danger into his home.

Babe gently pushed Malcolm away to avoid a confrontation and leaned against the wall, weeping. One by one, family members came out of the ICU.

Malcolm couldn't handle plans for the burial, so his mother did it for him. A small graveside service would be held the following Tuesday.

Back at Pappa's, they discussed Josie's death further. The last they had heard; a man went to purchase some drugs. This man had been told that he was not welcome there because of the way he conducted himself, but Josie let him in. That's when he brutally beat her with a tire tool and escaped with drugs and money.

It seemed strange that Josie would even allow him in her house. Malcolm suspected that someone else was with the junkie, who was an accomplice. Malcolm was the one who found her when he came in late that night. He had another friend with him.

Saturday, Babe returned Malcolm's car and saw the children. Malcolm's mother was keeping them. The children's minds were shattered with confusion. Josie's little girl ran into Babe's arms, crying that she wanted her mother. The night of the murder, they saw their mother lying in a pool of blood, with part of her head and skull crushed. The memory was still vivid as she asked if her mother's head hurt.

After making sure the kids were alright, Babe talked with Malcolm's mother.

"I'm ready to go to church now, one that would be right for me."

"That's good," she said.

Babe embraced the kids before she left and told them how to get hold of her if they ever needed anything. They all cried and hugged one another before leaving.

Sunday would have been Josie's birthday. Since Malcolm's family didn't acknowledge special dates like that, the family didn't even remember. But all Babe could think of was how sad it was to die before your birthday and not know whether you will be going to heaven.

The loss of an immediate family member allowed an employee automatically three days off at work. Babe thanked God because it was a difficult experience she was facing. Josie's death was affecting her worse than people realized; she thought it should've been her in that grave. Josie had everything to live for—a family and a husband—then Babe realized maybe she didn't have all those things to live for, especially if it continued the same way. Something else would have happened. Babe still felt that Josie should've lived long enough to see her children grow up and have grandchildren. It seemed like Babe wouldn't have missed any of that since she didn't have any children.

Malcolm's mother made all the funeral arrangements, and Babe prepared the obituary for print. The week after the burial was Thanksgiving. Since the family was still in town, Babe's mother asked her to prepare Thanksgiving dinner. Babe dreaded preparing a big family dinner; she couldn't find much to be thankful for. But within a couple of days, she realized she couldn't continue to be sorrowful, so she agreed to prepare dinner.

Everyone knew that Josie was the expert cook in the family and Babe was only her helper. Yet the dinner was so good everyone was sure that Josie had passed on her cooking abilities to Babe. Malcolm brought the kids over. To see them break their tradition to join the family that day made it all worthwhile.

Going back to work helped Babe put the past behind her. It was no secret how her sister died, and her coworkers were comforting with words of encouragement and love. Babe used to call Josie every morning at work to wake her up; that was a habit that was hard to break, and she caught herself dialing the number only to hear it repeatedly ring.

Babe found it difficult to stay in her own house. A second attempt was made to lease it. James, her oldest brother from California, was staying a while longer than the other brothers since his job wasn't as pressing. James stayed with Babe, and she thought it would work out fine if James decided to stay on, but

James didn't want to work while he stayed; he just wanted to run around with his old high school buddies.

When Babe and her mother realized that James wasn't going to seek out a job while he stayed, they decided to chip in on his airfare since that was another reason why he hadn't left.

Finally, Babe's prayers were answered when a young lady answered her ad to rent her house. Babe had moved some of her clothes over her mother's and stayed with her when she didn't feel like staying there.

Now that Babe was going to lease her house out, she decided to stay with her mother until she found an apartment out south. Every night, Babe wondered about the children, wondering if Malcolm could take care of them. He was still involved in drugs and needed to get his life straightened out.

Babe thought about Josie's request before she died, about keeping her children if anything ever happened to her. All she could think of was to commit to what she told Josie. The thought of raising three kids left Babe worried and concerned. Babe called Malcolm's mother and told her she would be glad to keep the two smallest children as soon as she found an apartment big enough and she could keep the oldest since he stayed with them most of the time anyway. She thanked Babe and said if Malcolm approved of it, she would consider it.

Malcolm must've thought the invitation was for all of them; he called Babe and asked her if he could stay with her since he felt uncomfortable staying at his home after what happened to Josie.

It was the only way she could prove to Josie she wanted to help. Malcolm was making it mighty difficult. Without hesitation, Babe refused Malcolm's offer since she knew he was still involved in drugs and the very fact that he was a brother-in-law made her uncomfortable. Babe hadn't even known that Markie was missing assume dead, after talking to Malcolm about keeping the children, he never told Babe anything it was mother that told Babe about Markie, Mother said that the policemen said it was too deep to deal with all the circumstances behind Markie's disappearance, yet Malcolm never said one word about it. Babe was so upset to hear that.

New Year's Eve was a quiet moment spent listening to fireworks from a bedroom window and sipping a glass of wine. It was a time of peace and New Year's resolution. As Babe fought the urge for drugs, sympathetically, she cried that the craving would leave.

"God, deliver me," she moaned, as she restricted herself to solitary confinement. The fact that she wasn't around the environment made the most difference. It didn't take long before the urge to do drugs disappeared, and the people that did drugs were never around.

Malcolm got back with Babe, letting her know he didn't want to separate his children, so his mother ended up with them. Babe knew it was a blessing that he didn't want them separated. It would have been more than a notion raising two kids already set in their ways.

A day didn't go by that Babe would not think about them, crying out to God that he would shield them with his love and protect them with his peace.

After the New Year, Babe remembered she had agreed to go to church. Staying with Mother was the best thing she could have done. Her mother was a great inspiration in directing her to church as well. Babe didn't want to attend her mother's church, but she was open to her mother's suggestion about a new church on the south side. This church on the south side was growing by leaps and bounds. Babe thought the least she could do was try it out.

The second Sunday in January, they made it to an evening service. It was different, and Babe could tell. It was nondenominational, with a mixture of races. From the very beginning, Babe was intrigued. She had heard that variety was a spice of life, and the variety there was beautiful.

The songs sung brought tears to her eyes. The congregation stood up for about an hour, praising God. That took some getting used to. People were singing and dancing. The music was upbeat, with a soulful expression. After singing the praise songs, the congregation was invited to shake someone's hand or hug them. Babe withdrew, hoping no one would discover her, but several people embraced her with hugs and handshakes until it didn't matter that she touched them. It seemed to relieve her of past hurts.

The sermon was about being obedient to God. What the preacher said seemed real and made sense. After preaching, he asked if anyone needed the strength to be obedient, and if so, to raise a hand. At that time, Babe thought, *what is it like to be obedient? Was it really what I Wanted?*

Before she knew anything, she felt an urgency to thank God for all she had lived through, and if it was time to be obedient, she wanted that for her life now.

Still a little reluctant, she slightly raised her hand, hoping no one would see her. Then the minister asked those who raised their hands to please come to the altar. Babe knew she had to go or become a liar. Hesitantly, she sat there deciding whether to go or not. The scripture said if you're ashamed of Jesus before men, he'll be ashamed of you before the father. The words were so loud in her thoughts that she jumped up and told her mother that she had to go.

Babe's mother knew she was scared; she stood also to follow behind her. At the altar, a feeling of peace covered the area as the preacher prayed for those standing and for others that needed prayer.

Upon returning to their seats, they were asked to hug someone before leaving. Mother and daughter both embraced and repeated a phrase from the song:

"I have a feeling everything's going to be alright."

Chapter 9

Being a Living Testimony

After a couple of visits at church, Babe felt a need to rejoice in the Lord over the new directions her life had taken. Finding a good church made a difference; the little church Mary told her about didn't compare to the one she was attending now.

Babe knew she would be moving out south as soon as she found an apartment, and a church in the same area would be more convenient.

Babe felt good about church and wanted to get her entire life on the right track. She placed another ad in the paper, and pronto, a tenant came to her rescue. Immediately, the tenant wanted to move in. She was on the government-housing program with two daughters. After all the preliminaries were handled Babe had to downsize because she was moving into a smaller apartment again, and she knew all too well that she would have to get rid of some of the things she had. What Babe couldn't sell, she got rid of by either donating or giving to someone in need.

Since Babe didn't want to be rushed, she decided to store her things in storage until she found an apartment comfortable to her needs. That way, Babe could stay with her mother while sorting through her decisions.

Mother stayed in the same neighborhood, and some of the neighbors were still there. Glenda, one of Babe's best buddies had lost contact, but she ended up doing time in jail for some kind of vandalism at her job. Babe had heard about it but didn't know the details. Then several years after she got out of jail, she had a heart attack and died, at the age of forty-three. Babe was devastated after hearing about Glenda's death since they were really close back in the days. Glenda's mother had already died, and it must have taken a toll on Glenda as well.

Babe knew that she had to search for an apartment. As she began looking in the area where she worked, she remembered the apartments directly across the street from the church. They were newly built and had a taste of elegance and luxury, but that always added up to expensive, so Babe decided not to even check them out. There were several apartments near her job, but Babe was undecided as to where to move.

One evening after work, Babe decided to check out some apartments. A couple of miles down the street were some apartments called the Lounge. They seemed to be older because they had been there awhile. They gave Babe a tour of a model apartment that had a den with a bedroom. It was nice, and Babe appreciated the extra room. She was preparing to give a deposit to hold the apartment when she decided to check out the one across the street since neither had a washer and dryer.

Babe asked a receptionist where she could find an apartment in the same area with a washer and dryer or the necessary hookups. The receptionist described two different apartments, one Babe could remember because it was named after a street, and she drove to it first. When she looked at the apartments, they were nice and had everything a person needed, but they were quite expensive. Babe knew the place was too high for her.

It was getting late, and Babe couldn't remember the name of the other apartment the receptionist had told her about, so she asked the receptionist at these apartments for the apartments in the area that would have a washer and dryer. When the lady mentioned Creekwood, it rang a bell, and Babe remembered it was the name of the other apartments. Quickly, she left to find Creekwood Apartments before they closed, and according to the directions she took, she was directly across the street from the church she had been attending.

Babe remembered how she shunned the thought of moving across the street because they seemed expensive, but actually Babe was surprised to discover that these apartments were only five dollars more than what the ones with the den. It had a built-in microwave, fireplace, and washer and dryer, not to mention the Creekwood Apartments had a Jacuzzi and workout room. It was a total shock to realize there was only a five-dollar difference.

Her mind was made up, and to think that maybe God had something to do with it all made Babe even more excited. Anxious to share the news with her mother, Babe rushed home to start packing as well. Payday was that Friday, and it was planned that Babe would move then. Babe's mother was glad that she found a place to move into; she was happy if Babe was happy.

After Babe got moved in, she noticed how convenient it was to attend church more regularly, and she actually enjoyed it. She eventually joined the church.

Even though she found herself wanting to find another outlet, it seemed like the church was the only door that opened.

The church services were great, but Babe wanted to keep a distance and avoid the holier-than-thou attitudes. Since it seemed like her life was back on an even keel, now seemed like the best time to begin considering outside activities.

Working part time was always a good resource for Babe; she began to apply at several department stores without any success.

Yet a desire to know God was stronger now than before. Going to church really settled Babe's spirit, and she looked forward to Sunday morning and evening service.

Staying across the street from the church led to more regular visits. The excitement at the church was that the minister was single and still young enough to arouse most of the single women that attended the church, not to mention there was an abundance of fellowship. It wasn't long before Babe began meeting friends and volunteering for other areas of the church. She felt her worries were behind her, and she had God to thank. She slept better just knowing her sister's children were in responsible hands. Their grandparents were Jehovah's Witnesses. But Babe figured it was something good in every faith, and she felt there was something to learn in every denomination. As long as she continued to pray for God's direction in their lives, she knew he would be faithful in caring for them.

Life's destiny began to change for Babe as she slowly opened up to God's better plan for her. Going to church wasn't as bad as she had expected and finding an area to volunteer in church gave Babe something to do.

The thought of serving God wasn't quite a reality until one morning, about 3:00 A.M. While Babe slept, an audible voice awakened her. The voice gently and clearly said, "You will be my living testimony."

Babe was alarmed at what it could have been. Then she remembered the prayer her friend suggested she pray for Josie—that she be a living testimony. Babe sat in bed, trying to figure it out, wondering if it could have been God while half hoping that it wasn't God because she didn't know what she could ever do for him when she was feeling inadequate.

A week went by, and Babe was afraid to tell anyone about her experience for fear they would think she was cracking up.

One day at work, Babe was walking with a friend during their lunch hour, and Babe decided to share her experience. Betty laughed and said, "That only happens to movie stars."

Since the idea of preaching didn't quite turn Babe on, Babe was relieved when she said that, now hoping she could convince herself the same.

Only a couple of days later, Babe was sitting up in bed early in the morning, about to get ready for work. Without a thought on her mind, again she heard an audible voice say, "They need to know!"

Babe's eyes lit up with astonishment, and her heart rejoiced with laughter to know that God had actually spoken to her. Babe truly knew that she knew God had chosen her.

At work, she couldn't restrain the joy from bubbling over, and her relationship with God began to take on a new meaning. Babe was the first employee at work, so when the others came in, they stopped by her office. Janice came by and asked how she was doing. Excitedly, Babe bounced up and down in her chair and clapped her hands.

"I'm going to work for God," Babe told her.

"If you're not careful, you're going to the funny farm," she answered with a smile on her face and moved on. Joyfully, she sat thinking, *God actually spoke to her.*

Janice and Betty liked the new change in Babe. In the days to come, Babe realized the thrill of hearing God's voice was behind her if she didn't know what God wanted her to do. Babe realized that she didn't know herself what to tell people about God. She had always believed in her own way, and that was enough for her, yet the Word of God states that even devils believe and tremble. To think that Babe was just as bad as the devil if she didn't do what the Bible said, that left her wondering how many more blind people the devil was tricking. It seemed like the short time Babe had been in church rekindled things she had learned, especially when scriptures came to her mind fast enough to answer her thoughts. Scriptures from the Bible began to convince Babe like never before.

"Harden not your heart when you hear the word of God."

Doubting thoughts occurred as she struggled with what she should do. It seemed that either way, Babe was doomed, knowing how much she feared God. Thinking back, when God pulled her through countless trials, regardless of her fears, she knew she couldn't betray him now.

Once again, God's Word reminded her that not only was God a god to be feared, but he was a god of love, and through God, you can do all things, for it's he who strengthens you.

According to the world standard, Babe didn't consider herself a super-bright person, just someone that worked hard and enjoyed being around people. She thought back to the special-education class she attended in elementary school, and how even now, the college courses overwhelmed her at times. But the Bible seemed to be a book of a different story; she was really interested in biblical history and how the love of God was shed abroad. Even though she considered herself slothful at times, she could already tell God's power was doing a work for her. God would also have to strengthen her because of some habits she wasn't quite sure she wanted to give up. The fear of being single for the rest of her life scared her. Babe had heard about some holier-than-thou lifestyles, and it all seemed like a bunch of bondage. She didn't want to be a hypocrite, preaching one thing and doing another, so she asked God to help her to do his will.

This church was one of a kind. The pastor was single, and a lot of single women attended there for that reason only. Many felt that the pastor would be their husband. It appeared a spirit of deception was at the church because they had heard a voice indicating that they would marry the pastor. Frankly, Babe didn't see anything special about him other than the fact that he was funny at times and preached a good sermon. She knew the women were drawn to him by his money and status, and he got the money from them, so that didn't prove anything. But as Babe thought about these things, she heard a voice say, "You can have him."

Babe wasn't sure that she even wanted him as a husband until she started to wonder if this was God's will for her to marry a preacher. Knowing that time would tell, she decided to carry on with the things of God until everything came together.

Everyone at church seemed to be living a somewhat straight life. Some Babe had met prior to church life, and she knew they were nothing but stiff necks. Others had been in church for so long, it was nothing more than religion to them instead of a relationship with God. Babe felt free from sin, delivered from herself and ready to win souls for the kingdom.

At church, they started on this testimony stuff. It was hard to believe what some people would share; they shared everything God had ever done for them.

One girl shared that she had been raped and was haunted by the rapist repeatedly until authorities finally caught him. The agonizing trial resulted in a forty-year sentence for the rapist. How courageous of her to share that before a large crowd. Babe felt the eyes of the people on her and wondered if God would ever want her to share her past. As she sat quietly, an impression in her spirit spoke and said, "The lost sheep."

Babe had already met people at the church that used to work in the nightclub with her, and she figured, with the help of Melody, the Word about her past had already hit the surface. Melody was also in the drug scene when Malcolm and Josie were circulating it. Of course, Melody had worked with Babe in the nightclubs, and she knew that Babe was quiet-spoken and reserved, not involved in anything rowdy or anything to promote trouble.

It was later found out that Malcolm and Melody got together after Josie's death and became a couple. Maybe that's why Melody didn't continue her fellowship at the church. It seemed that people could identify Babe wherever she went.

One weekday at church, Babe listened to the pastor as he looked directly at her, stating that they prayed for some people to come to that church. Babe thought perhaps, he meant after the rape and the justifiable homicide prayers were sent forth for her. *Amazing,* she thought, because she never let the situation get her down, and all the prayers that went forth to God on her behalf made her very thankful.

Suddenly, Babe realized the reason why the people prayed was because God prompted them to, and he would ultimately receive all the glory.

Six months after Josie died, Jonni was murdered by a man who said God told him to kill her. The news was devastating, and Babe couldn't understand since Jonni was living a Godly life, but the scriptures comforted Babe as she read, "Where it will reign on the just and the unjust." Babe wondered if Josie needed a guide to show her the light, and since Jonni died in Christ, she might have had to help Josie.

Reservation and fear rose within Babe as she thought back on what her past was like, knowing there were some things that would be hard to understand about her. She found it near impossible to share it all.

At work, she found herself crying in private as the old her died in order that the will of God could be done in her life. Babe not only believed for the sake of believing; she knew there was a love for God within that she never knew how to express.

"Oh, God, thank you for saving me." All this time, Babe never truly knew how much God loved her because she was too busy trying to do it her way.

After work one evening, in her apartment clubhouse, Babe was relaxing in the spa where she met a young girl in the sauna. Babe felt led to witness to her about Jesus. She told Babe that her brother, who was only thirteen, had spoken in tongues. Babe explained that the people in her church spoke in other tongues also, but she hadn't yet.

"It's in the Bible, so I believe it's of God when it's done properly."

She listened as Babe shared her faith in God, then she expressed how she dreamed of being married to her boyfriend, whom she lived with. Babe advised her to go to college and stay in church, and God would direct her life if she let him. They went their separate ways, and that audible voice within her spoke, "Fishers of men."

The spirit of God reminded her again of his commission to everyone.

At church they talked about fasting a lot. The pastor had fasted thirty days for his thirtieth birthday, consuming nothing but fruit juices. He said the Holy Spirit spoke to him clearly, and as time went on, the spiritual gifts manifested within his life. It all sounded exciting, and Babe wanted to fast, but it seemed hard enough just to diet.

One day, Babe had her mind made up and decided to fast. All day, Babe meditated on God's Word, and when she got home that evening, she snacked on popcorn and soda pop and prayed to God that his will be done in her life, and then she read the Bible all evening.

The next day after praying, Babe glanced at herself in the bathroom mirror and directed a statement to God. "How I'd love to hear from you, God, just a word of encouragement."

Within her heart, she heard a voice speak, "Faith,"

Surprised, Babe's eyes sparkled, and she asked, "Is that you, God?"

He didn't say a word, but somehow, she knew before the day was over, she would get a confirmation.

At work, Babe kept a daily word book on her desk. Upon arrival at work, she flipped open the book to the current day. To her surprise, the topic was *faith*, and the scripture was Luke 1:37: "Have faith in God." Babe praised God and couldn't wait to share with others her experience. They all thought she was funny, so this was just another cute joke to them.

After sharing her experience with one coworker, Babe joked that since God had answered her so fast, next she would ask him where the pot of gold at the end of the rainbow was. Her friends went on her way. Although Babe never asked about the gold, it was still on her mind. As clear as a doorbell, the voice within her spoke, "It's in your heart." With childlike joy, she ran over to tell her friends that the pot of gold at the end of the rainbow was in your heart. Now Babe knew there was something more to fasting.

Fasting became a part of her life. The pounds she had always wanted to lose began to fade away as a result of fasting in addition to spiritual gain, which strengthened her confidence and belief. All the farfetched stories she had heard about in ministries and read in the Bible were not only reality, but that power was still in the authority of believers today. The fact that Satan, the god of the world, has everyone blind by the power of darkness, and people weren't trusting God.

Babe's worries of ever marrying faded as her love for God grew more. She knew that she was married to God, and nothing could separate her from his love.

After fasting for three days, Babe found herself testifying before a small group at a Friday-night prayer meeting. She thanked God for strengthening her to make such a sacrifice. Babe recalled struggling with how difficult it all seemed to deny herself of things that would only result in worldly gain. As she worried about such things, she began to realize that she made it hard herself simply because of her own negative confessions. That revelation made sense, knowing that a person can make the best or worst of a situation; it's all according to that individual, and most of her problems came from listening to Satan-negative thoughts.

Services at church were on Wednesday and Friday night all day Sunday. Eventually, the church took priority over everything. A hunger for God's Word overtook her in her venture to do God's will.

Friday-night service was worth waiting for. At church, a woman of God ministered in a powerful way, operating in various spiritual gifts. The word of knowledge was spoken by

God through her. As she ministered one night, she revealed information regarding a woman's concern about having a child. Her statement quickened Babe's memory of the doctors that diagnosed her condition. Their prediction was that it would take a miracle before she gave birth. That word convinced Babe, but she didn't care about having children at this point; she knew that she couldn't play around in the Lord's house, and it was more of a warning than anything. If it was God's will for her to be a mother, she figured she would leave it to the Highest God.

Witnessing to others required boldness that Babe prayed for daily but working in a secular environment brought about discouragement that Babe battled often. Consecration to God allowed her to hear the spirit of God better.

As she sat on her living room couch in a state of melancholy, God's spirit spoke, "Joshua." Babe remembered that name was in the Bible; she reached for the Bible and began to read the book of Joshua.

The first chapter of Joshua was a good start; Babe read down and stopped. "Be strong and of good courage: Be not afraid, neither be thou dismayed: For the Lord thy God is with thee wherever thou goest." After reading the verse Babe felt uplifted and encouraged in the Lord. God's Word had strengthened her.

Understanding of God's Word was illuminated. As Babe began to grow in grace, she realized how omnipotent God and his

Word were; it was clearly understood that the Word was living and active and sharper than any two-edged sword. It penetrates even to divide soul and spirit, joints and marrow; it judges the thought and attitudes of the heart.

Messages from the pulpit had Babe seeking God for involvement. One Sunday, the pastor's message said that everyone must be doers and not only hearers of the Word.

Thoughts ran rapidly over the things she knew she couldn't do for God. But then an audible thought clearly said, "Prison ministry."

Prison Ministry? Babe thought. That's the last place she wanted to go, and then she remembered the audible voice that spoke, "Lost sheep," and she understood what it meant.

It would be difficult to deny when you know God has directed you and even if it wasn't what Babe wanted but doing the will of God mattered. Babe prayed for God's strength and direction, and she wondered how she could find out more about prison ministry.

Another Sunday went by, and the pastor mentioned different ministries in his sermon when he mentioned prison ministry. Babe listened closely. He gave no details; another closed case she felt.

At work Babe placed herself around committed Christians; one girl named Carol informed her of outside activities to take part in. A retreat was all new to Babe, but it sounded like fun. A group of women got together for a women's retreat at McAlester, Oklahoma. They gathered after work and carpooled, driving down Friday evening just in time for the last meeting.

After the meeting, they met in a hotel room where they discussed everything. Everyone had their prayer language but Babe. Babe didn't worry about it because it seemed like some were gifted with it, and she didn't want to make it seem complex. It took all the fun out of serving God when people would press you since it didn't make much sense to her. Everyone insisted on praying that Babe would receive the gift of tongues. As they prayed, she listened and wondered what to expect. Babe finally got tired and told them she was ready for bed. It was late, and everyone agreed that this was okay with them.

The next day, they had breakfast together before meeting for the workshop they attended. The workshop was good therapy; they learned to release what was on their mind. After the workshop, Babe wanted a break from the hard seats and a time to refresh on her own. She'd planned to skip the afternoon service.

While everyone prepared to leave, Babe had already discovered a sauna in the hotel to relax in. The sauna wasn't very warm, but she didn't care; she just wanted a place to escape to.

Patiently, she waited, hoping the sauna would warm up. A woman walked in and introduced herself. "Hello, my name is

Brenda Penn, I'm here with my husband for the prison ministry convention."

Now it was the third time the prison ministry had been mentioned, and Babe's reaction was somewhat startled. She asked, "How can I learn more about prison ministry? I feel that God is trying to direct me, but I don't know where to start."

Brenda informed Babe that her husband was the director for the Oklahoma County Prison Ministry. She suggested putting Babe on the mailing list to receive a monthly bulletin, announcing Bible studies and committee meetings at various prisons in Oklahoma County.

Babe shared with Brenda about her sister's death. Then Brenda told her about a prisoner who was led to Christ by a family member of the person he had murdered.

Babe's thoughts centered on the guy that killed her sister. He hadn't been arrested yet because he had left town, but charges were filed. There wasn't any remorse in Babe's heart for him, knowing that vengeance belonged to the Lord. Nor did it seem necessary to consider leading him to Christ whenever they caught up with him.

Upon leaving the sauna, Babe couldn't help but think of how God had tied everything together. She knew prison ministry was the ministry he wanted her in.

When the girls came back from the workshop, Babe told them about what happened, and they were astounded. They all left early Sunday just in time to arrive back in Tulsa and attend their own church service.

That evening at church, Babe inquired about prison ministry with an usher. He said he had been involved in it but was now enrolled in Bible college and hadn't the time. A lady nearby overheard and interrupted them. She explained that she had been active for ten years. She had a display of booklets, which she published and distributed in the prisons. Each booklet had her picture and her address on the back. She gave Babe a few booklets and prayed with her, and as they went their separate ways, her acquaintance left Babe wondering if she could write a book since her life was full of testimonies.

Another confirmation was just what she needed. Babe saw the assistant pastor's wife and decided to inquire with her. She informed her that the church supported outside prison ministries. She gave Babe the name and number of one of them.

On the way home, Babe recalled that the church bulletin announced a midnight ministry at a local nightclub. She was curious to know what could be going on at a nightclub since Babe was familiar with the clubs.

At the club the functions didn't begin until midnight, but Babe arrived early enough to meet the girl who had been raped and shared her testimony before the congregation. Babe introduced herself and complimented her for her bravery in sharing her testimony. She worked at the club but also had a desire to work in prisons. Babe explained her interest in prison ministry. Carol introduced her to the manager of the club, who also attended the same church. Her manager was involved in a prison ministry workshop. Babe was astounded at the connections. She practically told them her life history, and they were both shocked at what she had told them.

Around midnight, the band from the church set up, and the group started to play. Babe observed the customers leave while others stayed to hear the Gospel and the testimonies. Church members flooded the club in order to support one another. The Gospel songs stirred everyone's spirit with joy and prepared them to hear the testimony of a young man who had been involved in drugs, selling and using them. His crime caught up with him, and he was sentenced to serve twenty years in prison. His family prayed for him out of prison in three years. Now he's active in a prison ministry himself. Before it was over, Babe had met nearly everyone there.

It wasn't long before she was attending a workshop and orientation on prison ministry. Babe heard about a group that was preparing to go into a correction center for a prison invasion, which would last a whole weekend. It was her first opportunity to experience prison ministry, and she was excited to know she was in the will of God.

In the prison, she met different people and shared Jesus with them. Some received Jesus and others doubted. Babe shared with as many people as she could, realizing that the more she decreased, the more God would increase in her. Opportunities to volunteer in the prisons were infrequent, but Babe soon looked forward to more visits. She received a monthly schedule of committee meetings and Bible studies throughout the Oklahoma County prisons. A couple Babe met through another prison ministry asked her if she would join them in their ministry from time to time.

Nine months had passed since Josie was murdered. Mother had already claimed that they would capture the murderer and justice would be done. Babe never thought much about it, knowing that God would take care of it one way or another. While reading the paper one morning, Babe read that the guy had been located in Arizona and was arrested and was on his way to Tulsa, where he would be tried. Babe immediately called her mother to inform her of the news. She had just finished talking with the detective and already knew. Mother was sure this guy would be caught, and it came to pass.

With the guy accused of killing Josie caught, Babe thought back to what Brenda had told her about a family member leading the accuser to Christ.

At work, Babe found herself pondering on the thought of witnessing to this prisoner. She knew that she had no hard feelings toward him but didn't think it was necessary to confront him directly. She searched for the answer, knowing that God would direct her. Babe prayed to God for directions, and quietly, she listened as that still small voice spoke, "You must do what's right."

Babe had been in church long enough to know what was right. God's Word said that it's not his will that anyone perishes, and he that wins a soul is wise. After realizing how effective this man could be if he stood up for Jesus in prison, the idea of witnessing to him began to make more sense. If he turned his life over to Christ, he would be able to minister in prison.

When he arrived at the county jail, Babe wrote to him. After writing several letters without receiving a response, Babe continued to write out of obedience to God, hoping that God would turn his life around and that he would experience the love of God.

Babe knew he received her letters since they didn't come back to her. She trusted God that he would read them. The man's name was Billy Jones. Babe vaguely remembered Curt having an associate by that name, so she located Curt and questioned him. Curt said that he didn't seem like the type who would do anything like that.

Billy stayed in the county jail for at least six months before his trial. Babe wrote to him at least once a month to let him know she was praying for him.

One day at work, in the mail room, Babe was talking with an employee, and she informed Babe that Billy Jones' brother-in-law worked there. This man, named Barry, was a person Babe talked to nearly every day on his mail run, yet she knew nothing of this.

When he brought in the mail, she confronted him; Barry held his head down in shame and apologized for his brother-in-law. He didn't want Babe to learn of the relationship, but he couldn't deny it. Barry's wife's sister was married to Billy Jones. Then he told Babe that she knew Billy's wife because they graduated from the same high school. Sure enough, Babe remembered attending a few classes with her. She told Barry not to feel bad because all things work together for good for those who loved the Lord.

Babe shared with Barry her involvement with prison ministry and how she had been writing to Billy in jail. Barry told her that he went to see Billy and that he was changing. He was reading his Bible and seeking the Lord. It occurred to Babe then that perhaps she could visit Billy and let him know she was serious.

Babe asked Barry if he could arrange it. Barry agreed to talk with him to see if Babe could be put on the visitors' roll.

Eight months passed before Billy's trial. The attorney and investigators gathered all the evidence and issued subpoenas. Babe wasn't summoned, and she was glad for that. She didn't want to live through the horrible details all over again. Josie had been dead nearly a year, and Babe was living a totally different life.

The desire to do drugs was entirely gone now. Babe was thankful that God saved her to do his will. Malcolm and his father were subpoenaed. The hearing date was rescheduled several times before they went to trial. Babe was kept up on the news by various sources.

The paper published the outcome of the trial, and the verdict was guilty for Billy, and he was given a life sentence. Babe continued to write to Billy, but she didn't receive a letter from him, but one day, Billy decided to write Babe, and to her surprise, both Babe and Billy shared the same birthday. It was interesting to find this out as Billy had someone to help him write a letter to Babe. Babe could see that he struggled with knowing how to write, and all that he said made it all worthwhile to finally hear from him. He stated how sorry he was and that he would be glad to meet Babe.

After the commotion of the trial, Barry informed Babe that Billy had put her on the visitors' registration list. At one time, the thought of witnessing to this guy had seemed far from reality. Now Babe would meet him face-to-face. She felt sure God would express his love for Billy through her. The day arrived for Babe to visit Billy; she brought him several Christian workbooks as a gift.

In the waiting area of the jail, Babe prayed silently until her name was called. The heavy steel doors clanged shut behind her; private compartments behind a framed glass window secured the prisoners. Not knowing what Billy looked like, Babe turned to a guard to ask where he was. It was then Babe noticed a man waving for her attention, and she realized it was Billy.

Telephones outside the glass windows allowed them to communicate with each other. Babe introduced herself to Billy and explained what God had done for her and why she came. Billy was elated as they both talked about Jesus and what he was doing in their lives. Babe told him of the many opportunities she'd received to go into the prisons to minister; she hoped Billy would understand the commission to the whole world.

At first it was difficult for Billy to look directly at Babe, but as they continued talking, a sense of peace came over him, and he was able to express himself. He told her he was sentenced for life, but his attorney said he might be out in ten years.

At first Babe was upset to hear he would be out in ten years with good behavior. Then she had to repent to God, knowing she should be happy for him either way. Babe felt sure Billy could work for the Lord, whether he was in prison or out. Time ran out, and Babe had to leave, but she left the books she had brought for him with the guard.

Halfway to the exit, Babe turned to see Billy watching and waving with a smile on his face; she felt that her visit proved effective, and she had planted good seeds. That evening, she knew the strength of God had lifted her higher than any drug she had ever tried.

Billy would soon be transferred to a maximum-security prison, and she wouldn't be able to write to him anytime soon. The recent visit proved prayer does work.

At church, Babe became busier still. Working with the five- and four-year-old kept her pretty busy. The children were cute and teaching them brought on a real challenge. They asked questions that Babe wouldn't believe their small minds could think of. She found herself studying more, just to keep up with their ingenious little minds. Then she joined the choir. Since the church had three services every Sunday, Babe had a chance to participate in everything.

On Wednesday nights, she worked with the ten- through twelve-year-old girls, which challenged her to study the Word even more.

Time had turned things around, and Babe realized that everything was what a person made of it. She could make the best or the worst of a situation. It was entirely up to her. She loved being active, and it didn't bother her to have a full schedule. Helping people both in the church and outside filled the void in her life. She hadn't realized before how self-centered she had been until she realized how many lost and dying people there were in the world, and the good thing about it all, she didn't miss anything in the world.

Prison ministry activities continued to keep her busy. Another Prison Invasion weekend was coming up, and Babe wasn't sure if she could get off work. Everyone at work had seen the change in her life, so her supervisor didn't hesitate to approve the day off for her.

The volunteers met ahead of time to discuss the details of what to expect. Babe was appointed the photographer. Plans were to leave early Friday morning. They were to stay the weekend at the YMCA and minister at Mabel Bassett, a correction center for women, located a few hours from Tulsa.

Driving time allowed the volunteers to open up and converse with one another about their walk with the Lord. Everyone appeared much older in their faith. Babe wanted to learn from their testimonies. She had always considered herself a believer but didn't know enough about the Bible or serving God; she had been content to believe that he existed. She remembered when she thought she was strange when she found herself praising God for no particular reason, and now, she realized she should have been doing it all along.

They arrived at the YMCA late Sunday night, after settling in. Monday morning, everyone was anxious to get past the guarded electric fence to witness Jesus to the inmates. First, they met with the chaplain, and she reviewed the prison rules they were to follow. Refreshments were served to the volunteers as they prepared their packs with books and Christmas cards to distribute to the inmates, and then they formed teams; Babe was placed with Karen, who seemed mature in the Lord. They witnessed to the residents, who were given less than a year in the minimum-security house. Babe listened to Karen, and soon learned how to suggest prayer when needed.

Good preparations were made, and everyone was ready to give it their best shot. Babe had been warned against taking pictures if the inmates didn't approve. But to her surprise, most of them wanted their pictures taken. After prayer and fellowship, they're invited to the evening service and suggested they bring a friend to the gymnasium for the service.

After the morning mission, the volunteers gathered in the chaplain's office before the evening service started to exchange praise reports and replenished their book supply. Amazing progress had been made. Many women had changed their sexual preference since they're incarcerated, but the witness of the volunteers changed their hearts, and they were led to the Lord. Everyone was looking forward to the evening service. They prayed that the women there would come to God in a personal way, allowing Jesus to be Lord of their life.

That evening, women from the entire correction center gathered in the gymnasium. There were four separate buildings that housed the residents. The unit where Babe witnessed was minimum security.

Babe was advised not to take pictures for the service that evening. While helping people find seats, Babe recognized someone who looked familiar. It was Joyce, Josie's friend that shoplifted and exchanged stolen goods for drugs. Joyce recognized her as well. Babe sat next to her during the service and shared with her how fulfilled her life was without drugs.

Tears ran down Joyce's face; it was such a coincidence to see Joyce, now really going through a change in her life. Babe sensed the spirit of God taking effect. After a few songs were sung, a lady ministered, and there was an altar call. Joyce was the first one to make a move to receive salvation. Counselors waited until the prayer was completed. They gave each lady a packet explaining the new birth. The service lasted two hours in order for the residents to have a security check. That gave them a little time to fellowship. Joyce came over and told Babe she was ready to make a commitment. She asked her to visit her tomorrow in the east house dorm. Babe promised her she would.

That night, it was late before they went to sleep. At the YMCA, some of the volunteers went to a nearby hotel so they could sleep better. At the YMCA, others just sacked out on the floor with sleeping bags.

Time alone allowed Babe to cry out to God, thanking him that Joyce crossed her path once again, and she was able to offer her something better than drugs. Prison ministry wasn't so hard to accept after Babe understood what God meant by the "lost sheep," especially since she was lost in sin many times in her life.

The next morning, the volunteers ate breakfast with the inmates. Sitting with them helped break the distance they felt and established a closer unity. Babe was startled at how many inmates recognized her. Several were high school classmates. Conversation was sparse as Babe tried to think of what to say to them in such an awkward place, maybe mention a class reunion, but Babe didn't attend them, and she didn't think it was appropriate to ask why they were there.

After breakfast, the volunteers met in the chaplain's office where they had praise-and-worship service. Today, Babe was determined to visit Joyce; however, the volunteers decided not to rotate, but to minister to the same people as the day before in order to get better acquainted.

All that day, Babe worried how she would visit Joyce. After ministering to the same girls as the day before, Babe finished with some extra time. It began to sprinkle as she hurried toward the East Dorm. When she arrived, she saw a girl who appeared to be very lonely; she told Babe she was locked up for killing her husband in self-defense and asked for a prayer. After Babe prayed, the girl felt better. When Babe asked her about Joyce, she told her that Joyce was her neighbor, and then she showed her where Joyce resided.

Babe had to wake Joyce, but she didn't mind. The rooms in the East Dorm were like a luxury hotel compared to the dorm Babe had left. The rooms were more private, with walls and doors instead of open space. Since the lobby area was bigger, Joyce led Babe out into the lobby area.

Joyce had gained some weight since the last time Babe had seen her, which was shortly before Josie's death. Joyce explained that she had testified at Josie's trial, and she was sentenced because of a shoplifting case. She then began to share with Babe what had happened the night of Josie's murder.

She explained that night she was going to make a few runs with Josie. Joyce and Billy were together buying drugs. Billy came over to Joyce's house later to find out if Josie was alone. After that, Billy left, and Joyce didn't find out until 4:00 A.M. The morning Josie had been taken to the hospital.

Babe never knew about Joyce's involvement until now. Joyce and Babe both thought it was strange how it all happened. They suspected someone else was involved, but they couldn't quite put it together. Joyce excused herself to go to her room while Babe waited. She brought back some papers, which she presented to Babe. It was the transcript of the trial on paper. Babe didn't go to any of the trials, but the transcript would help her to understand what really happened.

Babe told Joyce that she saw Billy at the county jail; she was shocked. She knew how close Josie and Babe were. Babe explained to Joyce that life was behind her and the work of the Lord was more important to her. Joyce could see that God really made a difference in her life and shared how she wanted to experience what Babe had. Joyce asked many questions concerning salvation. Babe explained that she needed to be patient because God rewards those who diligently seek him.

They talked so long; Babe almost forgot about the service in the gymnasium.

Babe invited Joyce and told her to invite her friends and enemies. Before leaving, they joined hands and prayed. Joyce began to cry, and Babe could see that most of her problem was over.

That night, the residents packed the gymnasium. A local church held the service, and the volunteers were on standby to counsel the new converts.

Back at the YMCA, they packed their bags to leave early Wednesday morning. Babe tried to hold in her testimony, but while packing, she couldn't help but tell Karen.

The transcript was on her mind, and she was bursting to tell someone. When she explained to Karen about the transcript, she didn't believe her until Babe showed her the papers. Karen reached over to take it, but Babe held it back until she agreed not to tell anyone.

On the floor underneath the covers, Karen read the transcript aloud. Babe listened until she couldn't take any more. Babe excused herself to find a hiding place. The transcript brought back memories of how terrible Josie's death had been.

When Babe returned, Karen had finished reading and wanted to discuss it. Babe apologized because she didn't want to discuss it. Karen understood and told Babe she would keep her in her prayers.

On the way back home, the group sang and praised God. Everyone felt that God's will had been done. It has been a wonderful week. The residents at the correction center had received all the volunteers with open arms. Babe shared her testimony with a few of them, and some she promised to write.

Weeks passed before Babe forced herself to read the transcript. The fear of reading it upset her, yet despite her fears, she sat down one evening and embarked upon it.

Listed on the transcript were all the names of those who had testified. Babe tried to fit the puzzle together. Some of the names she had heard Josie mention. One name she didn't recognize and couldn't picture him as anyone she knew, so she decided to call the phone number on the transcript. Willie William was the name on the transcript. Willie thought Babe was a detective. After identifying herself, he remembered her as well. When he told Babe, his nickname was T-Bird, she then remembered him. He was a friend of Malcolm, Josie's husband.

Willie advised Babe to leave the situation alone before she found out something she couldn't handle. After confessing to Willie of her new life in Christ, Babe assured him that she could handle all things with Christ. Willie informed Babe that most of Malcolm's friends were in jail. After their conversation, Babe realized he had a point. "Therefore, if anyone is in Christ, he is a new creature, old things are gone and the new has come, this is from God." Babe was refreshed in her change and hoped to help change others.

Back at church, she met a friend who was involved in street ministry. Joan told Babe that she ministered to winos, prostitutes, and vagabonds by herself. Babe couldn't tell if Joan was crazy or brave to take on a ministry like that by herself.

Babe realized she could use some help, so they agreed to meet after Friday-night service to pray before they went to the Red-Light District, as she called it. At midnight, they arrived at the corner of Cheyenne and Boston, where the homeless and hungry hung out. Babe couldn't imagine Joan going there by herself, but Babe supposed her angels were encamped around her.

Joan stood at the corner of the store while Babe stood in the center. They gave out tracts while talking to the people that walked by. For some reason, Babe captured the attention of the people. Joan said that it was because they thought she was a prostitute. Babe thought perhaps since Joan looked like somebody's grandmother that was the reason, especially since Babe wasn't dressed like a prostitute. Actually, Babe didn't care what they thought; she just wanted to lead them to Jesus.

Babe turned to a young man who received the tract she handed him. He seemed to show some interest as they talked, but then he said it was wrong to push Jesus on people. Babe explained that she wasn't pushing Jesus on anyone; she just wanted to talk to anyone who would listen. Babe realized this guy wasn't interested, so she went to another area to pass out her tracts.

A month later, she was invited to the county jail with a group from the church, where they would minister the Gospel. In the cell tank, the ladies came in for service, and there was a girl who once lived in the same apartments where Babe had lived as a teenager. Another girl came in and recognized her because she had worked at the same oil company as Babe had. Babe didn't remember Carrie, but Carrie explained that she was Billy's cousin, and she appreciated what Babe was doing.

Another girl in the back of the room said she saw Josie the night before she was murdered. Another girl who was sitting near the front said she used to buy drugs from Josie.

As the group was leaving, some men from another tank prepared for service. While walking by, Babe noticed an inmate who looked familiar. It was the man at the Red-Light District who had accused her of pushing Jesus on people. Babe stopped to say something to him, but he kept on walking. Babe thought, *If Only He Had Listened.*

Chapter 10

Doing It for Jesus

Serving the Lord turned out to be more of an adventure and a privilege as Babe kept abreast on other activities. Different groups out of the church would plan missionary trips, and the thought of going to the Bahamas sounded like a different type of vacation that she could appreciate. Plans were being made to go to the Bahamas for a two-week missionary trip. There were seven who met at the church and planned for the engagement. Preparation for the trip included meeting periodically to practice singing praise songs and writing short sermons for the trip ahead. Everyone was excited, knowing that seven was God's perfect number.

In order to afford a cheaper trip, the group drove to St. Louis where they caught a flight to Nassau, Bahamas. Babe had never been to Nassau, and she looked forward to the visit. As the plane flew over the clear blue water, she could visualize herself ministering to others in Jesus' name. At the airport, a few men from the Bahamas Faith Ministry were waiting with welcome banners. They loaded the church van going to the hotel. There was unspeakable joy bubbling over. It was Saturday afternoon, and their destination was Andros Island, where they would go on Monday. But the group had the weekend ahead of them, and they looked forward to sightseeing.

That evening, they went to see the sights, and when they stopped a lady for directions, she surprised them by offering to take them anywhere they wanted to go. Then she offered to lend her iron from home since most of them in the group were worried about having packed wrinkles in their clothes.

Suzanne was her name, and everyone thought she was a blessing. It was like the Bible said: "Some strangers may be angels unaware." Later that evening, she took them to a restaurant, and everyone made a contribution to Suzanne's meal. Suzanne accepted only a love offering, and everyone thought that was neat.

On Sunday, it was prearranged that the group would attend Bahamas Faith Ministries. At church, they all stood when the pastor identified visitors. After service, several church members offered to take one person each to their homes for dinner. Babe wondered what she was in for. As the pastor coupled off the groups, he coupled Babe off with a lady that was noticed earlier coordinating a dance group, but the introduction wasn't very clear. After service, Babe joined the lady. In her car, Babe introduced herself again, hoping she would do likewise. Her name was Josie.

"Josie," Babe said. Her eyes sprung open with excitement as she shared her sister's name. Instantly, Babe felt a bond being established.

Josie picked up fresh conch from the fish market. Her four children welcomed Babe as they opened up and talked to one another. After dinner, conversation continued about what God had delivered them from.

Josie's background was similar to Babe's; she was a dancer in a nightclub and used to sell drugs like her sister. Babe enjoyed dancing in the clubs, but she never got paid to dance. Together, they agreed her vision to televise her exercise program would come to pass. God always turns experiences into opportunities, and Babe just wanted whatever God would have her do.

On Monday, they left for Andros Island where their missionary work would begin. As the plane landed, they knew there wouldn't be much sightseeing in this remote area. The airport was quite small. Men from the Youth Revival Missionary House met them. Wide open space of undeveloped land covered miles and miles of territory before they finally arrived at what was considered a rural area.

The small island had only one church and one pastor, but from the small church extended a missionary's home—a small three-bedroom and one bath where the volunteers would be staying.

The group consisted of seven people from Tulsa and one from Africa, whom the group met up with in the Bahamas. Saul was from Africa and would be assisting the group since he had been there many times before as a guide for missionary groups and would show them around. Altogether, there were eight in the group, so they called the team New Beginning because that's what the number 8 represented. Saul from Africa shared awesome stories regarding miracles and curses that took place in Africa, and he had everyone in rapt attention.

Every day, the group was up at the break of dawn, praying an hour or two then exercising before breakfast. Afterward, they went from door-to-door, inviting the residents to accept Jesus as Lord in their life and inviting them to service that evening. One night, they parked the van on a residential street with the speakers outside. The group started with dancing and singing to God. The Bahamians joined in, praising God, and later came to church for service.

At service that night, Ron from Tulsa ministered under a powerful anointing. God's Word of knowledge flowed through him as people came forth for their healing. Ron revealed that someone wanted to become a mother, but no one acknowledges it. Ron continued to minister God's Word.

By the end of the week, the team leader, Linda suggested the ladies write notes to the men and fathers there since Father's Day was that Sunday. Only one couple traveled with the group; they didn't have children. Babe wondered if Carol wanted any children; she asked Carol and Carol responded, "Sure." It dawned on everyone that the Word of knowledge that came forth in the meeting was for them.

Visiting the high schools was fun. Liz from the group sang beautifully. She led the praise and worship, and everyone shared a short testimony. Babe felt apprehensive as she wondered what she would say. As she walked before the hundreds of students and shared with them how much time she wasted working in the clubs, looking for excitement and fun, she assured them that the best thing in all her life was serving God. Babe encouraged them to seek God early so they would know his will for their life and would flee youthful lust.

Carol and Mike renewed their wedding vows after the word of knowledge revealed their desire to be parents. Ron married them since he was an ordained minister. Babe caught the bouquet of flowers.

Ministering God's Word was rewarding as they witnessed the young and old hungry for the Word of God. They planted good seeds in every heart they could; it was definitely working, and before long, you could see a certain glow on the ones who had received.

Close to the end of the week, when the group had accomplished their mission, which had been set forth for them, they began to seek out some pastime. They made sure to find time for snorkeling and spearfishing as they traveled in a motorboat the pastor provided; they traveled from one island to another. The two weeks in the Bahamas were nearly over. They had met a host of friends and had planted many seeds of righteousness.

Saul was planning to move to Tulsa with his family to attend a university there. It was agreed that they would all have dinner together as soon as he arrived.

Within a month, the entire group was together again, looking at pictures and eating home-cooked meals at Linda's place.

Chapter 11

Growing in God

At home, a desire to serve God grew deeper as the concern for the lost increased.

The weekend of Mother's Day at church disturbed Babe. As she listened to the pastor go on and on about abortion being murder, Babe didn't feel that she was condemned because of her past experience with an abortion, but she knew in her spirit some immature Christian from that background may not be strong enough to grow on.

After church later that day, Babe couldn't stop thinking about what the pastor said. The church was the biggest supporter of Life Alternative, a ministry that outreached toward single mothers, in hope of preventing them from aborting their unborn fetus. Babe hadn't given abortion much thought up until now. Her view on the abortion stand was an individual matter simply because she felt thankful that she didn't have to give birth to an untimely pregnancy. Babe had always thought the abortion was a blessing that she didn't have to raise a child she wasn't prepared for, and she never regretted it.

Regardless of what other women's excuses were, Babe felt the grace of God was for them also.

Yet as she gave thought to the voice that led her to believe God had spoken to her about the pastor, it gave Babe more reason to be concerned if this was all of God. With all the confusion at the church about the pastor being single and several women believing God for him, it wasn't long before a notion to test the spirit was in the making. This way, Babe would know if God was in the voice that led her into the same deception as the other women. Also, Babe needed to know how God felt about abortion; she knew she couldn't go alone with others' view just because she was a Christian; there would have to be scripture evidence.

After much thought and prayer was given, a notion to write the pastor a letter concerning her views on abortion was in the making; it was difficult finding an appropriate way to write it, so Babe wrote it like it was.

Dear Pastor,

I like this church, and I hope you receive this letter in love. Your Mother's Day sermon prompted me to write. I believe God is judging the many people that flippantly call abortion murder.

"How can men know?"; especially since they've never experienced one and never will, and the women that refer to it as murder are so religious, they have lost sight of reality.

In a sense they're judging, knowing there are many situations behind abortion. Now who made them a judge?

My memory goes back to when some denominations didn't even believe in doctors until they finally got a revelation.

My experience with an abortion left me thankful to know and understand the grace of God.

There was only one pregnancy that appeared to be out of wedlock that was God's perfect will, which was the virgin Mary who borne our Savior! who has come, and we need not look for another, even then God provided a physical husband for her. Just because a woman conceives doesn't mean it's always of God, especially when it's done in sin.

I also believe in fasting and praying, but all the fasting and praying in the world can't help me to be in one accord in this matter.

Excuse me for saying this, but I'm a pretty strong person and what you say doesn't bother me. I've learned to drink the milk, chew the meat and spit out the bones.

Pastor, there's a lot of emotionally disturbed women here in your congregation, that are already guilt ridden today because of how Christians handle the abortion issue; I see a need to be more compassionate in this area.

Honestly, I'm afraid that if God calls me to minister in this area, the only thing I can do is pray with the person in this situation, that God would direct their decision.

As Babe proceeded to sign the letter, a driving force impressed upon her to sign, "The Heart of God." Not wanting to sound corny, Babe opted for another salutation until an action from the Holy One signed through her "The Heart of God."

It wasn't long before her letter was received, but not quite accepted. Nothing was said from the people on staff. If looks could kill, Babe would have been dead on sight. Darts were coming from every area. Word got out about the letter, and many in the congregation were reacting as well.

Sunday night, the pastor addressed the letter after he dedicated a baby.

What a cheap shot! Babe thought, knowing everyone would be more sensitive about this issue after they saw a baby.

The pastor said that abortion was murder, and that the individual was not welcomed at his church if she ministers anything other than that. Babe had signed her name on the letter because she wanted him to know who she was, to make sure he wasn't deceived about other things at the church.

Although Babe never suspected that he would put the individual out of his church, reacting like a kid who couldn't have his way and so he tells his friend he can't play with him.

Deep down inside, Babe knew it wasn't his church; it was God's, and she had already read in the Bible How God warned the shepherds: "Woe to the shepherd that scatters the sheep." At first, Babe felt hurt that the pastor would respond that way. Afterward, she realized at least she knew that God couldn't be speaking to her about the pastor being her husband or, at least, she hoped. Her letter to the pastor proved that the voice she heard wasn't of God, which really made it all worthwhile.

Shortly thereafter, a plague hit the church. A several teenagers and single women became pregnant, the pastor called a seven-day fast to strengthen the church's spiritual walk, but the pastor was still ignorant to the abortion issue and was now reacting as if Babe needed to be delivered in order for them to see eye to eye.

It didn't seem necessary for Babe to see eye to eye with that minister; she knew she couldn't deal with him as a husband type for her, and it didn't seem to matter that he was the minister. Where in the Bible does it say that people in church are not to think for themselves? Babe was glad she didn't have to be in bondage like the other women in the church.

In the apartments where Babe lived, she found her neighbor to be friendly, and occasionally, Babe would try to witness to her from time to time.

One day, while Babe was showing her vacation pictures of the missionary trip to the Bahamas to Tori, Babe thought the pictures made good conversation and helped her witness. Tori's mind seemed a million miles away. When Babe asked her if anything was wrong, Tori confessed that she was pregnant.

Tori wasn't married and felt this pregnancy was terribly untimely. She had already had two abortions, and this was another unwanted pregnancy. Babe suggested Life Alternative outreach at the church for single mothers that care to give their baby up for adoption. Life Alternative would assist the unwed mother with some finance or provide an adoption. Tori couldn't see herself carrying the baby only to give it away.

Prayer was the only way out of the conversation for Babe. In praying for Tori, a moment of silence covered the room. As Babe waited for a word from God, she uttered a few words of God's love for her and closed the prayer. Babe lost all ability to pray, and upon leaving, she told her that all things worked together for good for those who love the Lord. Babe could see her heart was tender and tired of the same old mistakes. Babe suggested she attend church with her some evening. Tori agreed to attend church with Babe, but she had already made an appointment with an abortion clinic on Tuesday. Babe remembered the abortion she had and knew she was thankful for that outlet, yet Tori had already had two abortions and this one would be her third. Babe didn't want to get caught up in the number thing, but a burden for Tori led Babe to fast as she thought about what she was going through. Her boyfriend didn't want any more children, and he wanted her to have an abortion. The thought of having a child always seemed wonderful until you realize that you can't give the very best for your child and you feel that you have cheated the kid.

Adoption, on the other hand, is totally up to the individual. To trust a total stranger with the caring of your child requires some degree of strength. Many girls' resort to adoption when they find out they waited too long for an abortion, except for the ones in church that have been brainwashed to believe that it's murder.

After considering a concern for the unborn fetus, Babe decided to fast that weekend. She fasted with such ease. Babe knew it had to be God; she didn't war with her flesh at all. And still she prayed a simple prayer that Tori would do God's will in the matter.

On Tuesday, Tori went ahead with the abortion and said she felt much better, at least mentally. Tori's body had some healing to do, and it would take a couple of days before the soreness left. Though you could see that she had the peace that passed all understanding, and she did the best things for herself, knowing her relationship with her boyfriend was on the brink. After that experience, Babe prayed God's direction and understanding the abortion issue. It didn't seem fair to try to convince Tori that she was making a mistake. From looking at life and other women that fell short in the same area, Babe felt she had a lot more to be thankful for. The second most important commandment in the Bible is to love your neighbor as yourself, and like herself, she didn't want to see Tori go through that all alone.

"Lord, give me guidance," Babe prayed. Her feelings were quite sensitive toward the abortion issue after that, and she couldn't understand men claiming God told them abortion was murder. *What God are they hearing from?* Babe wondered. *There are women going through counsel now because they cannot handle it, and to listen to these* slanderous accusations in church that beguiled unstable souls.

More concern led Babe to see what Life Alternative had to offer single mothers. Maybe there would be some enlightenment in that area for her. At the first meeting she attended, they showed a movie called *Silent Cry*. The film seemed slightly exaggerated to say the baby experienced pain and cried. As Babe watched the movie, she reflected on her abortion. There's no way that the baby could have cried because Babe knew now the drugs, they used to numb the pain and also numbs the pain the fetus feels as well. If anyone was crying, it was Babe. Babe realized afterward they were tears of joy, crying that she didn't have to live through a stupid ordeal like that because she was too impatient for love, which turned out to be lust. Babe wondered what the people thought of miscarriages. She wondered, *Is God the murderer?*

When the film was over, they prayed for women who had abortions to be forgiven and informed women of the different areas they're needed in. Realizing the many circumstances behind many abortions, Babe withdrew her interest in this area; she had seen too many hypocrites, and she didn't want to add to the number.

Within the same month, a missionary from China came to America for a sponsored banquet. The banquet was organized by the church and was held at a local hotel to raise money for the cause. At the banquet, the missionary talked about women in China who were forced to have abortions if they had more than one child per family. Babe had heard that in China, they would abort the baby if the parents violated China's law, even if they were married.

It grieved Babe as she thought about Herod, Pharaoh, and the wicked kings in the Bible who tried to kill the baby boys so the will of God wouldn't be done. Tearfully, she thought, *God has blessed America.* She knew that it would be difficult to have an abortion if one really wanted a child. Softly, she heard the spirit speak, "Render unto Caesar the things that be Caesar and the things that be God unto God."

Babe realized that was a scripture from the Bible. In her quest for understanding the scripture as it ran over in her mind, she reached for her Bible and studied the story pertaining to the verse. Knowing that God speak to us by his Word, she prayerfully searched for an interpretation, and even though the situation pertained to money, common sense and God's revelation helped her to understand.

Most people value money on the same scale as life, and to some degree, it's right, but to some degree, it's corrupt. Yet another scripture plagued Babe: Psalm 90:3, when God told Moses to instruct the children of men (unborn) to return in order that the sinner be saved. *Return* in that writing meant to give back to God (abort). It appeared that God was saying give those unborn fetuses back to him if they're untimely. That sounded like what a loving God would do.

While watching the Christian Network on TV that evening, a well-known evangelist interviewed a prophet from New York. He asked the prophet for a Word from the Lord that he'd like to share. The prophet spoke, "Render unto Caesar the things that are Caesars and the things that are God's unto God." That's exactly what God told Babe as she questioned the abortion issue in China. It bore witness with what God had already told her, and she felt sure God had spoken. Babe also understood that China was already overpopulated, and this was one way of reducing the number of untimely pregnancies anyway.

During Babe's life, she had heard that God did all the evil things in life. Despite the fact that she was just a sinner, she stood her ground. Now that Babe had been washed by the blood of Jesus and walking in the knowledge of his love, she knew how important it is to tell others.

Jesus came to give us life and life more abundantly, yet people are settling for only life instead of life abundantly. God's Word says your children will be priests in the Bible; you'll find the priests of God were selected people, non-unhealthy or blemished in any way.

Babe's understanding of God's Word had been broadened to the point that, regardless of how a scripture is used, if the situation discerns it, then she knows where sin abounds, grace abounds much more.

Even though China is a communist country, the love of God is extended to every nation, and because China is already overpopulated, their laws appear just; whereas in America, the laws can be unjust when people are forced to accept other people's standard of living. From then on, Babe knew she was to treat Tori with the love and patience of the Lord.

It appeared that Tori had better sense than the people in church regarding abortion since the women in church were following the leaching of the pastor instead of researching what the Word of God said. Sure enough, as Babe thought that her diligent studying of the Bible confirmed it: "The children of the world will be wiser than the children of the light" (Luke 16:8). Jesus referred to it as worldly wisdom. After the abortion, Tori felt like something good did come out of it. She realized she was in the wrong relationship.

As time went on, Babe encouraged Tori to join her at church. She slowly came around, but Tori struggled with the desire to party. She wanted to meet someone to love her. Babe could relate to Tori all too well; she knew that she was the same way until the time was right. She knew not to press Tori. As Babe witnessed to her, she reminded her how much God loved her, but Tori wanted the love of a man. The Lord reminded Babe that he would give the growth, and she was just to plant seeds in Tori's life.

That didn't resolve the abortion issue easily. Babe's heart went out to women caught in the dilemma she'd experienced. Still upset overhearing the word *murder* as opposed to *abortion*, and to acknowledge it as murder is judging, which is a sin. Disappointment overwhelmed Babe as she prayed for God to enlighten people in this area. At church, Babe still felt adamant in standing for what she thought was right.

After Babe wrote the letter to the pastor, a concerned elder mother had heard about Babe's view and thought someone needed to point her in the right direction. Babe didn't know if it was coincidental that the elder mother was related to the pastor, but she agreed to attend a speak-out on the subject. The speak-out was arranged by the elder mother and lasted thirty minutes.

It was basically for women, with the exception of one ex-convict bragging about how many women he had impregnated at the same time, then goes to them with threats that they better not abort his baby while he was on his way to prison for selling drugs. Babe thought if he had to sell drugs to support all his children, what are they going to do when he's in jail? Babe didn't want to seem self-righteous because she knew that many of the children can rise above these circumstances, but she also knew that if it's only to glorify themselves, it would be for the wrong reason.

Every last one of the women took a stand against abortion; Babe felt outnumbered and sensed she would be stoned if she voiced her opinion. She sat back and listened. One woman said that she didn't feel abortion should be done unless God does it—meaning a miscarriage. That seemed rather naive, as if one refused to seek medical assistance for a tumor or any other sickness that can be healed by a doctor.

"Don't they know that is testing God?"

Even the Word of God says, "Thou shall not tempt the Lord your God." If a person demands a miracle as such from God, they may be stuck holding the bag since the Word of God states that all power has been given to his believers. Furthermore, most abortions stem from obvious sin, which takes you back to the Bible. Jesus told the Pharisee that asked for a sign, they were an evil and adulterous generation; the only sign they would get was when Jonah was in the whale's belly for three days, so will the son of man be on earth for three days; we have all the signs we need in the Bible.

Also, the book of Moses tells the people that some people will have to live with the consequences of their sin. But God still loves them, just like some people want to push their consequences on other people. A young girl at the speak-out shared with the crowd how she had become pregnant out of wedlock, and because she had been adopted, she decided to give the child up for adoption, but the horrible dreams that she had afterward left her seeking medical help and medication to deal with it. Babe thought she should've redeemed herself when she had a chance.

It's difficult to say who will need an abortion in these trying days. A couple at the church spoke out regarding their mentally and physically handicapped son. The woman shared her encounter with a difficult pregnancy.

First off, the husband didn't want any more children at that time since they already had one, but when the wife became pregnant, they had to deal with it. During the first trimester, this lady experienced hemorrhaging and suspected something. When she went to two different doctors, they both told her that she needed to abort because her fetus was at risk for deformities, then she went to a third catholic doctor, but he told her that he didn't believe in abortion.

At least this prepared the couple one way or the other. After the baby was born, it was discovered that the child had cerebral palsy, a long-term nonfatal intramuscular disease that caused those affected to be mentally retarded. The couple has learned to live with this and love their son. Their son was eight years old at the time, and their adjustment hasn't been easy with mounting hospital bills and futile therapy sessions; their situation sometimes devastates them.

The couple left the church shortly after the pastor addressed the letter Babe had sent him regarding abortion. I'm sure this couple was hurt by it as well, knowing that things could have been different if they had listened to the first two doctors' suggestion. Still they had hoped their little boy would someday be normal. That brought up more questions about abortion. Knowing the procedure for abortion was the same, regardless of the reason, left Babe aware that the prolife view is pretending to be the judge, especially when they justify one reason over another. Abortion procedures all basically have the same purpose; they end the growth of the fetus at an early stage.

Though there are various reasons, it appears that people categorize them all the same. The fact that one chose to have an abortion because she couldn't afford a child would be no different than a woman who chose not to have a defective fetus. The bottom line is that most abortions are from obvious sin. The situation discussed earlier may have been that the woman sinned when she disobeyed her husband's desire not to have any more children.

Just when Babe thought the abortion issue was fading away, a commercial on adopted children was viewed, most of which turned out to be pretty successful people. It seemed good that they had achieved something in life, and Babe thought, *Adoption isn't so bad.* Within minutes, her fine-tuned ear listened as God quickened her spirit, saying, "God gets the glory, and He will share it with no one."

That was scripture, and Babe began to realize that whatever is highly esteemed before men is an abomination to God. Upon realizing this, Babe was way off track with her concerns about abortion; she decided to leave the abortion issue behind. God had called her to other things, and abortion was not on her list.

Patrick, Jonni's brother hadn't been in town for quite a while. It surprised Babe to see him at the church altar. Talking to Patrick encouraged Babe as she listened to him; the Word of God was like a river of living water springing up from his soul. Patrick had accepted his call into ministry full time.

He didn't get to meet Jonni face-to-face before she died, but he did talk with her over the phone. He had met Joni's husband and the rest of the family and had accepted an offer to minister at his church. They both thanked God that he brought them together.

Back at work, Barry kept in touch to see how Babe was doing, and when she told him she recently wrote to Billy, he told her that Billy's birthday was the previous week.

"What day?" she asked.

"July 31."

"You're kidding. That's my birthday."

That evening, when Babe picked up her mail, there was a letter from Billy. What a breakthrough!

Dear Juanetta: I received your letter, and I was happy to hear from you as always. God has turned my life completely around and for the first time in my life, I'm free. I was in prison for many years before I was sent here and locked up. All of this is God's will. I do not consider this as punishment because this has been a learning experience. I have found Jesus Christ who has always been with me. I guess I was going so fast I didn't have time, or you might say I didn't take time to give God his praise. But I know I will never go back to living in the flesh. One of these days

I would like very much to sit and talk with you. There are so many things I would like to say.

The letter went on to explain about his friend in Christ, who encouraged him to write. The letter really touched Babe, but she didn't know the next step.

"Lord, tell me what now," she cried.

Billy's wife crossed her mind, so she decided to send her a card. The card was delivered to her by Barry. She called the same day. They talked for an hour and a half. Babe could tell that Mary hadn't forgiven Billy for what he had taken her through. She talked about divorcing him. It wasn't easy convincing Mary to trust him since she didn't know him herself. Mary hadn't seen Billy since all this had happened. She agreed to go with Babe to visit him. Before visiting Billy, Mary and Babe had breakfast together and enjoyed their visit. Mary appeared to be understanding and kind, and she counseled Babe about some issues in her life.

The next letter from Billy included visitor forms, and he explained about family night at the prison. He extended an invitation to all of them, especially his daughter, Sheila, whose birthday would be the same day as family night. October 20 was a special day to remember. It occurred to Babe that not only would it mark a family reunion, but it was a birthday as well. Sheila was eight years old that day. Luckily, Babe kept gifts for the spur-of-the-moment occasion, which she presented to Sheila. The prison was only an hour away, and they felt they should have planned this visit much sooner, but it's better late than never. They ran a little late and had no time to visit before the service started, but Billy seated them up front anyway.

The prison choir sang, and Billy and his friend Don were on the front line, singing. Babe couldn't help but notice the inmate who performed sign language for the deaf. A scripture was read from 1 Corinthians 13. They all held hands while they had devotion. Billy beamed at his little girl as they sat together, talking and laughing during the service. They were so glad to see one another. After the choir sang, a guy performed a pantomime of Jonah. The storm on the boat and the scene when Jonah tried to run from God reminded Babe of the storms of destiny in her life. How they changed her life by knowing the living God within her to do his will. "Surely I'm thankful that God never gave up on me."

Chapter 12

We're Only Righteous in Christ

Victory in Jesus was visible as Babe kept in touch with different ones that had crossed her path and miracles had already taken place. God's promises were being fulfilled everywhere she went. The team that went to the Bahamas, named New Beginning, met periodically to share God's good news. To hear that two couples were expecting parents blessed Babe. Babe remembered when the prophecy went forth for one of them; the other couple was just an added bonus. Babe's involvement with the prison ministry encouraged her to write to Billy regularly.

Babe managed to find a local ministry at the Tulsa Correction Center, an hour once a week; it uplifted her faith to minister to people who had once crossed her path. Transfer from surrounding prisons was sent to the Tulsa Correction Center. Several prisons Babe had already ministered relocated inmates there, which brought delight in seeing some of the same faces. Joyce came from Mabel Bassett prison for women. Babe truly thanked God for what he was doing in her life and many others. Joyce participated in the Bible Banquet periodically, but since she worked, her schedule wouldn't always permit it. After Babe told Joyce she sold real estate part time, Joyce asked Babe to help her get a house after she was released. Babe told her she would be glad to.

The residents seemed to enjoy her teaching and asked if they could attend her church some time, which left Babe wondering if the church would be willing to pick them up on Sundays for church. After asking the assistant pastor, she was told that it wouldn't be possible at that time. It wasn't long before the correction center approved volunteers to drive the state vehicles they owned for church functions, which gave Babe permission to take them to special occasions.

Still, time to fellowship with other believers added to her social life; a breakfast banquet was scheduled for Christian women. Babe and a friend attended together. There was a well-known pastor's wife who ministered and addressed an altar call for those wanting God to stir his spirit within them. Babe knew that she could always use a dose of God's Holy Ghost's power more than anything, so immediately, she made a stand for the altar call.

At the altar, a word of knowledge was revealed. That God wanted to use a woman in the abortion area. Babe listened but she didn't want to receive it; she had already told the church where she stood on the issue, and she didn't feel the church was open to the truth. Not only that, but God also already knew how Babe felt in this area, and it wasn't like he was telling her otherwise. She felt sure her views wouldn't fit in.

On their way home, Babe's friend mentioned how she thought about Babe when the Word of knowledge was revealed, for she knew Babe's view regarding abortion, and she understood because she had two abortions. Babe doubted that Word was for her and openly stated that those who worshiped God must worship in spirit and in truth. Babe would be untruthful to herself to stand prolife. The only way she could minister in that area effectively would be to women who had abortions already or who's going to need one and needed to know how to cope with themselves. Abortion, being such a controversial issue, Babe definitely couldn't imagine herself in this ministry. It seemed like enough persecution just preaching the good news.

At church one evening, a young single man sang a few Gospel songs. This young man was well-known but was not a member of the congregation. Just the mention of his name would cause Babe heart to melt. As he looked at her, he joked about chocolate chip cookies, stating the best thing about the cookies were the chips since he was Italian. Babe took it as if he might like her, and she wished with all her heart that they were one in God. He had visited the church all the time, and he was a good friend with the pastor, but on a few occasions, Babe got to talk with him. He seemed like a nice person that Babe wanted to get to know. Even though she was very leery of his friendship with the pastor, she still thought he was a man of his own. When he announced that he was joining the church that night, Babe rejoiced.

That night after service, Babe felt stirred up to pray that God would send him for her husband. Even though she found contentment in loving God, she knew it was normal to desire a husband.

Babe began to pray with understanding from her heart when, all of a sudden, in deep despair, a moment of travailing overtook her. While interceding with groaning and weeping, she knew the prayers were no longer anything she could conceive. Babe fell asleep to be awakened that morning by a song coming from her inner spirit. "We're only righteous in Christ." After repeating the phrase three times, Babe thought, *how strange*. She wasn't praying for that. But since Babe sometimes woke up singing a lot, she thought little of the matter.

Around noon that day, a friend knocked on her door, and to her surprise, it was Ron. They went to the Bahamas together on the mission field. Ron seldom visited, but Babe was glad to receive him as a guest. They talked about everything, but the most important aspect of Ron's visit was his visits at the abortion clinic. Ron shared that he felt God had led him to visit the abortion clinics in the area, where he sat for seven hours praying in the spirit for women that came in for abortions. Ron told Babe he said nothing to these women, yet he was very sensitive to what their spirit felt. It was a very humbling experience for Ron, and now he knew the women didn't want to go through with this, but they knew they had to.

While listening to Ron, Holy Ghost chills ran down Babe's spine. *What's The Meaning of This?* Babe thought. *Surely God is not leading me into this ministry?*

As they continued talking, Ron's words convinced Babe. These women really needed to be ministered to, and suddenly, that song Babe awoke to play through her mind again. "We're only righteous in Christ."

All along Babe knew it was only the self-righteous views that couldn't understand the abortion issue. God's Word says our righteousness is like filthy rags, and most pro-lifers try to enforce their law instead of God's grace, just like the hypocrites and the Pharisees the Bible warns against.

When they were in the Bahamas, Babe questioned Ron about her stand on abortion. He understood. A prophecy came forth from God through Ron concerning a couple having a baby, which came to pass later. Babe felt that Ron was walking close to God.

The ministry that Babe dreaded the most had come upon her. It began to be apparent when she wrote a letter to the pastor because she didn't want him to think she was playing the same game the other women at the church were playing, even though she felt the way she wrote. Also, she knew that she couldn't be his wife with a big conflict like that. But still, it was stirring this burden within her. Obedience was the only way out, and Babe had known the love of God, and she knew that he wouldn't put any more on her than she could handle. She thought that she avoided it long enough; how many times did he have to tell her?

Babe realized she would be out of place at the church where she was at. When she thought about it, she knew that, eventually, she would be moving on. She had a feeling it was going to get downright dirty. She knew she would have to confront the minister again and Lord knows who else. She didn't have a good feeling about it, and again, she did. Babe moved on to the furthest thing on her mind as she began considering what she was up against. She thought, *I Don't Want This Ministry*. Babe cried. Yet it seemed that the experience Babe had already had in life made it sure that she was going down the right road; she just didn't know what to do it.

Babe pondered on how to reach the world with the truth, and the only way she could do it was with the Word of God. Since she felt this leading was so strong, she knew she would have to look to God. Babe had learned how to fast at one of the churches when they went on a twenty-one-day fast, and it seemed like it helped her in hearing from God. She knew that she needed God's direction more than ever now. It seemed like many scriptures had already enlightened her, but one in particular they sang to was "Thou loving Kindness is better than life."

As comforting as the scripture was, Babe knew that she had to base the ministry on it. Yet Babe reviewed the entire chapter Psalm 63. As David praised and worshiped God throughout the chapter, he talked to God upon his bed and meditated on him in the night watches. Yet the portion of foxes that he mentioned reminded Babe about the little foxes that spoil the vine in the book of the Song of Solomon, which Babe related to in other studies.

Babe knew the entire chapter wasn't as vivid as Psalm 58. Psalm 58 described the wicked as the unborn, and Babe didn't want to be that direct since she knew that before abortion was legalized, women were forced to go through with untimely pregnancies, and they had no other choices.

Many of them learned how to cope with it no matter what, and from that stock, great men and women were born and bred in the United States of America. But there are also a great number of untimely pregnancies that went on to be burdens on society that reproduced after their own kind. A few of them became hardcore criminals that polluted and corrupted the land and increased the population in the prison community.

After realizing that this must be God, Babe knew that she wanted to be obedient; she began to envision all the billboards that said abortion is murder. Her questions were answered within minutes by scriptures in the Bible that said, "Satan is the god of this world." Babe knew then that Satan was the god that said abortion was murder. Babe finally realized it was time to drop everything and attend to the matter at hand.

Still unanswered questions stormed Babe's mind. "Why do they say that an abortion is murder?" While thinking on this, a scripture came to mind: "Heaven and earth will pass away, but God's word will never pass away." With that memory jogger, Babe reached for God's Word; she knew that the answer to any question would be there. God's Word is a light to our feet and a lamp to our path, and Babe knew there would be the truth. The Bible contains the truth.

Immediately, Babe opened the Word of God up to the book of Ecclesiastes 1:9, which states, "There is nothing new under the sun." Upon reading that verse, it dawned on her that even in the biblical days, abortions had to have happen, thinking back, Babe remembered the story of the woman that was accused of adultery and was going to be stoned to death; Jesus intervened and asked her accusers, "Those that have not sinned, cast the first stone." No one could cast a stone; they all left, and Jesus asked her, "Where are thou accusers?" He then told her to "go and sin no more." We have all sinned and fell short of the glory of God; why then are others pretending they are without sin?

Line by line and precept by precept, an in-depth study of the Bible was done, and because of the many translations, Babe found KJV the most original and accurate. Few people knew that in the Biblical days, if an unwed woman was found to be with child, they would stone the pregnant woman and the unborn to death.

Babe couldn't imagine Jesus allowing this to go on, so intently, she searched the Word even more so. In reading the book of St. John 21:25, John said that Jesus did more than what was written about. If every one of them were written, we wouldn't be able to pack the Bible. Babe knew in her spirit there was more in the Word of God pertaining to this issue. With abortion being a touchy subject, Babe knew the details were going to be sketchy instead of full-blown.

Babe's understanding of God's Word made more sense now, realizing that the Bible was not only for men but women as well. She had also heard that two-thirds of the Old Testament was in the New Testament since most scriptures were used repeatedly in the Bible, and a good study Bible helped to prove that.

The scriptures began to stand out when Luke the physician wrote about the teachings of Jesus: "Woe unto you also, ye lawyers! For ye lade men with burdens grievous to be borne, and ye yourselves touch not the burdens with one of your fingers" (Luke 11:46). Jesus talked about burdens too grievous to be borne; we all know the word *borne* is associated with the unborn, and it seemed like Babe was finding that the scriptures were easier to understand when she earnestly sought the truth.

As Babe studied the Word of God, she found more reasons to justify abortion than condemn it. Even the Old Testament gave directions to prophecies by King David in the book of Psalm. Profound revelation opened as she read and understood the literal meaning of God's Word. David prophesied in Psalm 7:14: "She who is pregnant with evil and conceives trouble gives birth to disillusionment."

As Babe interpreted the scriptures, she prayed that only the women that really needed to have an abortion would receive the truth because, first and foremost, women needing abortions are openly admitting that they made the mistake of sinning against God. The fifty-eighth chapter of Psalms describes an old-fashion abortion, as David describes what to do with an untimely pregnancy. How ironic that David describes the unborn as the evil because of the prediction of how they turn out when they aren't raised and nurtured under the upbringing of God.

Of course, extenuating circumstances surfaced as people referred to it as a murder ministry, but as Babe thought of the army and the military men that's on the battlefield killing or being killed, she knew that it wasn't the same thing, but if women cannot defend themselves against an untimely pregnancy, our nation would only fall prey to the enemies in our own camp.

As Babe struggled to fight the fears, God's Word became her constant comfort. Reading the New Testament was always assuring when she remembered Jesus telling the women right before he was crucified that the barren would be blessed. While Babe reviewed the Gospel, she couldn't overlook what Matthew and John wrote during the triumphant entry: "Tell the daughter of Zion, behold your King is coming to you, lowly, and sitting on a donkey, a colt, the foal of a donkey" (Matthew 21:5).

As Babe read what Jesus the prophet said, her faith was restored. In the Gospel of John, he wrote, "Fear not, daughter of Zion; behold, your King is coming, sitting on a donkey's colt" (John 12:15). When Babe read these scriptures, she understood that Jesus would go before her, and no weapon formed against her would profit and every tongue that tried to judge her would be judged.

At the church, Babe confronted the Pastor with a scripture 2 Peter 2:14. Babe forewarned the minister about the false teachers and how they're beguiling unstable souls, a heart they have exercised with covetous practices, cursing children; Babe knew that some of the ministers were cursing themselves as well as the women they were misleading and how the churches would be judged first. "For it is time for judgment to begin with the family of God and if it begins with us, what will be the outcome before those who do not obey the Lord our God" (James 4:17).

By now, Babe had made herself known to all the local churches she could, but she could tell some looked at her in a joking way. Babe sent letters to the churches as well as the congressman and the presidents, and while she was at it, she decided to send a letter to the Pope even though Babe didn't get much of a response. She just did it out of obedience. Babe wasn't surprised that no opportunities to minister opened up because she knew that it was too difficult to preach on, and Babe had already thought about writing a book. She thought she would help people to understand the Bible by breaking down the scriptures so they could understand the abortion issue better. This sounded like a much better idea since it was God's Word that would not return void. Discussions about abortion strengthened Babe's awareness in this area. With scriptures to justify abortion, a friend that believed the opposite gave Babe several scriptures to consider.

Upon reading Jeremiah 1:5, "Before I formed thee in the belly, I knew thee," what they overlook was the fact that Jeremiah's father was a Godly priest himself, which meant that God had already established a covenant with him, not like many situations in the world conceived in sin. Babe noticed in the New Testament book of Acts chapter 19; it talked about the seven sons of Sceva. Sceva was a Jew and priest of evil spirits and witchcraft. That proved to Babe that some false priests will be right in church. In Psalm 51, David wrote, "I was shaped in iniquity, and in sin did my mother conceive me." Many thinks David was born illegitimate because of this saying. There's no proof that David was born illegitimately.

Although it was customary for men to have more than one wife, which was contrary to the law of God, God allowed it because he also allowed divorcements eventually. David was referring to the Adamic nature that we all have; this is totally different than being born under the curse of sin. Even though God is a miracle worker in these situations, we must remember the truth. In Psalm 1-13, David said, "For thou have possessed my reins. Thou have covered my mother's womb." Again, David was in a situation where a covenant had already been established with God through his father, Jesse. Babe won't argue the fact that God knows all, yet he gives you a choice to love his law and do what he has prescribed. He knows when you are in sin.

Babe knew that Old Testament scripture that every minister likes to use to pressure women is to choose life; that's easy when you haven't sinned, but when a person is living in sin and they are hiding behind their lies, they need to know what sin really is. Now Babe realized that the word *murder* was a scare tactic, and if they would scare the women into having children any kind of way, Satan would begin to think he would win the world over. Unfortunately, it looks like it has already happened.

The scenario became mind boggling as Babe began to think how she could reach the many people that were still caught up in the ignorance of history. As much as she didn't want to deal with the abortion issue, she knew she couldn't avoid God's warnings. It was taking such a toll on her mind, and time away made Babe think she would be ready to grasp the situation better. When a chance to take an excursion with a group from work arrived.

Babe thought she didn't mind, even if it was to the casino. Babe didn't gamble much, but when a chance to take a weekend trip to Mississippi with a few coworkers was offered, Babe thought it could clear her mind from thinking about abortion.

An event was being made to join some coworkers one weekend at the casino. It all seemed innocent, and Babe didn't have a gambling problem, but she sure was looking forward to winning if she could. Everyone was going to meet at the bank's parking lot, where they would leave their car and join the group. Mississippi seemed like long ways from Tulsa, and after they got started that Friday evening, they didn't arrive in Mississippi until early Saturday morning, and they had caught a deal where they would be in at least two different hotels during the short time they were there. The long trip on the bus made time to be familiar with one another or, at least, be cordial.

The Hotels were beautiful, but it seemed like all of them were. They passed one nice hotel after another, and Babe thought, *How can they all be in such close distance without competing with each other?* Nevertheless, as they pulled into the Fitzgerald Hotel, all waited anxiously to unload the bus. While they all waited on their luggage, the planners matched up roomies. Babe didn't come with anyone, so she was okay with whoever they gave her, and since she brought her laptop and a few books, she figured when she got burnt out with the gambling, she would resort to reading and writing.

Most people knew each other, and even though Babe knew of her coworkers, several people joined them from other jobs. Altogether, there were about sixty people on the bus, and when Babe was matched with an older lady from another job, Babe didn't mind. They all gathered their luggage and walked through the casino as a group. Nearby you could hear the ringing of the machines and the sound of money clinging. As they walked through the crowded casino, one lady rejoiced over the big win she had just made. Tightly the group walked together, and Babe mentioned aloud to her new roomie, "That machine is hot." As they continued walking, a voice from behind her said, "Do you have some money? I'll play it."

Babe looked surprised at the young girl and said, "If I had some money, I would play it." They all shuffled along.

Babe thought about it and wondered, the nerve of some people asking her for money to play on that machine.

After washing up and checking their luggage, Babe and Monica, her roommate, decided to have a bite to eat and later check out the casino. At the hotel's restaurant, they had coupons for free meals; that went with the package. As Babe and Monica were grabbing a table, the young girl from the casino who wanted money to play the machine approached Babe and told her she lied about the machine being hot. Babe didn't know what to say. Finally, Babe told her, "I didn't swear about it."

Apparently, the girl must've gone back to the machine thinking it was hot like Babe thought, but Babe didn't know; she only saw a girl cashing in on a win and said that. Babe felt bad because the girl had lost her money, but she didn't know what to tell her. She didn't expect the girl to go back and lose all her money on the machine, then suddenly Babe began to feel uncomfortable about the girl. First, she wanted money to play the machine, then she wanted to blame Babe for not winning. Babe didn't know for sure, but she was beginning to wonder if the kid was just trying to make it difficult for her.

Babe decided, *It's Only a Couple Days, I'm not going to let this kid ruin my trip.* So, Babe decided to avoid the young girl after that. Although on the way to the other hotel, the chatting in the bus proved she was just a young kid trying to have a good time. Eventually, Babe had a formal introduction with Katie and Kerri, her twin brother, who had joined the group for the weekend outing. They were loud on the bus as well, but after a while, Babe didn't mind since she knew they were just a bunch of young kids.

The weekend ended, and most people had run out of money as well, so the long trip back was full of giggling and laughter, even for the sore losers. A few people won and a few lost, but Babe broke even since she had planned on not spending much.

On the way back, they didn't stop much, and it was close to midnight when they arrived at the bank where they left their vehicles. Gathering outside the bus and loading their cars with their luggage took some time, but they all looked forward to being at home before long. Babe loaded her luggage in the bed of her truck and unlocked the doors.

As she approached the door to get in, three people approached her and questioned her. It was Katie, Keri, and their friend. Surprised by their approach, Babe just waited to see why it seemed like they were blocking her. Suddenly, Katie asked Babe if she killed such and such. Babe didn't believe what she was hearing, then she realized they're asking her about the justifiable homicide. Babe didn't remember the guy's name, but she assumed he was who they stated. Then Babe took a deep breath and admitted she did, not knowing what to expect. Surprisingly, they responded with a "Thank you!" Babe couldn't believe her ears until they explained that the rapist, she killed had killed their father years ago and left him to die in their front yard. Then they started asking Babe all kinds of questions about the guy, and Babe could only tell them that she didn't know anything about the guy; she was only defending herself. All left with the joy of knowing. They didn't win big that weekend, but it put closure on things Babe had never thought about, and it gave Katie and Keri the peace of thanking her for her story.

Driving away, Babe wondered if it would be that easy in convincing people about abortion. The thought of warning people reappeared in her mind. Babe thought all these years had passed, and it seemed like people still wanted her to know that she did the right thing. Now serving God was taking her to a level that even Babe didn't fully understand. But since it was God's Word, she felt sure those that God loved would understand.

Chapter 13

Opposition from the Enemy

Babe could tell this wasn't going to be easy. She knew the power of fasting, and since she had learned how, she looked for God's strength to take her on a twenty-one-day fast. She had fasted three days and lasted. Nothing miraculous happened, but God's peace began to comfort Babe more. She knew that twenty-one days on liquids would be good cleansing spiritually and physically since she needed God more than ever. Babe knew the Word of God revealed the truth that would lead the people out of darkness, and the only way she could share it would be through his divine revelation.

At the church where Babe experienced opposition, she would listen to how the minister would fast and pray, and he was still in error simply because he hadn't tempered his ego to understand the Holy Spirit's teaching through a woman. Babe knew that the Holy Spirit would open her mind to deal with the opposition that she would have through fasting.

As Babe prepared for her fasting, she decided she wasn't going to get into bondage. Her liquids would be to satisfy her hunger and thirst, and she would feed off the Word of God. Near the end, she gave in and joined some friends out for dinner, where they also encouraged her in her desire to know God deeper.

After Babe fasted for twenty-one days, she noticed a peace about it all. She knew some wouldn't like her and some would appreciate her truth as well as honor his Word through her knowledge. She also knew there were many people that felt the way she did, yet they didn't understand how the Word of God revealed it. Babe was also touched by a dream she had shortly after the fast was over. In her dream, she envisioned herself crossing a sea, and while in the water, a song played, an old hit from the 60s, "Drowning in the Sea of Love." Babe crossed the sea, and her head bobbed as the song played: "I've been down one time, I've been down two times, I've been down three times."

Then the melody played again, "Drowning in the sea of love." When Babe woke up, she sensed God was telling her that he was baptizing her in his love, and his love would carry her through the trials of life. Babe knew in her heart that true love was willing to open up to understanding God's love and grace through abortion. But the haters of the world were making it difficult for the love of God to be shed abroad.

As Babe began her exhaustive study of the Bible, she began to unravel the mystery behind every chapter in the Bible, yet Babe had wanted the government's approval, but she was beginning to wonder if something was hindering her. One letter she sent to one of the late presidents made her think that he thought the book was a threat. After Babe informed the president of the book, he wrote her a letter and told Babe that he wouldn't endorse the book. But Babe didn't ask him to endorse the book, and she thought since he was pro-choice, he would be glad that Christians could stand on the Bible to justify abortion.

The letter made Babe wonder, but she continued with her study because she knew that her directions were coming from God now, and she knew it was better to obey God than man.

However, it was beginning to make Babe wonder about some of the sermons from different pulpits at different churches; also, Babe noticed how the sermons were too direct and how people came into Babe's life haphazardly, and Babe didn't feel the spirit of God within them. It was then that Babe realized she was being watched. Babe remembered when Josie and Malcolm sold drugs; Babe used to tell Josie that a star was following them at night. That same star was following Babe now, but she wasn't doing anything illegal. Later, Babe found out he had more skeletons in his closet than carter have liver pills.

That's when Babe realized the object that she thought was a star was actually a satellite. When Babe realized this, it meant that they had been watching her long before now. Looking back now, Babe remembered things that triggered her memory all the way back to the justifiable homicide, which meant they were there when Josie was murdered as well.

As Babe thought about it, she began to feel that they must be watching her for her protection, assuring her that they were her friends and she had nothing to worry about, but it wasn't long before Babe could sense they were also in her apartment and everywhere she went. Babe didn't understand how the government could do this, but she knew for a fact that it wasn't God. Many times Babe knew that she was being bugged, once.

She was disconnected when she was talking about abortion. This upset Babe so bad that, one evening, when she tried to redial the number, her phone became dead, upsetting Babe even more. That's when Babe realized these people were trying to shut her up. Babe ran to a local convenience store to continue her conversation.

Babe had switched churches, and she recalled the new pastor joking that if the Bible said that Jonah swallowed the whale, he would believe it since the story about Jonah being swallowed by the whale had many people thinking the Bible was just a book with nonfiction stories. Babe liked what the pastor said, meaning he believed the Bible wholeheartedly and taught it with utmost respect. Babe loved to sit under his teaching.

Babe had the most difficult ministry in the Bible because now Babe realized that the disciples could only hint around to the subject because of the controversy, and the Old Testament prophets were very direct in many cases even though it was OT English. Written centuries ago, it had to be translated in a way that people could understand. Babe was convinced that most of the Bible was centered on the abortion issue because God told Moses to write the law, and the law against illegitimate children was never done away with, but people misled others because of the evil and wicked nature of men.

Now Babe had to contend with all sorts of evil in the world; many had good intentions, but Babe had also been told that hell was bought with good intention. Like the adoption ministries, Babe knew that someone had to care for these orphanages, and she didn't want to discredit their good intentions. She had once supported a television ministry for children in other countries, and she knew the need was always there, with international adoption being a trend for Americans because it's less stressful. Many know the books will be closed, but in America, there are usually a few loose strings.

Either way, adoption can be unpredictable. Making God's Word safer than anything. In Matthew 23:15, Jesus said, "Woe unto you, scribes and Pharisees, hypocrites! For ye compass sea and land to make one proselyte, and when he is made, you turn him into twice the child as hell as they are." Like many that hated the abortion clinics and doctors who performed them, Babe knew this evil was unbearable and quite scary. Now that Babe knew the Feds were watching her, it was difficult to determine if they were the good guys or the bad guys.

Some clues encouraged Babe as she made time for television and new movies. Then the movie *The Bodyguard* came out, with Whitney Houston and Kevin Costner. Kevin, a former FBI agent, played as her bodyguard; Babe gave it thumbs-up because she thought the producer actually had her in mind.

Babe loved Whitney Houston in the movie and only wished she could sing that well. Word had traveled about the books or more so about Babe because the books really hadn't been published yet, but at the first church Babe committed to, a few famous Gospel singers had performed there, and Babe remembered taking pictures at a dinner, which included a few memorable ones. Babe knew that they all stared at her and wanted to hear or read about her testimony because of her background.

All Babe wanted to do was translate the Bible, whereas everyone could see the truth about abortion. Another movie Babe took a liking to, was the movie *Babe*, about a little pig that learned how to lead the sheep. Babe, the pig, and the sheepdogs took a liking for each other; and when Babe, the pig, successfully led the sheeps, it was an inspiration to Babe because of her name, and the sheeps were like people that would eventually find the truth and be led the right way. A movie that Babe had not watched was *Baba Kid's* because as funny as it sounds, Babe hadn't made up her mind to have children and the fact that many scriptures led to the success of women having families that God blessed.

It was then that Babe realized the only reason the Feds were watching her was for the simple fact that she didn't have children. That became offensive because Babe thought she didn't want the entire world in her bedroom making a big deal about her sex life. If this was the only reason, they were watching her, it became disturbing because it didn't seem like they cared about women that needed to know the truth or other countries that needed assurance in God's Word.

Babe's job had downsized where she had worked for seventeen years. Citgo moved to Houston, she now had her broker's license to sell real estate, but this was a slow market, and Babe had been working in the nursing business on the side as well. She did agency work a lot because they paid more, and there were a variety of jobs. Babe loved working in the hospitals; she would work in different areas all the time. Once, Babe was working in the intensive care unit, and there was a redheaded registered nurse. He seemed nice at first, but when he asked Babe what kind of birth control she used, Babe thought that was kind of personal, and why would he need to know something like that? Babe told him that it was none of his business. And they chuckle about it. That's when it seemed like most men's approach was about having a child, but none talked about marriage, nor did they seem like the kind that Babe wanted to be with.

Some guys that she would meet out of the blue seemed like they were attracted to her, but then, Babe would realize that these men were already informed, and Babe could tell they were only users. Babe still enjoyed the company of the opposite sex, even if it was just platonic. She liked to have a balance in her life. Her mechanic, for the most part, was very agreeable with Babe on the abortion side, but when it came to talking about God, he couldn't relate. He told Babe that the Bible was written two thousand years ago, which made it outdated since we have cars now and the only thing, they had in the biblical days were horses and carriages. Babe couldn't believe a grown man had no sense how God was present in this day and age as well. Babe knew since he wasn't brought up in church, he couldn't relate, and he didn't want to relate to any of it.

At this point, men were only a diversion because Babe had been there and done that. She knew her focus now was to do the will of God, which was to write the book, and she dedicated herself to that.

One movie that Babe had once enjoyed was the *Passion*, produced by Mel Gibson. Babe was torn apart at the way they crucified Christ, and there was a scene in the movie that became disturbing—the way the devil was portrayed as a female, dashing in and out of the scene, especially at the end when she appeared to have a small child, but the child looked like a dwarf. *Was it a hidden clue?* Babe wondered.

It seemed like Babe was experiencing opposition from the enemy, and she couldn't go anywhere without someone sending a baby and a woman to try to spook her. Babe didn't quite understand the nonsense behind it because she really loved children. People anxiously awaited to stalk her just to say rude things or make an appearance that she would see.

Once, when Babe was in between jobs again, she went to apply for a job, which took about one hour to fill out all the paperwork, but when she finished and was ready to leave, there was an older car parked next to hers that had this handwritten note on it, stating: "If your momma had aborted you wouldn't be here." Babe was flabbergasted because she knew she didn't have a chip on her shoulder like the many who tried to accuse her of. But whoever was bugging Babe could track her every presence. Another time, when Babe had lost another job, it seemed like a small red truck dashed out in front of her with more handwriting, and this time, it stated, "Only the strong survive."

Babe was upset because it began to seem like she was being targeted by hate bullies. Babe began to think the government was behind everything; they're the only ones with tracking devices like that, but Babe didn't understand why they worried about her. Finally, Babe had to remove herself from church because she didn't want to hear any sermons about herself. Babe missed the fellowship of the saints, but she knew it would be better to finish the books and get them published before committing and attending anybody's church because too many people had heard about her, but she was determined to let his Word guide and direct her. She was blessed to understand Psalm 45:10, "Hearken, O daughter and consider, and incline thine ear; forget also thine own people, and thy father's house." Babe couldn't believe what she was reading, but she marveled over the excellence of her Lord and Savior. She knew this scripture meant that if she had to leave the church, so be it, and even if her family or her race didn't approve, she would have to leave them also.

The entire chapter of Psalm 45 gave Babe directions as she read about the daughter writing, even though the author of the chapter stated he was writing. It gave stronger hints for Babe to write the revelation down. In that same chapter, it seemed to be saying God was more worthy to be praised than the children of men (unborn). At times, Babe really didn't mind being a loner because God's Word was very fulfilling. Babe began to understand numerology as she studied the Bible; she knew that reverse numbers have the same significance. Transposed, 45 is the same as 54; it was awesome when she realized Isaiah 54 and

Psalm 45 was referring to the same woman. They both had seventeen verses in them.

Most people thought Babe was way out there, and she was compared to the world's standard of living. Babe's mother became offended when she said anything about the word *bastard*.

One girl she knew said the same thing about her mother when she heard that word. Babe was offending people she had no intention of offending just because of that word. It didn't make any sense to Babe because she couldn't change the word, and she just wondered if people thought God was going to change the word. *Don't Count on It,* Babe thought. Babe could see how God stated, "You might have to leave your own people as well."

Just about everybody in Babe's family had their children before their marriage, and even though God blessed them despite their way of doing things, it didn't make it right, and it looked like most of them still struggled financially. Babe's older brother didn't have any children, and he seemed to regret it, but Babe felt thankful she never had children.

While Babe waited on a better time to get the books out there, it seemed like it was never going to happen. The IRS got into the picture, and no matter what, they were determined to make Babe owe them. Babe knew they were scamming her, but it was hard to prove if you didn't get a certified tax accountant.

Babe felt IRS was upset because she cleaned out her retirement with the oil company, and she sold the rented houses because it all got to be too much of a hassle, especially when the housing authority supervisor had the nerve to tell Babe that she needed to get married. Right about now, Babe was getting tired of people trying to match her up and mate her. She was also fed up with the Feds telling everyone about her finances, and she began to think most of the time that she was getting scammed because of the spies hanging over her head telling others her business. Maybe they got upset because Babe cleaned out her money right before the economy dropped.

Nevertheless, she tried to pay them when she could. After she was forced to file for bankruptcy, it seemed like her job situation was up and down, but now that Babe knew who was behind it, she began to question the government. Babe figured they were probably growing tired of watching her and there was no action. So, they had to create some action; it seemed like Babe blamed them for everything, even when she couldn't prove it.

Babe had her problems, but around the world, the earth was shaking. While working at the hospital one night, Babe knew the weather looked scary. Babe was on a private sitter job. They had predicted a bad hurricane even though it wasn't near Oklahoma. Babe was tuned in because it was on the top of the weather charts. After the night had passed, the aftermath of Katrina surfaced. It was horrible, and it wasn't getting any better. Babe thought about her old friend she had met while on a cruise; they stayed in touch until Babe found out she must be somebody the government was using. Babe thought she might have been an informant because this girl called Babe when Babe was cleaning out her retirement to restore some rent homes, and this girl called Babe out of the blue, telling her about her son using up her retirement. Babe figured this woman wouldn't have called her to tell her this if someone hadn't told her what was up. Babe didn't want to have anything to do with her afterward.

The government became so possessed with Babe's life she couldn't believe they were that annoying. But Katrina was real, and the cleanup was devastating. They couldn't get help fast enough, and people were all battered and beaten. If it wasn't the hot drenching days, it was the danger of being alone at night. The crimes were fierce, and the people were in a panic. FEMA, the federal government agency, couldn't save them fast enough. Nursing homes were killing some of the people to keep them from dying a worse death. Babe couldn't believe the disaster happening there. They said it was a category 6 hurricane. Babe just knew it was the worst she had heard about. Then again, she remembered the Red Sea and how the people were all swallowed up in the water; she couldn't help but compare it with the Bible story because it seemed like God may have been saying something to the people—or was it the government? —was not hearing. The Katrina crisis cost the U.S. government a lot of money and lives as well.

But it looked like, all around, people were having difficulties in maintaining life. One morning, Babe was lying in bed trying to wake up. Sometimes she would leave her television on at night and sometimes to be awakened by it. Babe rolled over and noticed the commotion going on the television; she couldn't believe her eyes. People were jumping out of the twin tower building windows, dying on impact. It scared Babe; she didn't know what her country had done for the terrorist to attack her country like that. Babe grieved for her country, but she was still preoccupied with getting her business and book out of the way. She wanted to help in some way, but she didn't know how.

After 9-11, Babe seriously began to wonder what was happening. She had heard that some well-known evangelist blamed the homosexuals for 9-11. Babe thought, *What the hell did the homosexuals have to do with this degenerate act?* Babe had thought that some people had labeled her a homosexual since she had noticed everybody seem to be trying to test her sexuality.

Babe didn't have time for a husband because, for one thing, she didn't trust the government since they couldn't knock on her door like they had some sense. Babe didn't like accusing the government, but she figured she would rather accuse them instead of God. She felt they were trying to hide behind lies like everybody else. Babe wasn't homosexual, but she sensed they're bugging her 24-7 for some reason. Babe had grown to understand why people were like they were. Maybe the government wanted her opinion about everything. If it seemed to be that valuable, why did they have to act like she was a criminal of some kind? Babe thought it would've been nice to work with them if they had approached her the right way. It seemed like Babe couldn't make friends without the government using people, or was it because the town she lived in was considered the Bible belt?

There was this one girl that Babe had met; when Babe told her about the ministry, she asked Babe if she would ever have another abortion. Babe thought it was weird. *What Does That Have To Do With Anything?* Although Babe was living closer to God than she had before, she knew the devil could slip in and put a bad seed in any conception.

Technology had come a long way, and sometimes, Babe would notice how she would be listening to television and the program would be communicating with her as if they knew what she was doing, and they would respond accordingly.

Sometimes Babe thought it was funny because she knew they were trying to give her a word, but this became old, and Babe had to limit herself from watching television, especially if it was a live program. She knew the government could use certain devices to bleed through the channels.

The way they were doing things, Babe couldn't help but wonder if they were playing with the media through the satellites. She would turn on the television, and she would swear that it appeared even the newscasters and celebrities were saying things to get her attention.

The auditor claimed she owed money for 2003 taxes, and that was the year of 9-11. Now this evangelist was like all the other preachers that were coming against Babe to get married. She didn't understand why, all of a sudden, it was any of their business. She was tired of the scum-of-the-earth men approaching her. When they discovered the evangelist had a heart attack in his office and they discovered his body the next day, Babe wondered if it was a sign especially with the fact that he was seventy-three years old, and abortion was legalized in the United States that year.

Ever since Princess Dianna and Dobie were killed in the automobile accident, it was said Americans might have been a target. But our government was too busy trying to make Babe look crazy. It also dawned on Babe that her brother had a birthday on 9-11, and she could never remember his birthday until what happened on 9-11.

After 9-11, the American president went on a rampage, destroying anything and everybody in sight, causing the United States deficit to plunge in the sight of American investors. Even the president predicted that America was on the verge of bankruptcy.

Before Babe's finances were downsized, Babe ventured out, taking a trip to Egypt. Babe had heard about a collection of scrolls discovered while some pheasants were preparing the soil for harvest. This was in 1945, and when the scrolls were discovered and translated in English, they named the book the Nag Hammadi Library.

Some predicted that these scrolls were written after the ascension of Jesus, when he walked the earth for forty days before returning to heaven with God. Babe had already taken a trip to Israel. Since this new birth began to stir up some deeper issues, Babe purchased a copy at the bookstore. They were referred to as the Gnostic, as in knowing.

Babe browsed through the collection of books, some known as mythology. Some of the readings where so deep Babe knew that she would have to fast and pray over some of the writings and read other reference books as well. However, when Babe got to the book referred to as Thunder, it seemed like it appeared to be saying something. It was written in the female order, and it had a striking similarity to Isaiah 54 as well as Psalm 45, but more bold and brash as the description of this woman was revealed. Babe's visit to Egypt was just as interesting as she sought out the truth of the matter.

It seemed like when Babe realized how many countries still didn't have legalized abortion, she couldn't believe it. At a printing facility, Babe was getting some copies made, and she decided to ask questions about their country. That was over fifteen years ago, and they still don't have legal abortion.

While she discovered that, she couldn't help but notice other places on the map weren't legal as well. When Babe saw that Venezuela wasn't a legal place for abortion, Babe thought about Vince and how he wanted Babe to return with him. Babe didn't know it at the time that God would call her to stand for abortion. She couldn't imagine how it would happen in a place where she would have been outnumbered and Lord knows what else. Babe began to think that, even then, she must have been in the will of God.

Fifteen years later, Babe was sitting in front of the television with a friend at work, and the riots and fireworks were all going off in Cairo, Egypt. As Babe tells her friend about her visit fifteen years ago, she tells the friend, "You know, they didn't have legal abortion then, and they probably don't have it still." In the news, it was stated that the leader they had had ruled the country for over twenty-five years, and they wanted to remove him, but the leader didn't want to go.

People were fighting in the street, and over eight thousand people had already lost their lives behind the riots. In a flash, Babe saw a guy with a T-shirt that had the number 54 on it, and Babe shouted, "Look at the shirt, it has the number 54 on it!" Immediately, Babe thought of Isaiah 54. Babe knew these people were suffering because of the tyrant leadership. It only took our presidents eight years, two terms, to screw up our country; she could only imagine what twenty-five years in office would do to a country. Babe knew these people needed the liberty of God's love. Babe prayed that night that God would help her to tell the entire world about his grace through Jesus Christ.

When Babe thought about it, she kept thinking that it's sure bondage when people were constantly trying to hook her up with a man. As much as Babe thought it was good to have a mate, she had grown set in her ways, and she knew her commitment to God was stronger than the desire to have a man.

Furthermore, the men these days were also burdened with the care of the world. But as she was studying the Bible, she veered into the book of Revelation and read the prophecies regarding the two witnesses that would be killed for their testimony.

In another chapter, the woman that gave birth to the man-child and how the devil was there trying to take it; made Babe realize. Rev. 12:17 describes that child was caught up to GOD. Babe begins to understand it sounded like her abortion, because that is what happens when abortion is done. Babe also recognized it had 17 verses in that chapter also. How these things are happening every day to women in prison. Some are in prison in their minds, but the ones that actually go to prison while pregnant end up turning their children over to child custody. Even when they try to do the right thing, these children end up going from bad to worse.

Work, work, and more work; it seemed like that's all Babe was doing. Every job she got she was working as much overtime to resolve issues with the IRS. Between losing jobs and struggling with bad vehicles, Babe couldn't seem to get back on track. Babe almost felt that it was a bad thing to have left the church, but she knew that with IRS hanging over her head, she couldn't commit to giving the church when it seemed like they were both in cahoots.

Recently, a neighbor moved into the house next door. The tenants were on section 8 and had plenty of kids. Babe had a chance to meet her neighbor when she came in from walking one evening, and she saw her on the porch. Babe always tried to be nice to the neighbors when she could, but Babe could tell that this one was going to be interesting. She had eight kids, going on nine, and she asked Babe if she wanted her ninth one.

Babe jokingly responded, "Do I get a check with it?" But before the girl could respond, Babe told her she was joking. The girl's name was Sharon, and they had lived in Arkansas. She and her mother stayed together. The girl told Babe that she gets $900 in food stamps if Babe knew of anyone that wanted to buy any; they went for half of what they buy. That was interesting; Babe told her she would keep it in mind. Seven boys and one little girl, and she thought she was pregnant with another boy.

The neighborhood was full of little mouths chattering all the time; Babe never had time to be bored. One of her kids was always knocking on the door for something. Babe didn't mind the kids, but it wasn't long before different kinds of people were in and out of the girl's house.

It didn't take long before Babe realized that the girl was selling drugs. Babe had been twenty years clean of drugs, and it seemed like when Josie died, that lifestyle died as well, and it was replaced with something more fulfilling. Church was the replacement, but now that Babe wasn't going to church, her curiosity made her wonder.

It seemed like since all she was doing was paying the IRS; the more she made, the more they took, and Babe was beginning to feel that she could see why people did drugs. They were forced out of their jobs and then the pressures of the world. Yet in reality, it only made it worse, at least, for the ones that really had a goal and a vision.

Although Babe was drawn into a friendship and even though Babe knew there was something about these people she couldn't trust, there was something about them that made Babe wonder. Josie used to joke about writing a book about drugs, and Babe would just listen, but after losing a family to drugs and a society, Babe couldn't help but wonder if it's something in the laws that could be changed. Eventually Babe found herself picking up Sharon's kids from school and keeping them. Sharon would give Babe a few dollars in food stamps in exchange for small favors.

Babe seems to be on a roller-coaster ride; it seemed like ever since the IRS claimed that she owed all this money, Babe didn't know if she would ever get back on track.

One day, frustrated as hell over the Feds still watching her and the problem with getting things fixed the right way, Babe gave in to her curiosity and asked Sharon for something different in exchange for the errands; Babe really didn't know what she was doing because even when Josie was doing it, it always seemed redundant and stupid.

But this stuff that Sharon had made Babe wonder—an eye-opener and a head-opener, not to mention that it seemed like it cleaned your system. Babe knew that most people didn't want to be fat, and the street drugs helped to prevent this, but Babe had frequently would go to the weight doctor when she became stressed out, so she didn't need to rely on street drugs.

Even though Babe knew she was being watched, she didn't care; she was fed up with them constantly trying to set her up with a man, so this became her way of showing the Feds, and she knew people do not get pregnant behind drugs.

But before long, it seemed like Sharon had turned on her, and she was trying to find friends for Babe to use with. Babe wasn't comfortable with this. Sharon's mother acted like a street hooker, and their crowd was the same way. Babe had taken a liking to the stuff because it seemed like they had the real stuff, then Babe looked back and wondered what Josie and Malcolm had been doing, but it was a different and time.

Babe thought they must've stepped on it too much, causing real dope feigns to kill and become strung out. Afterward, Babe realized that she couldn't join with others in this lifestyle because she only wanted to vent some frustration, but she didn't want it to be a lifestyle. Even though Babe came to her senses about the drugs, Sharon still kept trying to find friends for Babe. Babe insisted to Sharon, "Don't bother. I'm not comfortable with others."

One weekend, Babe stayed over at her mom's, trying to help her since she had just gotten out of the hospital, and when she returned home, she couldn't figure out why everything was so quiet. Sharon wasn't around and neither were the kids. After a day or so, Babe noticed that Sharon was back and so were the kids.

Babe asked, "What's been going on?"

Sharon was surprised that Babe hadn't heard that she had been busted. Babe being away for the weekend, had missed all the action. Now Sharon had to move because she could no longer stay in the section 8 housing. With the need to move, Sharon's mother became quite persistent with Babe.

They wanted Babe to let them move in with her, and Babe knew that it was a trap. None of them worked, and Babe didn't want that kind of traffic in her home.

After Babe went back and got her real estate license, she purchased a fixer-upper home, and she didn't want to lose it behind drugs. Finally, Sharon found a place on the other side of town, and Babe helped move her. Babe was so glad when they moved. After Sharon and her family moved, Babe began to wonder if they had been sent by someone from the government, especially when Sharon told Babe that her grandfather was in a insane institution in Arkansas for cussing out one of the former presidents. It sounded like the same one that sent Babe that letter about not endorsing her book.

As Babe broadened her studies to understand that some psychics were not all misleading, she began to have a better understanding of the Bible and the story about the psychic in the Bible, when Saul went to the witch of Caldor and asked the witch to bring up Samuel, a prophet and priest of God who was dead. Whatever form of sorcery it was, this witch brought the image of Samuel up, and Saul wanted to know if they were going to win the fight the next day. The image of Samuel told Saul that they would lose the battle, and they lost the battle. The witch didn't lie, and some image of Samuel did appear telling Saul that he would be defeated in battle.

After hearing all sorts of stories about the spiritual world, Babe couldn't help but understand the psychic views about life after death. After she listened to a tape series from a well-known psychic regarding the underworld and the secrets of high society, Babe was astounded at what she heard.

Babe believed this psychic because this psychic always gave God his righteous place and even wrote a book about God. Babe knew what the psychic said about the presidents and how some of them were on drugs and funded their campaign with drug money. Babe knew that one of the presidents pardoned a drug dealer in his last days in the office.

Babe was glad about this because now she was beginning to see another side to this drug business, not like when Josie was murdered. The governor of Oklahoma stated that he believed that a drug dealer should get the death penalty. Babe thought about that and knew that she had forgiven her brother-in-law, and now that she passed medication in the nursing homes, when she worked in the prison, Babe began to realize that drugs were drugs.

Her experience with her neighbor Sharon also left her thinking that it's bad to sell drugs, but people were going to get them no matter what, and the way the government was letting them into the communities, it seemed like they only wanted to penalize poor people the most.

But now, this only gave the Feds something more to hang over Babe's head. Even though Babe wasn't an alcoholic, Babe began to notice when she went out to eat before going to work on the second shift that if she had a drink with her dinner, it seemed like the coworkers would all know about it because this was the kind of stuff they liked to talk about, and eventually they would use it against Babe. But then, Babe realized her coworkers would joke that way because someone was informing them of everything Babe did. Babe couldn't believe it; she knew that it wasn't a crime to have a drink before work, and she didn't make a habit of it, but just knowing that the people where she worked were getting a full report of everything she did before she went to work was annoying.

Malicious and evil were these people, with every intent to destroy what they couldn't control, but Babe decided she would leave it to the Lord.

When Babe wasn't working, she was busy reading and writing. Babe would get updates from pro-choice organizations daily because they knew of her vision. Babe would go through her emails, and more and more stories would strengthen Babe. One article stated that 40 percent of women have had, or will need, abortions in America.

After reading the statistics, Babe realized that many women were hiding behind their hypocrisy, but if they could see the truth in the Bible, they would come out and support the women in other countries as well.

The Bible gave more evidence than anything. When Babe read there would be seven women to one man, Babe knew that these women will finally realize that men in America cannot afford one wife, and to think that the women outnumber the men gave Babe reason to believe it's the women's choice to be a slave to sin or face reality about childbearing.

Babe had met a guy while looking for wood to burn; this man had served in the military and was disabled now because he had a blood disorder. He also had a drug habit that he couldn't beat. When he found out about the books Babe wrote, he started talking like she had to have children, whether she wanted them or not. As a matter of fact, just like her mother. Babe thought, *We'll See About That.*

Chapter 14

The Elect Lady

Evidence in the Bible was beginning to stack up so high that nothing could convince Babe she was wrong. As a matter of fact, one evening, Babe passed by a rally in a church parking lot, and they were holding a rally for prolife. There were quite a few people, and Babe began to wonder how all these people could be wrong. Babe heard the spirit of God speak to her. "They didn't come to worship me." Babe knew it had to be the Holy Spirit because a scripture confirmed it. In Matthew 21:13, Jesus said to himself, "It is written. My father's house shall be a house of worship, not a den of thieves." Jesus said this because in the book of Zechariah, adoption agencies that referred to abortion as murder were considered thieves. When their intention overrides the truth, it makes it erroneous. But if a woman chose to give her baby away and they receive it in the spirit of love, God will bless both. Some women have given their babies away grievously and still regret it, but at this point, they must rest in God.

By now, Babe had searched the Bible backward and forward, and she knew there were clues throughout the entire Bible.

However, now that Satan, the god of the world, had infiltrated the world with his lies, she knew she had to make sure those that missed the mark and sinned would also have the hope that they could be saved since there are different degrees of salvation.

For sure, Babe's eyes were opened as she read a book near the end of the Bible, when she read the book John had written to the elect lady. This book hit Babe like a thunderbolt. It drew Babe in while she sat on the edge. As Babe read all thirteen verses, Babe realized that the book was written to her personally, speaking of Thunderbolt it also had a striking resemblance to the book called "Thunder Perfect Mind" found in the Nag Hammadi Library, near the back of the book, just like the book John wrote to the Chosen Elect Lady, close to the back of the Bible, also they were discover 1945, indicating the figure nine when transposed.

For some reason, Babe couldn't take her eyes off this book, and as she reached for her study Bible, it became clearer that she was the elected lady. The two key words were *love* and *truth*. One of Babe's name was Juanetta; it had to be split in order to verify its meaning. Juan was the root name of John, meaning" God's gracious one," and Etta meant "truth."

The fact that Babe collected hearts is symbolic of love. In the first verse, John wrote, "The elder unto the elect lady and her children, whom I love in truth; and not only but also all that have known the truth." To Babe, John was speaking not only to her but to the elders of all churches, preaching under the name of Jesus Christ. Babe liked to look at the word *elders* as those that are old enough to understand the truth. The children were others who stood with Babe in their belief that women should have their choice. Jesus referred to believers as children many times.

In the second verse, John wrote, "For the truth's sake, which dwelleth in us, and shall be with us forever." Babe knew that the Word of God meant truth, and truth also meant law as well, and God's Word was telling her something more about abortion. "Grace be with you, mercy and peace, from God the Father, and the Lord. Jesus Christ, the son of the Father, in truth and love." In the third verse, John emphasized the importance of truth and love, along with mercy and peace. All of this sounded good to Babe. The grace of God seemed to be taken for granted by some, and since she was born in Mercy Hospital, she thought maybe it was ingrained in her and this was the kind of mercy God was speaking of.

John wrote in the fourth verse, "I rejoiced greatly that I found thy children walking in truth, as we have received a commandment from the Father." This made Babe feel that John knew that it's very important to walk in truth.

As Babe read the Word of God, it seemed to come alive. John wrote in the fifth verse, "And now I beseech thee lady, not as though I wrote a new commandment unto thee but that which we had from the beginning, that we love one another." These words reminded Babe that even though some will not understand, she must continue to love them.

Since Babe had named the ministry "God's Loving Kindness Ministry," the sixth verse said it all: "And this is love that we walk after his commandments. This is the commandment that as ye have heard from the beginning, ye should walk in it." Another point John was making was to walk after God's commandment, which meant his laws as well.

After reading the seventh verse, Babe became perplexed at what John was saying: "Many deceivers have entered into the world, who confess not that Jesus Christ has come in the flesh." This is the deceiver and Antichrist. Now Babe knew that the word *flesh* also meant God's Word, and if people deny that the fifty-eighth chapter of Psalm prescribes an abortion for an untimely pregnancy, and all the other prophecies describing Jesus' plan of salvation through abortion, it means they are denying that Jesus Christ came in the flesh as well. John was quick to recognize the spirit of Antichrist recorded in 1 John 2:18: "Little children, it is the last time; and as you have heard that Antichrist shall come, even now are there many Antichrists that denied the father and the son."

The Old Testament has been referred to as the Father, and Jesus represents the New Testament. Yet John was emphasizing the importance of both. Moving on to the eighth verse, John went on to say, "Look to yourself, that you lose not those things which we have wrought, but that we receive full reward." When she read this verse, she knew she had to stand on the Word of God like never before because many people would try to change her mind.

As Babe read on, she compared scriptures with the New International Version for the ninth verse because the translation hit home better: "Whoever runs ahead and abideth not in the doctrine of Christ, hath not God, He that abide in the doctrine of Christ, have both the father and the son."

This scripture quickened her to many things but mainly on the importance of Jesus dying on the cross for the lost sinner and the fact that you cannot say an egg is a chicken or say a fetus is a child. Even if the OT describes abortion as children at times.

The tenth verse warned her of the false teachers. John wrote, "If there come any unto you and bring not this doctrine, receive him not unto your house, neither bid him God speed." After reading the verse, Babe had to pause for a moment to thank the Lord for showing her that the first church she attended was not the right one for her.

John continued in the eleventh verse: "Anyone who welcomes him shares in his evil deeds." It didn't take Babe long to realize that other ministries claiming abortion was murder were the Antichrist, and they probably don't know it. It's one thing to help a girl that waited too late for an abortion, but it's deception to tell the girl it's murder when God said it's his grace.

Babe read what John wrote in the twelfth verse: "Having many things to say to you, I would not write with paper and ink: But I trust to come unto you and speak face to face, that our joy may be full." It seemed like John hadn't really seen this lady in person, but he hoped to someday. Wow! How Babe wanted to see John face-to-face also, although Babe knew that God's Word was the face he was referring to, and that was good enough for Babe until God wanted her to see more.

By now, Babe knew this was a prophetic book that John wrote because it was very close to the book of Revelation. Scriptures throughout the Bible proved that a woman was prophesied right after Jesus' prophecies, Isaiah 53 and 54. John ended the book of 2 John with the thirteenth verse, telling her, "The children of thy elect sister greet thee, amen." Time seemed to be repeating itself, and Babe felt like she was a part of history, along with other women that knew the truth and stood for righteousness.

Giving thought to her sister John mentioned in the last verse, Babe wondered what she was like. Babe knew that her heart longed for the women in other countries that were forced to live with an untimely pregnancy, how some were raped, beaten, and sometimes killed at the hands of malicious and hateful men. Babe knew these women were her sisters as well, no matter what race; she knew that God wanted these women to know his love.

Some theorized that this book was reversed for the church, and most churches have sister churches, but the Old Testament and New Testament scriptures proved the prophecies pertain to a woman. Because of the diversity of God's Word, this book also applies to the churches of Jesus Christ that uphold the entire truth and believe and obey.

Blessed assurance left Babe confident that if a person cannot see the truth in her testimony, it would be because their eyes have been blinded and their ears closed by the ignorance of their sins. Babe wanted so much to show the people the truth because she knew that another part of the Antichrist was the beast. "A man that lacks understanding is as a beast that will perish" (Psalm 49:20).

Now Babe tried to understand the government part better. Babe thought she would give them the benefit of the doubt when Babe realized that they had been watching her. Now she wondered how far back they had known; Babe knew they were far better educated than she was, and for all she knew, they might have sent the rapist just to test her. Babe didn't study the Bible until she finally realized she couldn't delay her calling anymore, but Babe began to believe others had known all along, but they couldn't tell the world until the elect lady received her calling.

Just when Babe thought she had summed it all up, she couldn't stop reading 3rd John because it seemed to reveal the character of the minister at the first church. His name was Demetric, just like the character in 3 John. Basically, John wanted to encourage Gaius, also in the Lord, to emphasize the truth and how important it was to walk in it and how it was important to teach his children (followers to walk in the truth as well).

John commented on how good it was for him to take the strangers into his church and share the love of God, and it's good even if it is a godly sort; the church shall still do well. But he cautioned him to take nothing of the Gentiles. (Not to make his father's house a den of thieves.) John told Gaius that, in the name of God, do not mislead these people, only teach what is the truth that we might be fellow helpers of the truth. John told Gaius that he had written to other churches, but he sensed opposition with them because Diotrephes, the arrogant one, sought authority over everyone who received him not. As Babe read on, she knew beyond a shadow of doubt that this was what happened at the Antichrist church.

In the tenth verse, "Wherefore, if I come, I will remember his deeds which he doth prating against us with malicious words; and not content therewith, neither doth he himself receive the brethren and forbiddeth them that would, and casted them out of the church," John reminded Gaius to follow that which is good, not evil because "he that doeth evil hath not seen God."

As Babe read the twelfth verse, she knew that pastor middle name was Demetrius, and even though the scriptures stated "he hath a good report of all men, and of the truth itself," Babe knew that the Bible warns you to beware when men shall speak well of you. "Yea, and we also bear record; and we know that our record is true." The word *yea* is a caution (but); the truth is a question, but John knows the truth from God.

Also, Demetrius was mentioned in the book of Acts, known as a craftsman, who made silver shrines for Diana, also known as idols. Then John tells Gaius, just as he told the elect lady that he had many things to write, not with ink and pen, but face-to-face.

Somehow, Babe still felt that it was possible to actually experience a deeper relationship with God, but she knew the world had her stressed out, and it was difficult to actually do the miracles that Jesus did, but she was still glad to know that his Word was the face that would lead her and others to victory.

As God's face was revealed, God began to show Babe many more scriptures to stand for women and men that needed to seek an abortion. Babe compiled another book titled *Forbidden Fruit* in hopes that no woman or man would ever feel condemned behind an abortion.

Chapter 15

Salvation for All

As Babe gathered information for the factual book on abortion, *Forbidden Fruit* sounded like a perfect title. Scriptures after scriptures were translated, and some of the scriptures made Babe fearful of the way the Old Testament described some things, and Babe had to leave them out, but she had gathered enough information to help people understand. Since the world was infiltrated with all kinds of people, Babe knew that she had to take the angle of love as opposed to the law. That was easy when she researched other countries and knew how bad the children in third-world countries were—millions of babies are dying at the hand of starvation and poverty as the famine gets worse, yet the leadership would rather see innocent children being born into situations like these.

Even though they have ministries that travel abroad, these countries never see the money that's being raised for them. It's sad to think that many organizations secretly hide behind the cause but never confront the cure. If abortion was legal in some of these third-world countries, they would be able to help themselves, but some countries like to keep it this way; that way, they will have reason to raise money and delegate it their way.

Just think of how many people are blaming God for children like these. Since they blame him for retardation, maybe they don't know that blasphemy is an unpardoned sin. How can people blame God for children born into poverty and sickness when he warned the people of their sexual sin? Poverty and sickness are a result of sin, especially sexual sin.

We all know people haven't been taught to abstain from sexual sin and fornication, and those that know the difference at least have the sense to use birth control. In some countries, women are forbidden to use birth control of any sort.

Men and women are all suffering behind untimely pregnancies.

For the men that are man enough to admit that he cannot afford a child or another child at this time, we take our hats off to you. At this date and time, someone is being penalized for delinquent child support or not paying child support at all, or someone's license is being revoked because they failed to pay child support.

The system is making it more and more difficult for men and women both to write off taxpayers when it comes to child support. Back in the day when most women had big families. The government bore the weight of many homes that couldn't support the many children they had or for women whose husbands left them without any financial support. Our government has been there because there was no other way for these families to survive; that's exactly why some people look up to the government now, but the government is providing ways for people to become productive taxpayers. In other words, it's time to put it back in the system. Some that have lived off welfare all their lives are going to school and rebuilding America—at least, that's what the government's aim is.

We have children in America just like the ones in the third-world countries and if we didn't have legal abortion, it could be a lot worse. So, when someone tries to put women on a guilt-trip because she doesn't want to put her baby up for adoption, there's something wrong with these people.

When people are barren and want a child that bad, apparently, they're the ones with the problem if they cannot open their homes and hearts to some of these children already in state custody who're in need of a family.

Our country has been blessed to the point that their eyes are blinded by the world's needs, and some couples are consumed with having a perfect home that they don't see until reality hits them with divorces and other problems, causing another shift in the family plan.

It would be difficult to preach abstinence in a world that is overrated by sex and the pleasures of sexual sin. It probably wouldn't matter how many scriptures warn the people of fornication, adultery, and idolatry, and they are in the OT as well as the New Testament, which leads me to the preventive measure of birth control, and abortion is the ultimate birth control.

The word *bastard* and *illegitimacy* have offended many people, and some want to take it out of the English vocabulary, which might work in some families, but God will not allow his Word to be changed or altered. If a woman knows that having an illegitimate offspring would cause the child to resent God because of his Word, she should think twice about it. If a person chooses to have a child knowing he has birth defects, causing people to blame God for this, they should also think twice about it. Surrogacy could replace adoption since in the OT some women would have children for other women.

False teachers will take the blame for many of these cases because they beguile unstable souls. But for the situations already in the world, we must trust God but never blame God; God will give us the strength to endure what we have to, and the government has many programs to help.

Sometimes I believe the government and God go hand and hand, but we must put God first because the government has been guilty of causing the problem before it was legal in America.

Thank God for leaders in America that could foresee the problem with illegal abortion.

Now we have to focus on cities and states that would rather let the Antichrist's spirit corrupt them, however they are under the umbrella of the government, aiming to destroy and corrupt the entire principles of justice. We have children right here in our country that's suffering from poverty, starvation, and lack of support that are in need of a family to care for them.

Many are offended over the word *bastard*, but further in the Bible, it informs the strangers that embrace themselves to the new covenant of God that they can become children of God. This is told repeatedly, but warnings are stronger because the curse would be upon some for generations upon generations, making it difficult for all to receive the inheritance of all that God has for them unless they are reborn. Sure, the generational curse can be broken, but it takes a lifetime before some people finally get real with God.

When the Bible talks about the sinner living one hundred years old and still being cursed, it's because God has allowed them to live through things to help others, but he knows that some have lived for the devil most of their lives and they're only going through the motions. Most people get real with God when they're too old to live in sin as they did when they're younger; for many their health begins to fail, reminding them that they don't want to take those kinds of chances anymore.

As Solomon talked about during his dying days, it will all be vanity; all the children he had and all the wives he had only made him turn his heart from God, and during his old and dying days, he knew it was all vanity. Some of the wild oats people sow in life may allow them to live longer, just to do the right thing by them, but in the end, it still might be vanity.

God is merciful, knowing that he will allow many people to live a long and prosperous life just to get their house in order, and the old saying that God will not send anyone to hell, he gives us plenty of time to be redeemed.

God welcomes the strangers and the bastards and the misfits in his Kingdom, but it's conditional that they become circumcised of the heart and live according to his commandments; otherwise, it will be a strict and harsh judgment for the churches that don't teach and emphasize this. Judgment will begin in the house of the Lord. Some people know they cannot live according to the Bible yet attend church and live any kind of way while attending; they're only fooling themselves. That is why birth control cannot be emphasized enough.

Still yet, as Babe reasoned with the truths in the Bible, how many deceivers have come into the world denying the Word of God prescribes an abortion in Psalms 58. The kingdom of heaven suffers violence because the love of God is waxed cold. Some are saying the Antichrist has not come yet, but most will admit that the Antichrist does not believe Jesus is the Son of God. Then there are those that admit that he's the Son of God but have been misled due to false teachings.

It began to make a lot of sense since most religions started in Europe, and when the deception became obvious, many key leaders left Europe to establish Utopia, as described in the novel Thomas More authored, the small paperback titled Utopia, an ideal place, to sound like Ethiopian connecting with the prophecies in Zep. 3:10 about the Ethiopian daughter. Unfortunately, Thomas More was executed alone with John Fischer for conflicting with the Popes teachings, and that's why we have different denominations. Now it seems like what they left in Europe has surfaced in America.

Translating the scriptures in the Bible proved to be more of a challenge than Babe thought because of all the symbolisms that needed to be explained, as well as relating it to the types and shadow scenario. Many of the scriptures were simple enough to just explain, but she took a different approach to every book.

As Babe prayed that the people would understand, it seemed like the Lord began to show her how practical and basic common sense is the biggest example. If they refuse to accept the sufferings in other countries and harden their hearts to helping the poverty-stricken babies there, neither will they reason with sound doctrine.

Many people don't try to read the Bible because it can be complex, especially since they have many translations, but some people have hardened their hearts to certain sins, like a friend that refused to believe that it's not okay to have premarital sex.

Whereas when two people make a commitment, it's between them, and that's fine if that's the way they want it, but for the ladies that have lived for a wedding all their life and they don't mind including God in the picture, it's their personal choice also.

The only way a person can be saved is by acknowledging that Jesus Christ died on the cross for all, including that woman that needed an abortion. Governments will play an evil part when certain cities have to go by local votes, and then they get others to bribe city and state officials.

When they can bribe doctors to start lying about how abortion causes breast cancer, things are getting too drastic. To see how deceitful, the Antichrist can be made, Babe realize that this book is for a greater cause. These people actually think they are doing a good deed by controlling women laid with heavy sins, only to eventually dig a ditch for both of them. If they succeed in their wicked and malicious plot to save the unborn when the unborn cannot speak for themselves, that's when we know that mother knows best.

Chapter 16

The Elections from Hell

After completing the two books, Babe was waiting on a good time to revise them, because it seems like the government was doing nothing but telling people that she needed to get married and have children, for a minute they had Babe believing them, many men would come around acting like they wanted Babe to have their baby, why waste time if a man only wants to have a baby by you? Babe was getting older, and she didn't want to mislead any of them at this point. Not only that; it seems like the government had ways of knowing everything about her, so it also seemed like a plot...

Babe knew she got a bogus ticket that she never knew she had, after picking up a sheet of good plywood that someone had left on the south side. She was on her way back home. Less than halfway there, a lady was flagging her down, trying to get her attention. After Babe saw her, she pulled over and asked her if everything was okay. The lady told her that debris flew from her truck and hit her car. Babe saw she had a nice new red SUV. She walked around her car to see if she had hit her and she didn't see anything wrong. So, she told her she was lying and trying to scam her. So, Babe drove off.

About time Babe got home, 30 minutes into her rest a policeman knocked on her door and asked her if that was her truck in the driveway, and Babe told him that it was. She tried to explain to the officer what had happened, but he ignored her and then he left.

The job Babe had finally landed ended up letting her go after they claimed she made a medication error and that was that. Since she had worked a double shift, Babe believed she could've been tired and overlooked something, but since she never had a warning of any sort, she thought she would get her unemployment.

Knowing that the government was always there hanging over her head, looking to report anything she did. They seemed to be trying to control her one way or the other. Babe had to leave the church, because Psalm 45:10 told her to leave the church and her people, because of the false doctrine already established. Babe was kind of glad to leave the churches, because many of the people looked at her like she was an alien, her interpretation of the Bible begins to offend many, because many were already brainwashed by the governments and the Popes, although she doesn't know how the government had access to whatever she did; but she could tell they were up in everything she did; they would be communicating with the media.

On television when she tried looking at it, and the feedback was incredible. One popular actor was on The Late-Night Show, the actor told the host of the night show that he liked Leo women and Babe just responded right there without anyone present, "I don't like you," just being sarcastic with him. Then he said, "You don't have to go and write any letters. "She thought the government was sending waves somehow.

Babe thought it was funny, who wouldn't have wanted this actor? He was so gifted, playing the piano, acting and singing. She finally figured out that the illuminati's were the ones that specialized in witchcraft and sorcery and what they were doing was demonic as the devil. Working overtime just to get her in bed with anything or anybody.

Their presence alone was too annoying to even want a man, and knowing that this calling was really testing Babe, she knew that many men wouldn't understand, and since she had already met too many that was only trying to use her. It made it easy to focus on the bigger vision about the world-wide problem that whoever was present they would do something because she was tired of them trying to get her to date.

Later on, Babe found out that the actor had a sister with Down Syndrome, and this was their way of trying to get Babe to accept this condition, in case she had to decide at her later age to have children. That was nerve-racking, because it seemed like they only cared about her having children whether she wanted them or not.

Whatever this thing was hanging over her head, it wasn't crazy about Babe, because now she knew the government didn't like the message she was conveying.

After losing her job, she thought she would be able to fall back on unemployment, but they dragged it out and never paid her until she was behind on her bills.

While waiting on her unemployment that same policeman stopped her and told her that she had a warrant for her arrest. Babe asked him for what, he told her a hit and run. Just so happened he told her he was the one that gave her the ticket, Babe told him she never got a ticket, and he told Babe he left it in her mailbox. He told her that she needed to go to the county prison and surrender.

Surrender, what the hell? After thinking about it Babe knew that it was a setup, because she never got the ticket, because she would've disputed it, but Babe mine was on so many things. She should've known that she couldn't trust the government and they were over the pig's patrol. The government had everyone acting like puppets on a string. Every job she worked, she would see some man come right behind her and wanted to speak to the DON at the nursing home. They were just miserable bastards, trying whatever they could do to get Babe in trouble.

Nevertheless, Babe decided to go to the police department and surrender since she didn't have any money and she didn't know what they were even up to.

At the police station, they threw up a ticket that Babe knew well because she was traveling through the casino in her little Ford Escort wagon. The window broke out the back, after trying to scrape some ice off it shattered on her. Babe remembered the incident and she wanted to make it right, because she knew that she had insurance. She just didn't want to go all the way to Pawhuska County to prove it. Babe was very overwhelmed at the time, because the government was doing nothing but making her life a living hell. Later on, Babe found out that the Sheriff could have verified that she had insurance by the records, but since it was an off-brand insurance company, maybe that's why she had to go through that hell.

Most of the places Babe worked at were already being used by the government to cooperate with them.

After surrendering at the police station, they took her phone and used the pictures to flash on public media. Babe didn't realize that until after she was out of jail. Babe sister Candi picked up her car for her. Babe found out that the bogus charge would have cost about $3000.00 to clear up, and she would have to go to Pawhuska to clear up that other ticket.

It seemed strange being in the same prison she used to work at, the same prison that she once passed medication at.

It gave Babe a good reason to call on the Lord, knowing she didn't ever want to get used to being in jail. Her roommate was a young white girl and she told Babe parts of her life history, to think her and her mother were sharing the same man sexually Babe thought my God, Babe assumes it's more women to go around than men, if you need one that bad.

While crying out to God at night, Babe found herself just seeking God to get out as soon as she could, although when she had a dream that her dog was pregnant again, Babe thought, *Dear God, I should've gotten her fixed. Yet God must've been concern about Babes' dog, Sheba, a mixed terrier that a co-worker let her have at the nursing home she just got fired from. Sheba was just a baby when Babe got her and they had grown together, Babe had left her with her mother and her sister would come by and feed her, Babe couldn't find smokie her black cat of 7 years, and since her mother didn't like cats, Babe prayed she was okay. Linda, a girl that owned a lot on her street, had an empty lot where she fed stray cats, so Babe hoped Smokey would be alright. Linda was nice enough to get Smokey and the other kittens fixed after they were born.*

After spending about 7 days in the local prison, then Babe went to Pawhuska for about 3 days total, talking to the judge and public defender; they decided on a payment plan.

It was planned that she would get out on Sunday. Babe was lucky to find someone that was going to Tulsa, and she was able to get a ride with them. Babe sister had her car, but she had her sister in-law staying with her. So, Babe's mother wanted her to come and stay with her until she got her electric turned back on. Babe's house was too big to move back into because the electric and gas, everything was going to be too much.

Staying with Mother was great. It seemed like she was always there for Babe. Her mother. had a three-bedroom house and she loved having Babe over most of the time. Now she lost 10 days of her life spent in jail, which was worse than overnight because of a DUI. Babe lived and she learned. Things just never seemed the same after realizing the government seemed like they were really working against her.

About a week after getting out of jail, the news hit that Whitney Houston had died, and someone said it was foul play. Babe couldn't believe it. Whitney became an icon to her when she did *The Bodyguard*. She reminded Babe of what they wanted her to think of them, whoever they were hanging around. Babe began to doubt that simply because of how they were acting. They seemed to be upset because Babe saw no need to date or marry because that would mean that she would have to put up with more of their shenanigans, because whatever these idiots were waiting on, Babe felt no need to oblige. Later on, knowing the world was being controlled by the Illuminati and it was said they had Whitney's drugs spiked.

Babe had already been staying at her smaller house, because it was smaller, she was so glad to see Sheba, but she was thinking where are these puppies that she had dreamed about, Sheba had been over at her mom's while she was in prison, and Babe couldn't tell if she was pregnant, she thought she still had sagging tits because of the last time she had puppies.

One evening Babe had to go check on things at the smaller houses where she had been staying during her transition she decided to look around, thinking she knew God was trying to tell her about the puppies, but since Babe didn't get any phone calls, her mother put money on the books, but Babe didn't have anyone to call to check on things and she wasn't sure what to tell them.

After looking around, and seeing nothing, Babe heard a faint cry and she thought that must be the puppies, Babe searched everywhere, until she found the puppies, hid under the porch deck, she had to open up the pooch steps, and there they were 4 cute baby puppies, Babe couldn't believe they had been there for almost 10 days without Sheba feeding them and she thanked God for that dream, she was able to bring them to Sheba at her mother's house and Sheba was able to feed them and nourish them. That was a miracle within itself. Babe was so glad she could save the puppies, and they were soon ready to give away. Mother had a neighbor that kept his niece in the summer. She was the first to take one and Babe's friend Kelly took one and Kelly's daughter took the last 2. That turned out to be a happy ending after all. God still answer prayers even when you don't know what you are praying for.

As Babe was wondering why this government would try to set her up, she was counting some money, and looked on the back of the dollar bill sign, and she recognized the emblem of the Illuminati. The triangle with the eye, people refer to it as the all-seeing eye... Babe guesses they must be the ones involved in watching her because it all seems like witchcraft and sorcery. After finding out that the Illuminati were associated with the Catholic faith, Babe realized why she had reservations about all of this.

According to most of the teachings she had been reviewing, the Catholics were the ones that started that heresy about abortion being murder she knew to steer clear of any of them. One guy Babe dated was Catholic, and his sister wanted them to get married. He was spoiled, he was too cheap to buy her a ring, then he let his electrical license expire, but he liked smoking his weed and playing in the band with his homies, but nothing else would he do. And the other Catholic that wanted to date Babe; had too many kids and had never been married. So, Babe became uninterested by Catholic men because for one she didn't believe in their faith.

Now Babe was baffled because the United States is in cahoots with the Catholics, then looking back at history, America didn't even exist, but a Pope back in the 1600's made an Ethiopian man his slave.

Soon after the United States was developed and the Popes of Europe had conspired to bring the slaves over to America, that is when the first conspiracy started. They raped the women and lynched the men, making it seem like it was okay to procreate any way that it happened.

Now knowing that the illuminati were a part of the Catholics, and the Catholics were very much still a part of guiding the leaders of this country, Babe thought she better not even think about trusting them.

Settling down with Mother gave Babe time to think about what she would do. She attempted to find work, but it seemed like every job the troublemakers had already made sure they were in on this, and they would control her every disappointment.

Babe got a job as a med-aide at a small nursing home, it was small enough that she didn't think it would be a threat, but then the DON had to be informed and the next thing Babe knew they had some girl retraining her. She was a seasoned med-aide; they put her up to making Babe look incompetent to get rid of her, then one of the girls from the office was hanging around talking about dating. Then Babe knew that was the problem; the government had been hanging around hoping that she would get laid. Hoping she would get pregnant. It seemed like this would happen over and over, and they were simply trying to ruin her life, because she didn't see a need to rush into anything with some man that they were using.

When mother suggested Babe signing up for disability, Babe didn't want to, but it seemed like the government wasn't going to stop, no matter what, harassing her and sending bullies or trying to hook her up with a man.

Babe was able to file on the grounds of depression, after filing for disability. Babe was relieved that it happened so fast, but she didn't like being on disability, so she continued to work, and enjoyed it when she got a job at an agency. The agency turned out to be God sent. She could work where she wanted and she could pick and choose where she wanted to work. She knew the snakes were still around, but it helped her avoid some that only wanted to bully her. They even allowed her to work on disability, but she could only make a certain amount.

This gave Babe a perfect time to get the books out that so desperately needed to be done; however, she threw them together and used a self-publisher to publish them.

However, after they were done, Babe sensed the publisher didn't understand the significance in the books, so she passed them out to her friends. Some of her friends thought the first one was great, but they shunned the second book because it taught women the importance of having a child that they wanted, giving all the reasons the Bible would warn women also.

Even though the books were done, there was still something missing about them. They hadn't been distributed to the 3rd-world countries, where they needed to be informed, and the government was still hanging over Babe's head trying to make her look like the enemy.

Still, the disability gave Babe a chance to work when she wanted to and decline other jobs that would have too many sitting devils waiting to be used by the government.

Babe still had to work for a living, so she decided to put the books on the back burner until God said so.

Way before Facebook was around, Babe remembered reading the Bible and the scripture that tells the Chosen Elect Lady that John said he would come to see her face to face. Wow, to think about seeing John, Jesus or God face to face would be a thrill worth waiting for, but since she knew, it was referring to the word of God, Babe began to seek the word of God like never before. Facebook became a source to speak out.

It finally came time for Babe to move back to her place. Mother had gotten tired of Babe, and she would always send her brother from Texas to get Babe the hints. Babe was ready to go back home anyway, her mother was helpful during her transition. Going back home turned out to be A better way of having her independence.

Babe decided to move back in the smaller house, she had been staying over there since it was total electric and the bills wouldn't be as much, she like the neighborhood also, she had already met most of the people in the neighborhood, they were nice except for the one-man next door, when Babe had tenants in the house and his mother was still living, Babe had to cut off a Rose bush that was protruding over the drive-way scratching up the neighbor's car. The neighbor's mother was living at the time and she was upset with Babe about it, so this carried on even after her death. Frankly Babe didn't think the guy ever liked Babe because he claimed he wanted the property to make a parking lot of it. Because it was in need of repair, but Babe had everything fixed.

While staying there Babe was glad when she met Mary, she used to frequent the neighborhood where Babe had a house. Mary mother used to live across the street, but it was in such a bad state of repair that Mary stayed around the corner with a friend of hers. She was really fed up with her living conditions and she talked about moving. Babe didn't know how long she had been jobless, but without a car or a desire to drive, working wouldn't be an easy task.

Babe offered Mary a room in her other house when she got ready to move back. It was big enough to have a few roommates and she was glad to accept the offer. At one-time Babe wanted to take in foster children, but it seemed like the idiots couldn't be trusted. Even during orientation for foster parents, some moron started joking about being a pedophile. Babe thought she would never want them putting her in a trap like that. So, Babe decided against it, not only that the bastards only wanted Babe screwing and that was just turning Babe off of even dating. Even more to think about what kind of hell they would try to take the children through. "They just didn't care about anything but Babe having a relationship and all the men they sent seemed like dogs.

Isaiah 56, begin to warn Babe about the dumb dogs, it was bad that the government had taken on that image.

After writing one president about the book and he wrote a letter and told Babe he wouldn't endorse the book, Babe didn't ask him to endorse the book; since he was pro-choice, she thought he would understand. But later on, when she started writing the book on drugs, all kinds of information were revealed about that president; Babe was told he was the illegitimate love child from a previous president's father. This president also had the nerve to tell Babe through some word of familiar spirit that she wouldn't have a fairytale life.

When he said that Babe knew what he was talking about. The sad thing about it was he was a Democrat, and Babe was also, but the way the presidency was, most of them would tell you what you wanted to hear, but they were still like wolves in sheep's clothing. This president managed to move a neighbor next door to her when she moved back to her bigger house and that's when Babe knew all the rumors, she had heard about him were true.

Reagan put the drugs in the family when Babe sister died, now Bill Clinton was trying to start in on her again. But that's when Babe started the other book, *God's Pill for the Gospel,* so this time Babe would know how to justify the ones that were ruining lives and didn't care.

The neighbors that moved next door to Babe were from Arkansas, this happened before Mary had moved in, Babe found out they were selling drugs, and since Babe had already started writing a book about drugs, since they kept bringing them to her... Babe realized the drugs the neighbors had were real drugs. Talking about a "master blaster"

After months of staying in the rented house, Babe was ready to move back into her larger home, and since she would have a roommate to help out, that would be a good start. Mary had a friend that she had known, Randy had a truck, so we paid him to move us, Randy also became the handy man that Babe needed to help restore her home after she moved back, some of the panels on her patio needed to be replaced and Babe bought a portable building that needed to replace the storm damaged one that needed to be hauled off. Randy being between retirement and unemployment, the money came in handy for Randy also.

After Mary moved in with Babe, Babe saw how distant she could be with her family... It was like Mary was an outcast. Her brother lived in Oklahoma City and actually the house was willed to him, so Mary felt no need to repair it. Years of neglect had set in so badly in need of repair. It was terrible, Babe wondered if they could restore it, but the city tore it down before Mary could get any money to save it. Babe had started restoring houses ever since she was at the Oil Company. They were a good source of income after they were rented. But at times the repairs were troublesome, but after a while Babe started learning how to do the repairs herself. After she knew the Feds were hanging over her head, she got rid of them, except for the one across the street from Mary's mother's home. Babe liked the neighborhood and she was still making repairs from time to time if it wasn't rented.

Mary had an impressive background. She was in the military for about 5 years, so she was able to benefit from the benefits they offered her, but Babe thought she told her that because she had Indian in her, it helped her with college, but she claimed she had to go through hell to get it. She had a college degree and was a veteran, yet she was near home, less and destitute of basic needs, Mary seemed to have a love-hate thing going on with her deceased mother, and she never met her father until she was 40 years old. That might have been the reason why she seemed moody most of the time.

While Mary was staying with Babe, Babe cousin returned from California. He used to hang out with James Babes oldest brother, but James claimed that Tank drank too much. Since Tank was in need of a place at first, Babe knew he had hepatitis and she was leery about that because they put people like him in isolation in the hospital, but later Babe recanted and asked him to move in with her and Mary. She would just make sure everything was sterilized. The thugs hanging over Babe's head probably told him things she said, because Tank was a veteran.

Tank was also an alcoholic, and because Babe lived across the street from a liquor store his brother didn't like that idea.

Tank also had cirrhosis of the liver, and he was in a bad state of health. Babe was beginning to look forward to nursing him and the extra money would have definitely come in handy. But it just wasn't meant to be. He finally got him an apartment in the new apartments they had recently built for people with disabilities or low income.

Before long Tank was receiving the maximum amount for being a veteran and disability, and he still liked getting high. Babe would hang out with him and from time to time they would get high, since that's what he liked to do, it gave Babe a break from putting up with Mary, because she had her grouchy moods.

Tank knew Babes oldest sister and how she died. Babe told Tank that since she wrote the first book and the closure on it wasn't good enough, so Babe decided to write a book on drugs, especially since it seemed like they just kept bringing drugs around. Babe told him about the last neighbor from Arkansas and you know what president came from Arkansas. The thing about it, Babe hadn't done drugs in 20 years, but when she decided to write the other book it gave her an excuse to experience drugs since she really didn't know anything about drugs when Josie and her husband were selling them.

This girl from Arkansas had the real deal. Babe didn't know if it was the strength or the cut. She didn't understand how many times, it would just seem like wasted energy and money before, but this girl had some stuff that must've been a master blaster, because after that hit Babe thought now, she saw what's behind the drugs, and the government is putting it out there and trying to ruin people's lives behind it.

Everyone that was telling Babe about the president that was putting the drugs out on the streets and increasing the penalty for those that used it or sold it. But he was partaking of the drugs himself. Babe thought that was a chicken-shit bastard for you, then when Babe found out that they had prison stock, most of them had an interest in it. Babe told Tank the name of the book and she told him that she decided that now knowing that they brought drugs into the family to bait her out, and she thought about how Josie used to joke about writing a book on drugs. It began to weigh heavy on Babe's heart, also knowing how Whitney Houston died, and Josie also. It's like these idiots have nothing better to do than go around putting drugs in people's lives to ruin their life, then go around tainting the drugs to kill them for the hell of it.

Tank started talking about going back to California, where the crack was worth having. He knew the stuff around town wasn't worth the trouble. He would invite Babe over every now and then with a treat and then Babe would treat him, but it wasn't worth the trouble. Babe told him she found out that Reagan was putting the stuff on the streets also, especially up in California. Babe told him that Reagan was the president at the time Josie was involved in drugs. And to think Nancy Reagan coined that phrase, "Don't do drugs," that's kind of a double standard, would you think? The Bible also tells us thou shall not tempt God, but they are tempting people when they bait them with drugs. Babe was told that they have a movie named *"Made in America'* she has not seen it, but it was based on a true story, how most of the presidents and politicians are putting drugs on the streets. Babe also told Tank that believe it or not, Babe believes that Nixon was the president that wanted to legalize drugs, because Nixon vetoed abortion and he wanted to legalized drugs. Babe believed that Nixon knew they had a double standard when it came to drugs, and he really was trying to do what God wanted, not the world. But the way they ousted Nixon, Babe thought surely; he couldn't have been that bad of a president. Nixon probably knew they would use drugs to bait Babe out and that's exactly what happened.

Babe knew that people that were in the wars, they were using drugs just to deal with the horrible things they had to do and see. Then they come back home only to be called a drug addict. Since Babe had been serving God, God had dealt with her about the number 37. While Babe was on a day job, they had to package envelopes and mail them. She was packaging them in bundles, Babe would just bundle them in stacks never knowing how many were in the bundle, when Babe counted them to account for how many she was mailing, they were all 37 in about 4 bundles. Babe thought that was neat because she never thought they would be the same amount. Babe was heavily involved in the church at that time. And she attended church that evening and the pastor mentioned Amos 3:7. Babe thought there goes that number again, and of course Babe had to read Amos 3:7: "God will not do anything unless he informs his prophets. "Now knowing that Nixon was the 37th president, Babe realizes that Nixon really was a prophet, but they made him look bad, because they knew that Nixon was trying to do the right thing. That Watergate shit was blown out of proportion.

For one thing Nixon vetoed abortion and the Supreme Court had to approve it. To think of the surveillance spies that were corrupting the world because of drugs, Babe could see if they were real crimes, but the surveillance spies couldn't even be compared to water gate. They are watching people to set them up for just about anything you could imagine.

Babe figured, had not Nixon followed his heart women would still be using back-alley abortions and killing themselves. But they hated Nixon for that, and they hated him because they knew he wanted to legalize drugs. Those 2 issues were the problems of the world that centered around the first conspiracy... Because the governments have used both to undermine people everywhere.

Tank knew Babe stand on abortion, and he felt that if he had been born with a hole in his head, he wouldn't want to be born that way and he could see why women would choose abortion. But since he was born out of wedlock, that was a bitter pill to swallow. Tank's mother never married either son's father, but back then women didn't have a choice.

My mother later told me that Tank mother had an abortion, and it must've been though the process of a back-alley abortion. I could see her point, after having children that the men wouldn't help out would be a burden, as least Aunty stopped at two children. Babe mom told her that Tank's mother lucked out and found a back-alley abortion and she survived, but other people's circumstances were different. Babe knew that she wouldn't have been able to depend on anybody, not even the baby's daddy after finding out about the other women. The baby's daddy had and after finding that out Babe never looked back.

Tank was a little bitter about being born out of wedlock, but when he had his daughter, he tried to rise above that, but it was his brother that took Tank daughter in as a family and made her a part of their lives. The war screwed Tanks life up, and the drugs, were strong and better when the men went to war, and it was okay for them to comfort themselves while in war, but they came back from war and realize, that Doctor's didn't want to help them with the cure that could have helped them, so some were able to kick the habit, but some died from the FDA drugs and the agent orange the chemical that was in the air.

At least when Tank had his daughter he was in the military, but he knew beyond a shadow of a doubt that his daughter was his, and he made sure that he signed the birth certificate, which would be just as important as being married. Now they go back and do DNA's, if they have to, because they aren't letting them get away without taking care of their children, but some of the men were getting women pregnant while they were in the war zone, that they never had to own up to.

About that time Tank understood why the other books were just as important as the first two. Babe let him read the books she had already written, he told her he thought they were good to read, Babe told Tank that after she finished the three books, she would like to put them all together and send them to the 3rd-world countries first, because it seemed obvious that they were hit the hardest with the deceptions.

Tank was making so much money. Babe wanted to be his personal assistant. He had a car that his mother left him when she left Tulsa to be with her other son after retiring.

She moved to Kentucky to be with her oldest son, because he was more laid back. He was well established, but he kept his eye on his little brother no matter where he was. Tank's brother, Truman used to be a football athlete, he had a relationship with his father, but Tank, never really had much of a relationship with his father, nor his half-brothers and sisters. Tank was a good-looking man though. Babe remembers meeting him in a club and thought he was a good catch, until her sister told her that they were first cousins. So much for that.

Tank struggled with being an alcoholic. His mother was the same way, but she was a hard worker, and it never seemed that way at all. But Tank going to the Army didn't help any, because the army bases made sure they sold them all the cigarettes and most everything they needed to cope with being there, making it more of a crutch to depend on the bad habits. Tank was drafted like his brother. Tank was exposed to all the good drugs and women that he could've had in the military, and his weakness for them took a toll on him.

Babe remembered when Tank was still living in town, he was looking for a job. He would do anything, but all he could do was paint, and that was the easiest thing for Babe to do, so she couldn't help him out. Now Babe looks back and regrets that she couldn't find a job for him, but painting was about the only thing she could do. Tank had tried to take an electrical course, but he couldn't pass it. Babe thought it could've been his intake of alcohol that kept him from being what he tried to be, some black people never had the chance at a real education, when they kept them from reading the Bible because of slavery. Truman, his brother, excelled in everything.

Tank was really struggling mentally. He would talk about the military and how he threw a hand grenade in the enemy's camp and probably killed about 50 people, now as he aged, he wondered if that was even the right thing to do. He would confess that he didn't even know those people but he killed them because, whatever. Babe told him that he had to do what he had to do because that's why they needed people to protect the country.

The turn of another election and President Obama and his wife were the best that Babe could relate to, they interacted with her. Babe prayed for that family, because she knew that President Obama was trying to do the right thing, he lost his mother to cancer of the uterus, so he knew women needed to know more about their bodies, he visited Planned Parenthood and supported them also. Babe was really impressed when President Obama fired the governor of Texas, when he tried to close all the abortion clinics. Babe knew that God had his back also.

Back to the election that was at hand, we thought Hillary had it, she was moving the numbers toward the finish line, but then this *Apprentice* actor, Donald Trump, was getting the kind of attention that only the radical right would appreciate. He knew how to throw his weight around. He was already getting on Babes nerves talking about reversing the rights for women, when God was showing Babe that women all over the world needed to have their God-given rights for their choices.

This man was so full of himself, talking about every race proved that he was very much a racist. Until it came to the men that were sex fiends and were proud about it. During the counting, Babe noticed how Mr. Trump left with his wife and returned about 30 minutes afterwards. Finally, the election count was over, and Babe could see that Mr. Trump was going to be the winner, but it all changed when he returned with his wife, Babe had a feeling, they were up to something no good.

Talking about feeling defeated, all the women felt like it was the worst day in their lives because this joker had already talked like he was going after the women for all the wrong reason. This man was really going to have Babe praying, she knew he was coming after her.

Right off, Babe wrote him a letter even before the inauguration to let him know the mission ahead of her. Babe knew that he knew, because they had a radar over her life ever since they knew that prophecies were being fulfilled.

As a matter of fact, Babe was beginning to think the government knew before God called her, she was beginning to think that was the reason the government went to buy slaves from Africa. Babe was thinking about how calculating they were, to go all the way to Africa and buy slaves to bring back to brainwash the entire world, so that when the Ethiopian daughter arrived, they knew she would have to submit to them.

Babe guessed those 50 years of freedom left her independent of rights and thoughts, so when this president stepped up to the plate, he thought that he was really going to show Babe a thing or two. During his election, one of the guys that was running for governor somewhere had the same last name as Babe had the nerves to say that he hated that they allowed the slaves to be free. Babe thought what kind of jerk he must've been. Then Babe realized that most of them were upset because they couldn't get her to do what the government wanted her to do.

It didn't take long to realized that slavery held up the truth of God's word, they knew that if the Ethiopian daughter testimony would set the women free, they didn't want the women to be set free. Now Babe was able to put the dots together and understand why they wanted her to get married. They thought if they got her married, they could control her through some man, and she thought, "I don't think so". Babe had her mind made up, and she wasn't really worried about having children, because if she did before she had completed the task it would affect the mission.

Babe wasn't the one worried about having children anyway, but she knew that if it happened, they would have a greater way of controlling her. They thought by making her get married and having children, they would be able to do things that just weren't right. Babe knew by now they would do anything they could to prevent the truth of God's word from being properly interpreted.

Mr. Trump didn't waste any time trying to put a border wall up to separate the immigrants from the United States. The wall was going to cost in the billions, and nobody wanted it. They kept fighting about it. Mr. Trump closed Congress, causing people to lose their jobs because they wouldn't vote for the wall. Babe thought it was unnecessary for people to lose their job over something that most of the people didn't want, at least we knew the Democrats didn't care for it. Babe felt that if it was because of the drugs, what difference was it really making, because they had tunnels they could travel through, and most of the drugs were being legally delivered and delegated by the presidents and the politicians. The weight of the president was one of much power and abuse.

After the last Republican president, they all found out about the self-inflicted nightmare they encountered with 9/11. It was the worst thing Babe had witnessed. She woke up to the sight of smoke and fire and the planes crashing into the Twin Tower, Babe thought. *Omg, what's going on in this country?* Babe couldn't believe what she was seeing. She had changed careers and she was working in the nursing business on the side and had a few rented houses.

Babe felt so bad, she tried to support them with a donation. at least what she could afford. It wasn't until all the commotion died down that the author and columnist Michael Moore was telling the world that 9/11 was instigated by the president and the Muslims. He accused the president of assisting the Muslims out of the States safely, then they set the blame on Bin Laden. That blew everybody's minds. This guy named Michael Moore was making everybody wonder, because it sounded terrible that a government would do their own people that way, and how they go over to these countries starting war, like Hussein, how they accused him of doing injustice to his own people, but they were doing their people just as bad if not worse. Babe thought this guy Michael Moore was pretty brazen to tell the world that information, not to mention that we had the same kinship name. It made Babe wonder since she had a God son name Michael Moore, and Babe also had a brother whose birthday was on 9/11. Babe couldn't remember her brother's birthday until that happened on 9/11. What a story, now she can remember her brother's birthday. It all seem too sad of a circumstance to even think about it. But when Babe thought about a scripture that stated out of the mouth of two or three witnesses, his word would be confirmed. Babe began to think that her two brothers were like the witnesses. Later Babe heard that one evangelist named Jerry Farwell was going around saying that God allowed that to happen because of the homosexuals, afterwards they found him dead in his office of a heart attack at the age of 73. Babe thought that's when abortion was legalized in 1973 and the reverse of 37, which identified Richard Nixon as the prophet of God that vetoed abortion. Poor Nixon, he truly was a man of God, and no one understood, because they didn't like the fact that Nixon put his foot down and vetoed abortion, and he wanted to legalize drugs at the same time.

Babe was still in high school when abortion was legalized, and Babe really wasn't involved in politics, so she didn't know if she was even old enough to vote for Nixon because she might've been a Democrats and Nixon was a Republican, but now things have flipped. Babe didn't know the events at the time, she just felt blessed that Nixon vetoed the abortion bill when he did.

That's another reason Babe felt this government was doing nothing but trying to get her married and she thought, the hell with that, they were using anybody and everybody, but they were too stupid to know that God wasn't leading her that way. Babe had been involved with living for the Lord for some time now and she could tell when she was talking to an imposter, and many of the men had one thing on their mind: sex. Babe had outgrown sex in the worldly way, God had given her another outlook.

After 911 and finally another election, Babe would just wait, we all just waited on a better place. President Obama Was a nice candidate he was going to be running against Hilary but Hillary gave in when she saw that Obama was going to be the favorite. The New President was Obama. A biracial man with two young girls, and only one wife, he was sending messages of justice and equality and a better plan for the poor people, but most of all he had a heart for women. His mother died of some female cancer and for that reason he thought supporting Planned Parenthood was the best thing for women. After Obama won, he went eight years of being the president. We had the best eight years of our lives, at least for the women, although my personal life was still somewhat of a struggle. I didn't hold it against the Obama's; as a matter of fact, Babe wrote to Michelle Obama and told her about some taxes that the government was trying to pass down on her and she mailed me a letter, proving that she was trying to help me resolve it, although the government usually would have things tied up and they couldn't do any more than what they let them. Babe thought it was nice that she wrote her and responded. Babe also sent Michelle some e-cards and wondered if she read them. Babe had printed the first two books by then: Betrayal of a Nation and *Forbidden Fruit.*

Eventually, the taxes would fall off at a certain time, and even though Babe went through several tax authorities, they would eventually beat her out of the money because they claimed the rent house was worth more than Babe could ever get from it. Those eight years of Obama's election were good. We all had something to be proud about after President Obama left. We knew that he did what he could, but before President Obama's terms were up Babe had gotten deeper into the fact that the government was behind a lot of these drug wars and her involvement with the prison left Babe to believe that many people in prison over drugs were in prison without just cause, before President Obama's term was up, he pardoned well over 1000 people in prison and Babe was glad about that. Babe told President Obama she was writing another book about drugs and how they weren't the problem, it was the government putting the drugs out there.

Babe would frequently get emails and letters from the Obamas, and she was glad that they finally got a president that cared.

Now the 2016 election is upon us, and it seemed like Hillary was going to take a stab at it. Even though Babe wasn't crazy about Bill. Babe wouldn't hold that against Hillary. This president would hold the title of the 45th president, and Babe was so hoping that a woman would be more fitting, because then Babe could explain the divine nine revelations that was beholding to women of every country. All the scriptures that were connecting to the women were in the form of 9. Isaiah 54 equals 9, Psalm 45 both transposed, both chapters were describing women in the Bible and their Chapter, both had 17 verses. God was showing Babe ways to understand and explain his Bible better. They were very encouraging when Babe read them because she thought these women were loved before and always. Yet these other countries were doing them any kind of way, and America finally got our breakthrough when Nixon put his foot down.

Hillary was in favor because she adopted much of President Obama's views and choices. Hillary being a woman would be automatically for her to fund Planned Parenthood. And even if she did let some jerk off for raping someone when she was an intern, Babe had to understand that lawyers are hired to defend people, even if the person did things we didn't like. Most would go by the money they were being paid, so now we know why money is the root of all evil.

President Obama wasn't well liked because he was black, but some people opposed of others as gays, homosexuals and the LGBT. It was President Obama's Vice President Joe Biden, the vice president that got the ball rolling for the LGBT and same-sex marriage. Since Babe didn't have to worry about being snubbed by the church members anymore, she could see why that would be fair. God called Babe out of church when he knew they were infiltrated with false teachers, and the government was helping them to brainwash the world. Some churches would act like Babe was an alien. It was beautiful when Babe first started going to church because God made himself very real to her. God was giving her orders that she knew were from God and she was understanding. But the deeper Babe got in God, the less people would understand. Psalm 45:10 eventually led Babe out of the churches to write the books, and it was then that she decided they needed to be circulated to 3rd-world countries. Because they seemed to be brainwashed the worst. Babe thought any country where the women weren't given choices were because the Bible wasn't properly interpreted.

China was on the same page as Babe was. As a matter of fact, China is the country that spearheaded the mission for Babe. After hearing Nora Lamb, a missionary from China, speak at a dinner at the hotel across the street from Oral Roberts, Babe was surprised to find out that China had mandatory abortion. Babe thought that's serious, she then heard the Holy Spirit speak to her and tell her, "Give unto Caesar, Caesar and give unto God's God. "Babe knew that was a scripture pertaining to taxes and then she realized that if God was the creator of life, so if we gave God our babies back to him, he would cleanse us and forgive our sins although our country had been baptized in false doctrine because of the Catholics; But the good think about Hillary, she was going to select a Catholic pro-choice vice president. And Babe was glad to know they had pro-choice Catholics, which was good because the Catholics have been around a long time, but we have heard about all the skeletons in their churches. So, this way Hillary could help save them this way. That was a good thing, because many Catholic schools were very well rounded and people would pay to send their children to a Catholic school, but many people also denounced their religion on their own when they realized the history behind them.

Now it seemed like Hillary had all grounds covered. She was open and honest about everything, but that event at Benghazi was trying to hold her back. Babe wasn't up on that until she saw where they based a movie on it, and it was about some men from the United States that were supposed to be protecting the United Kingdom's United States Embassy, but they weren't supposed to have any weapons, but they were attacked by some militants from Gaza that created a terrorist attack.

The men were outnumbered, and they needed a backup and Hillary, being the State of Foreign Affairs, wouldn't call in a backup and she had authority to do so, they claimed! Babe believes most of the men died, and Babe wondered why wouldn't they not allow them weapons? Nevertheless, that's why everybody wanted to blame Hillary and Babe thought she probably didn't have the authority that they thought, because President Obama would have had to send more troops over there, and it wasn't done, probably too late anyway. But they have been blamed by. Most people that don't but this thing probably could have been dealt with better.

Still, it looked like Hillary had an edge over the *Apprentice Guy*. Babe never did like his program, especially since those are the last words anybody would want to hear: "You are fired."

Now here it was time for the election, and the votes were coming in and Hillary was looking good. Babe watches it all on television, and it's looking good, but instantly this *Apprentice* guy takes about a 30-minute break and takes his wife with him and when he comes back the board takes a turn. Babe thought, what the hell did he do? she believed he left and had something done. Because suddenly, he was the winner. With much contention, nobody believed that he won fair and square. Babe knew for sure he didn't win. People protested everywhere; they knew this man spelled TROUBLE. They couldn't believe it, like the world's worst nightmare.

While Babe was working with co-workers one night and they were talking politics, which they shouldn't have been, because being in the red states, people would get pretty upset when you talked against their party. So, they tried to keep it to the minimum. One of the girls mentioned that before long women will lose their rights all over again, and Babe protested, "Over her dead body." Babe knew that she would rather die if it ever came to that, because it looked like so many people were just wanting her to try to have a baby, no matter what she was still pro-choice, and this government just didn't understand Babe don't think she would even trust a man the way they kept throwing any man and then Babe realized they were also using men to beat her if she didn't start a relationship with them. Since

Babe would use people from the day center, after that devil campaigned in her town, he started using everybody so he could go against Babe, one of the girls would braid Babes hair after Babe paid a homeless girl to braid her hair once, she asked Babe if she wanted her to be a surrogate for her, and Babe thought why in the hell would she think I would want a surrogate, Babe didn't want a Baby at that point because that's all the idiots were focused on that was watching her.

The idiots hanging over her head to see if it would happen. Furthermore, what makes them think Babe had that kind of money, while the government tried to beat her out of everything, and if they couldn't they would send others to short change her.

Shortly after that Babe heard a doctor talk about how they can inject a toxic into a surrogate mother and it would affect the birth of the unborn, as if they were going to impair the infant before it had a chance to live. That's Terrible, Babe thought, what doctor would do anything like that? It seemed like the doctor would violate their oath as a doctor, preventing them from endangering the patient in any way, the Hippocratic Oath, a policy that they were supposed to live by. But after switching over to the medical profession, Babe saw enough of that, regardless of the Hippocratic Oath, preventing doctors from doing anything unethical. Babe knew of many doctors overprescribing drugs and giving people the wrong medication just to keep them coming back, the cause of unnecessary surgery. It was Medicare and Medicaid, a guaranteed salary. Some of the people that had good jobs, they could easily be taken in also It seemed like it was safer not to have insurance, at least the doctors wouldn't be trying to get rich off the people, also creating more medical problems for the people.

Now that Mr. Trump was all up in Babe business like the others, they just tried to pretend as if they weren't Babe knew the satellites and the drones and whatever else they used to invade her privacy. They would continue until they could make her or break her... They didn't understand she wouldn't be taken down without a fight.

Babe had a hard time calling this guy the president, because of all the havoc he was creating. Many people were protesting because they didn't want him to win.

Hillary finally made a public announcement and told the people to stop the protesting because she would accept the defeat. Babe thought that was grand of Hillary, but Babe just wished they would have proved it. that she really won.

Looking back, Babe doesn't think that was the first time the Republicans cheated. Babe remembered once when Al Gore and George Bush were running against each other. Actually, Babe didn't remember it, but someone mentioned it and they told her how tight that race was and how they had to count it over and over again, and they told her they counted it 37 times. or either he won by 37 points. When someone reminded Babe about that, she knew they lied and they used that number because they had followed Babe back then and they knew the revelation behind that number but they were really unconcerned about Babe's mission. Babe remembered the elder Bush is the first one that she wrote to and never got a response, but to think they had been watching her before that.

As a matter of fact, Babe believes they were watching her before God had called her and then she realized they might have even paid that rapist to rape her, simply because when she thinks about it, the policeman told her that the man had a lot of money on him, and Babe didn't think to ask him how much. But now that she thinks about it, how the guy she was dating from Venezuela wanted her to return with him to go to Venezuela, Babe thought that would have been nice, but she couldn't think about leaving what family she still had here. Also, shortly after he left, how Babe bumped into a classmate and the classmate was stationed in Hawaii, with the military, how convenient for him to come to her rescue.

Clarence had the same last name as Babe's, he was biracial and they hardly knew each other in high school, but now all of a sudden, he came to her rescue.

The more Babe thought about it, she knew the government had it all planned. A lady from Nebraska sent Babe a check for 100 dollars and asked her if she wanted her to help Babe move, and Babe thought that would be great, but Babe couldn't expect a person to be that generous without even knowing her. She had read about her killing the rapist and she followed the story to know that she had been burglarized many times. As Babe thought about it, Babe wished she had taken the lady's advice because she was genuine.

Clarence turned out to be stand in. He had a momma baby in Hawaii, and Babe knew that it wasn't worth getting serious. But he stayed around long enough to help her move out of her house into some condos across town.

Just to think all this stuff that Babe went through was instigated by the government had her really thinking, what in the hell do they want from her. As Babe followed the scriptures, she realized that Isaiah54 describing the barren woman really was her life, and the 17th verse reminds her that no weapon formed against her would prosper. All the other prophecies describing this lady, made Babe realize that they had been waiting on her.

Vincent kept in touch, but her quick encounter with Clarence had her putting Vincent to the side, Babe remembered a keepsake that Vincent sent her and she didn't understand what it was. It was a wooden vase with floral print on it, and it had a stick inside of it. Babe thought it was cute, but it seemed to be saying something more, but she didn't think about it. Somehow, she lost the information with Vincent's address on it, but later she would come to believe that these creeps spying on her might have done something with it.

After the job had downsized and Babe thought she would change professions, since she had been working at a nursing home down the street from the other job, Babe realized that she liked the hours better because the hours were flexible and she could still tend to the rent houses acquired after becoming a real estate broker. It seemed like Babe didn't like the fact that it was difficult selling houses and one agency she hooked up with had one hell of a boss, he was very attractive. In other words, he would tell Babe about how he had an apartment aside from his house, where he would go from time to time and knowing that he was married she could see where it was going and she didn't want to be a part of it. So, she ended the part-time job with him.

Back to the gift that Vincent bought Babe as a token of their friendship. Babe had already written the two books before she finally realized that most of life had been staged by the government because the way the scriptures were describing this woman, Babe knew she wasn't crazy, but they really watched her like a hawk, and she thought about a movie, called "Truman," Babe remember it was played by Jim Carey and how they monitored his life like they owned him and now they must have been on Babe's back that way. And just to think, ten years or so after the ordeal, now working in the medical profession, after becoming a medication aide, and passing out medication, the gift that Vincent gave Babe appeared to be a pill crusher or would some use it as a cocaine crusher. 'OMG', Vincent was trying to warn Babe they were going to do this, because five years after killing the rapist her brother-in-law took it upon himself to start selling drugs on the street. But now knowing all the other stuff they have done, they brought it to him and made him some offer.

Even thinking back one day, her brother-in-law had the nerve to tell Babe, that she could still have children, even after the doctor told her that she wouldn't be able to have children. Babe thought what an idiot, here he had brought drugs into the family and put his family in harm's way, and all he could think about was her having children. Babe didn't even think twice about having children, why would he be worried about it?

Just remember, all this was making Babe very unsure of this government. Babe thought about the scriptures in the Bible, and she thought some describing these women would reassure her that she could have children but knowing that she was enjoying her time in God more only had her assuming that it would only mean spiritual children or women that wanted children, especially if that's all this government cared about, anybody that was consumed with Babe having children through all of this had to be crazy.

Yet this government was trying to make it out to be biological. Babe thought they must be crazy, why would she even want children knowing how demonic they were? Some friends only pretended to be her friends. They were so busy trying to hook Babe up with some man and finally she realized they were using her as well, before Babe knew anything, they had people believing that she was being disobedient. For a moment, Babe thought she would like to try, but then they became so persistent and annoying, Babe thought, this must be some trap, because they were always trying to put single mothers on some pedestal. That's when Babe realized they were straight from the pit of hell.

When Babe finally realized they have done nothing but tried to downsize her life and now they are telling people that she's being disobedient, and some were dumb enough to believe them. Babe started thinking, she was glad that she had the abortion when she and she didn't miss the fact that she didn't have any children, because she knew some people that were struggling just trying to raise their children without child support, and after seeing how her mother raised them, Babe didn't want to depend on the government, because whatever they tell the clients to do, they were inclined to do so, For instance, how they told her mother to put her daughters on birth control and she did so without even discussing it with her daughters, Too bad they don't worry about the boys as much as the daughters because both brothers ended up with children before they had planned them, made life miserable for the brothers; that got stuck in a marriage that was doomed before it got started, Babe began to see the government for what they really were, they wanted people having children to strengthen their economy. They didn't give a shit about the women or the children, and they sure didn't care about the races, how they brought the slaves over here knowing the Ethiopian daughter would come out of that race.

Wow, it almost began to take on the turn of a nightmare, but God word was the reassurance that Babe needed. Many people had already eaten of the forbidden fruit and the government knew that by bringing the slaves over here. They would have her race of people brainwashed before the prophecies was ever fulfilled and most of them were, how the case worker encouraged her mother, informed them that they needed to get on birth control pills when they weren't even having sex. It seemed controlling, since mother was in and out of adulterous affairs, so why would it matter to her?

That was one reason, Babe wanted to venture into her own place as soon as she graduated, thinking she wouldn't be influenced by her lifestyle, but Babe had to live through some things as well.

Now this government knew all this because of the scriptures and the prophecies, so Babe had to play along, but eventually it got old and now old enough to know that they couldn't take over her life anyway they wanted. Babe was determined to do God's will first, before she even considered a husband or a family. And she knew that women in other countries were very much in need of the truth of God's word properly interpreted. Most Catholic people didn't even try to understand the Bible, they were all spoon fed by the Pope and the Bishops. This was done like that in the Old Testament, but since the New Testament made the Bible complete, and we had to learn them both in order to fully understand the plan of salvation, Babe knew of all the cult religions as well.

Now Mr. Trump had already stated that he would close all the abortion clinics and Babe knew that wasn't right he started with Texas, since the governor there had already started shutting the clinics, Babe thought it seemed like she was going backwards instead of forward.

A mighty fierce of anger rose up within her, and she chanted, something like this: "Terrorists from the north, south, east and west. Arise and defend the daughters of Zion the very best. "Babe was so pissed with this man; she could have spitted nails. But all she could do was wait and pray. Babe knew God called her to help other women, since she felt they earned their rights in America, but now they were trying to close the abortion clinics.

President Obama had to fire the governor of Texas because he was abusing his power. Now this Trump dictator hired him in another area, but here they were at it again, trying to close the clinics. It all appeared that they were aiming at Babe with all this because they knew about the books and they didn't want the truth of God's word to go forth, but they wanted to use her to try to have children, no wonder the desire wasn't even there. Babe started thinking if a government would be that evil, her children wouldn't be safe.

Sure enough, as Babe read the 12 chapters of Revelation, she noticed it described a woman having a man child and how it was caught up to God and Babe Thought, oh, my, it sounded like the abortion she had and how it was caught up to God. And it became clearer that aborted fetus did return to God when the women didn't feel they were able to care for them and the pregnancy was untimely, like Psalm 58 described them. As Babe continued reading, that chapter of Revelations also had 17 verses and the 17th verse was the most important of all. It described the woman and how the devil went about chasing the woman to devour her other children. That's when Babe knew beyond a shadow of a doubt, she wouldn't even consider having children forever and not even consider a husband. because she now believes that the government fabricated the entire story up about her having children, because too many people thought the same way. But the 12th chapter of Revelation summed it up clearer.

Well into the first year of this tyrant of a president year, he was on the warpath and it was obvious that he was directing his hate at Babe, more than the innocent women that he was abusing their rights now, and Babe thought, Lord, "if I had never tried to reach out to other women, maybe our freedom wouldn't be jeopardized." As Babe began to even doubt her calling unaware, there was a flood of immigrants coming over from everywhere, from the north, south, east and west, Babe. thought about that chant she prayed, and she thought Lord, "what have I done, they aren't terrorist, they are just people looking for a better place to stay." They were coming from places that were poverty stricken, women were nothing more than sex slaves and baby barriers. It looked like most of the place where women had no rights to abortion, they were just sex slaves. If they were raped, they wouldn't let them have an abortion, but the men were free to move on in life without the burden or even the risk of paying child support.

Now something was happening, and Babe began to see God in it, he brought the terrorists in another form. These immigrants were a terrorist in the sight of the president, he talks about most races, and people still couldn't see through him. He didn't like

President Obama, but here he was calling on President Obama for his advice. Babe thought he had his nerves, needing President Obama's help. I don't think Obama had any answers for him, but Babe couldn't wait to put her 2 cents in.

As she would read the Bible on and on, she remembered reading somewhere in Psalms and she knew it was describing another abortion, but this one was a full birth abortion, So, she went back to review the scripture, it was one of a graphic nature, and Babe thought jokingly that must be her evil twin sister, this abortion was so graphic that it literally was describing a full-term abortion. Babe thought as she read over the entire chapter, Dear Lord, it was describing the entire scenario that was happening with the immigrants. Psalm 137 The entire chapter was describing the saga of what was happening with the immigrants, they were in a weary place in they couldn't sing the song of Zion, the good women that they referred to as Zion, but the ninth verse is the one Babe would zoom in on. Because it was God speaking to the daughter of Babylon, who ought to be destroyed, "Happy shall he be that rewarded thee, that taketh thy little ones and taketh them and dashed them upon the stone.

The ninth verse, is a prophecy of the Daughter of Babylon, who ought to be destroyed, knowing that Babe had lived a sinful life before she totally committed to God, not knowing how many times she escapes death. Chances are this prophecy ties in with the other prophecies, that lead to the Elect Lady.

"Babe also thought about that movie *Beloved* and how no one could understand the movie, because one of the women was haunted by some ghost of the past or even future, she would kill every baby that she had, and they thought something was weird about it, but then Babe realized that some of the slaves were raped and had to endure such things, but we never thought it could be that bad.

As soon as Babe realized that God was telling her that those women needed safe abortions just like the women in America had, so Babe got on her laptop and wrote the president a letter, and she told him that they need to allow them the rights to have legal abortions, because Psalm 137 was describing an abortion, she also told Trump, they also needed to legalize the drugs over there so the drug cartel could sell their drugs and help restore Mexico to their glory. Babe loved cruising over in Mexico. And she believes some governments have ways of making some countries look good and some look bad.

They were making America look good, and Babe thought every time she came from vacation she was so blessed. But when God called her to write the book and reach out to other women, the government started putting pressure on her to get married, and she didn't feel God in any of it, they were getting people to ostracize her for her stand on abortion, but as Babe stated before Planned Parenthood told her once that she was the heart of the mission, Babe thought at least they knew that she was real and her heart spoke louder than words. Babe didn't care about what the owner of Planned Parenthood said once about black people, they claim Margaret Sanger the founder of Planned Parenthood made a racist remark, claiming that black people were like weeds that needed to be cut out.

This woman could've been racist, but the fact that white women and black women were all needing legal and safe abortions, she probably only said that because she knew the prophecies described the Ethiopian daughter and most white people automatically started hating people on that account. Half of them had no idea what they were hating for, just the devil in them.

After writing the letter to the president, Babe knew God wanted her to do this because it confirmed the book that God wanted her to send to all the countries where they were still abusing women and girls. Babe knew he got the letter; she might have mailed it this time because it was the best way to know that he might read it. A few times Babe would send the letter certified, making sure someone would acknowledge the letters. Babe doesn't know why because everything Babe did these people would know and if she didn't even mail the letter properly, they would surely inform the president. Babe was determined to stay on track with God.

Even though the president got the letter, and he knew that God was telling him something, but he was stubborn, he didn't want to help them, he ignored their living conditions, and many of the immigrants were dying because of the living conditions, he could have set up a first-aid tent with antibiotics, at the least until they resolved the ordeal. That number 37 was still in the picture, now in a bigger way, 100-fold, assuring Babe even more that Nixon was the prophet God sent to legalize abortion in America and she's going to carry the torch that Nixon left. Also, that verse 9 connected to the abortion, like so many other scripture Babe had found in the Bible. Babe knew that the drug situation would have to be handled, but they were being stubborn and weren't defiling her but God by being ignorant.

As hell was boiling over with the immigrants, Texas was another place of hell where they enjoyed the ways of the unrighteous, Babe had heard about a few of the immigrants as well as her own black people coming to an untimely death because of her being outspoken and Babe grew angry so when they stopped a black couple that wouldn't stopped for them they claimed that they riddled their car with 137 rounds of ammunition, Babe didn't know if that was their way of saying to hell with that number And my people. The governments were more than one country, it was the entire world, and they were sheep in wolves' clothing. Now Babe knew what Nixon was up against.

Things just went from bad to worse with the immigrants, they were of great numbers, frequently they were coming up dead, a sixteen-year-old boy, all on his own, nobody even came with the child, they found him dead from dehydration, one of the children 2 years old died, crossing a river. Which explained the verse even more so because it talked about how they wept at the rivers of Babylon, it was too real, all this time, Babe never knew how that scripture really applied, Babe just jokes about the 9th verses, also the number 9 was back in her face.

Now the drug cartel was on the other side planning their attack, while 2 SUV sedans traveled through their territory with their family. The Drug cartel ambushed them and riddled the 2 sedans with 150 rounds of ammunition. These cars included families traveling through their territory. It seems like 9 people lost their lives, but a few of the children lived and were allowed to escape. Sometime it would seem like a retaliation execution because things had started happening back-to-back

Another incident in Texas had Babe very upset. One of their female policemen walked into the wrong apartment and claimed she thought the black guy was robbing her apartment, yet she was the one in the wrong apartment. She shot him. Babe thought that's crazy as hell, just because you walk into the wrong apartment, there's no reason for you to shoot the guy, If the key worked, it had to be some set up, these cops were just as corrupt as the governments, they got their orders from the government and the government was letting them get away with much of what they were doing. After she realized she wasn't in the right apartment, but she had shot the guy and killed him, they went and confiscated the marijuana he had.

That's bogus as hell, Babe knew damn well, after that 9/11 attack, they enforced some stiffer laws to violate everybody's rights, Babe knew they did this to justify watching her 24/7, Babe thought it was bad enough what they were doing to her, but to do her people any kind of way, just pissed her off. Babe knew this government was creating havoc on earth and she knew beyond a shadow of a doubt, that she wouldn't submit to a man, because frankly they had pushed too many buttons and Babe began to realize it was time for her to get her defense mode and they were stirring the pot. When they talked about man-made wars, and man-made laws Babe could easily see how it was done.

After realizing how they were doing her people, Babe would every now and then do some drugs just to piss them off, one-day Babe woke up in a bad mood, it used to be better. Babe had just dealt with them but as time progressed, they became more annoying Babe was still working with the agency and she had a job in Cleveland, OK about 45 minutes away, from the time she woke up to the time she had to go to work which was like all day long, Babe was bitching, her neighbor came over and wanted to borrow something but Babe didn't have it, Babe figured they put him up to coming over because they had everybody in her business and this guy was no different. Men thought they could draw me in when they did the kind of work that she was learning. So, my neighbors that were Mexican, the couple was great, but they had many repairs to do when they moved in, and they had some guy staying with them to help them out and he was able to stay without paying as much. Mexicans were resilient at restoring homes, Babe had seen them restore homes from nothing to something.

Being from Mexico, their helper Hosea would eventually get to know Babe, when she found out he had about 7 children, by 2 different women and her brief encounter with him, led her to believe that his daughter wanted another brother, Babe thought when he told her that, she wanted to tell him, maybe he should get her a dog or cat. Babe sense he was trying to tell her that he wanted her to have a child for him, that was just too stupid, Babe thought what makes him think she wanted a child by him, he already had 7 and now he's acting like he wanted another one. Babe thought what the hell is wrong with these people, they had everybody thinking Babe needed a child, Babe was getting tired of that.

That particular day, Babe was in a bad mood, and she was bitching from the time she woke up until she had to go to work that night at 10:00 that night. It was like Babe would be in her bipolar mood. It would happen every now and then, just knowing they were around, even though she couldn't see them, Babe just knew they were always around.

On Babe way to Cleveland that night, Babe was still in her bipolar mood, and right before she was to the exit, she noticed an ambulance was coming up the opposite entrance. Babe slowed down but there was no way to stop so she slowed down and when she slowed down to exit, about a ½ mile in the city she got pulled over by some sheriff, Babe pulled over immediately, he was asking her all these questions and wanted to know if babe had any drugs and if she had taken any that day, or alcohol. Babe hadn't taken any yet because usually she wouldn't take her diet pill until she got to work or when she would start getting sleepy at the job. He wanted to sit in Babe truck, but her passenger side was cluttered with stuff, so he had her to get out and he was playing these ridiculous games, walking a straight line with one foot in front of each as she walked she Couldn't believe this idiot, when she told him she take diet pills, but hadn't had any today, he told her that diet pills would stay in your system for over 24 hours, something like that, Babe told him she needed them for depression, also to help her stay up when she worked nights.

He was trying to scare Babe, telling Babe he could take her in, but Babe knew not to tick him off. After about an hour of dealing with him he let her go and she was about a few minutes from the job, when she got to work one of the girls said she saw Babe. He gave Babe 2 tickets that would have totaled about 400.00 dollars, but Babe knew she was going to fight them, because she knew the idiots thought they were teaching her a lesson apparently. Babe wasn't learning anything she would find herself getting more upset that they could use anybody they wanted. She knew they heard her and she didn't care, big pig belly bastard. just another idiot that the dogs used.

On the due day of the ticket, Babe decided to rent a car, because she didn't want to miss the court day. She disputed the ticket simply because she thought failure to yield to an emergency vehicle was crazy, because they were both going in opposite direction and being on a two-lane exit, that sounded like nonsense, Babe knew that satellite and the Illuminati were behind it because of her bipolar mood that day, it didn't seem like privacy matter to the dogs, some freedom she thought.

As Babe was leaving the witness stand, some white guy approached her and looked directly at her and told her, "Next time we are going to poison you. "Babe couldn't believe the idiot would say something like that and walk off. Babe was stunned, so stunned she didn't have time to even say anything. she couldn't believe he would say something like that, and then she thought, like Whitney Houston, because the talk was that's what they did, and Babe wish she would have thought to tell him. "Make my day". Babe had to pay 100.00, court cost, and that was settled.

Talking about ticked off, Babe thought sometimes she hate that she goes on and on in her bipolar mood, but then when Babe thought about what John said in the bible. John 10. That the thief doesn't come through the door, they come by the back door, or satellite or Illuminati. Babe knew the stupid government had assigned these people in her life and she had days that she didn't like it and they knew it; they would steal her keys and a few times she would find them.

What pissed her off worse when she went to the bank to get some money on the mechanic and the bank tried to cheat her out of 200 dollars, but when Babe brought it to her attention, she gladly gave her the money. But when she got to the mechanic shop the 200 was gone, it might appear to be amazing what they could do at times, but believe me, Babe wasn't amazed, it had become annoying. Babe knew they were doing these things, because of the truth Babe brought out in the Bible, but she couldn't undermine the word of God, they were the idiots for trying to control her.

Babe had to borrow 200 dollars to pay the mechanic, when she returned some white joker had the nerves to be talking to the mechanic about Karma, Babe thought immediately about 150 dollars she found underneath a patient's bed, at the time Babe was struggling, and she knew it wasn't the patient's money, but she also thought it could be a test, since they see everything and know everything. Nevertheless, Babe kept it anyway because she knew the idiots weren't God and frankly, she didn't think she had to impress them in any way.

That evening, a so-called friend that had helped Babe alone with her dead-beat husband had the nerves to come over and Babe told her, Linda had the nerves to tell Babe that money could've been some single mothers, and Babe thought they never cared about money they scammed her out of. The money Babe lost, or they stole or ripped her off for... All of a sudden, it seemed like they were trying to defend the single mothers, and Babe thought if she has to have a baby to get any help, they need to get the hell out of her face.

Because she didn't want to ever take a chance having children, because these idiots were beyond help. Linda and her husband Bill used to live in the neighborhood, they had property in the back of Babe and they let Jack, some hoodlum stay in the back with his RV that he drove on the back of his truck, Jack had access to their water and electric, Jack seemed to be a handyman, Babe paid him to fix her car a few times, Babe sensed they wanted to hook her up with him, and Babe thought, between them and devils hanging over her head, they seem bound to find her some piece of man. But God was flagging everything they did and everybody they sent... Bill was a veteran and they had been together since high school, as a matter-of-fact Linda got pregnant, while Bill was in the military.

Naturally they would always send me someone that had had their children before they got married, Babe didn't see anything wrong with that, but in this world, it seems like that's how it starts and Linda was lucky that Bill married her, since her parents had a little money, most guys would fall on that. But Jack didn't interest Babe at all, frankly not too many men interest Babe because she had reached a level with God that they couldn't comprehend and knowing the devil was hanging over her head 24/7, Babe just knew not to think about it. The book of Rev. 12:17 had such impact on Babe especially when she thought they had been watching her before she even knew it and to think they instigated most of the stupid stuff that she had to live with. Rev. 12:17 stated that the devils went about seeking to devour the women's other children. Babe just didn't want to go there with this country.

All her thoughts of even having children faded by the wayside, when she thought, the governments are the devil. They have done nothing but sent false fleeces, and why would she want to put up with their nonsense, because that's what it became, Babe had made a vow with God, that she would rather die, then to give these idiots a chance to exploit her children the way they are trying to exploit her, Then Babe thought, they must really be crazy to have persecuted an entire race just for this occasion, and as much as Babe begin to understand and regret about slavery, there was still something she couldn't even trust about her own people, it was the government's way of brainwashing everybody.

After that eventful day at the courthouse, Babe returned the rental car, it was nice, keyless. Took some adjusting to, in order to remember Babe didn't need the key, about time Babe returned it she thought had it figured out. It was a later model and it felt good to ride with confidence that the car wouldn't break down on her

Babe had many new cars with the help of hard work and God, or should she say vice versa. Babe knew that God was her redeemer in every way, but lately with these evil principalities hanging over her head, it seemed like her life had come to some serious issues.

Now these idiots had everybody thinking that she was being disobedient, and she thought how anybody would know anything about her being disobedient if they didn't know God or the Bible.

Babe knew all the signs, but later in life, she realized that the Illuminati and the government specialized in witchcraft and sorcery, so Babe discarded all the signs, and she grew closer to God. Because his word was showing her that they were the devil mentioned in the book of Revelation.

Some people had enough sense to know that the only person that can make that decision in your life would be herself and God. Now Babe felt thankful that the doctor told her that she couldn't have children and anybody that only wanted to have children, would be the wrong person, because Babe didn't really want to put up with a government that worshipped bastards, and denied the word of God. Still feeling that the abortion was a blessing from God, Babe just grew content, that maybe it would be better for her in the next life, for having a family. Because these wicked principalities in high places only wanting to use her as some sex slave, or some guinea pig.

They must be crazy and then that idiot telling her they were going to poison her next. It seems like they had people ready to do anything at any given notice, that's how close they watched her. Babe thought, if she lived through this She would move to Mexico, Canada or Switzerland. That might sound crazy, but at this point, Babe don't know if she would ever be safe anywhere. Especially if it was a man thing, some men got upset with Babe because she felt no need to date anymore, Babe wanted to take for the title of the nuns, even her mother claimed there wasn't nuns in the Bible. That's crazy there were several women in the Bible that committed to serve God, without a husband.

Mary and Martha sat at the feet of Jesus, she doesn't know if they ever got married Deborah the prophet, and even though Babe didn't want to be a Catholic Nun, it's just none of this and none of that for the time being, because the world only thought about sex, and the evil idiots hanging around was going there with everybody she met. It seemed like they couldn't wait to get her in bed with anybody, their presence was a turnoff, because some men Babe met just wanted to be friends with, but they started using them to try to seduce her. Babe thought what the hell, they never learned a damn thing during slavery, I guess they used the slaves anyway for this reason, and Babe thought she don't feel like picking up where they left off. The sad thing about it, half of the men they would send, had them thinking Babe was a whore, she thought it took one to know one. The way this government raped the slaves and lynched the men, Babe thought whore is nowhere near the evil in these bastards.

Whether Babe was a whore or not, they had the men thinking that way, and that made it even easier not to want them. Some had so many kids, it would surprise Babe that they think she would even want them. It seems to me that when a person has so many children that they don't know what to do. Like the old lady nursing rhyme that had all those children that lived in a shoe and didn't know what to do. Frankly Babe thought they must've been a bigger whore then her, even though the Bible states that a man with a lot of children is blessed with his quiver full. That was Old Testament, but Babe also believe David and Solomon proved that having a lot of children would all be vanity in the end.

Reminding Babe of some nurse trying to teach her a lesson on drugs, talking about why people do drugs, Babe told her the same reason people do sex, because they want to feel good. With her having 5 children and not knowing if it was a cut off or what.

Babe thought please! I don't have time to even hear that mess.

Knowing now that some people would take drugs to keep from having children they couldn't afford.

The world was getting brainwashed, and Babe was ready to expose the dumb lies the government made up about drugs, only when it's God's will. The idiots had the people thinking Babe was trying to commit suicide, if they saw her do drugs, just some dumb excuse to hang around.

After Tank died, Babe didn't have anybody to hang out with that did drugs, but really, Babe didn't want to hang out with people like that anymore, her neighbors that came and left showed her that most of them weren't about nothing but getting high. Babe had to work and make a living, and even when the devil would get on her nerves, she would do stuff to piss them off, Babe figured eventually they would poison her like they did Whitney Houston, and she could leave this world forever. Since they go around doing that kind of shit. Babe didn't believe half of those people that were overdosing was doing so accidentally.

Babe had already written the presidents and told them she would rather be a crackhead for God then a crack whore for the government. Whatever she did in the world, they tried to magnify it, and all it did was gave Babe more reason not to trust them. What kind of game where they're playing, the things they were doing only strengthened Babe desire not to trust them and rely solely on God's word and faith.

Now Babe believe The President was out to destroy her since they couldn't get her to fornicate or commit adultery and that would assure her that she wouldn't have to worry about getting pregnant, and since some thought Babe should at least make an effort, Babe thought hell no, because if it should happen like that, Babe said she didn't want to ever trust this government, they have played too many games and life isn't about games. It's about loving and helping other see and understand the truth of God's word, and apparently, they had been all misled by the teaching of the Pope and the Illuminati, being a part of their cult.

Even though the Pope told Congress to turn left when Trump was becoming President, Trump never acknowledged him, Trump was more than glad to present the Pope with a new Lamborghini sport car, very expensive indeed. Babe guess she couldn't blame the Pope for accepting it, even if the devil gave it to him, that's what they say about these charity cults. Heck, there's an old joke about that old lady.

The Pope seemed like he tried to wash his hand of all the errors of the past Popes and by faith, he blessed the same-sex marriage later and even though he seems to be a peacemaker and wanted to be, it was still a suspicion about the entire faith. Knowing they had a secret society, and all kinds of evil and demonic plans were formed during these meetings, and most of the presidents were involved. Babe found this out through Silva Brown, a psychic that she used to watch. Babe found one of her audio books at the library and checked it out. She was very enlightening.

Now that mother was a Seventh Day Adventist, she would share some things, when she told Babe that the Masons or Masonic were like a cult of some sort, and Babe's brother was a member of the Masons and they were always doing nice things for people.

Chapter 18

NOVEL 19 CORONAVIRUS

The presidency wasn't having a good time, after Congress didn't approve the funding for the wall to be built, The President was throwing a few temper tantrums and then the flock of immigrants came, he had his hands full, he had assigned some school administrator to handle the immigrants, and they were making it a money-making scheme, they had taxpayers paying over 400 dollars a day for one immigrants, and that was so high, they could have been in the best hotel for that kind of money, but instead they were caged in like animals.

Everyone thought the presidents were role models for the world but Babe didn't know who gave them the orders, because they never confronted her directly but over the years, they have let her know that they were there. Babe has to admit that in the beginning she thought this was awesome, and they must be like her "Bodyguard," like the movie Whitney Houston starred in, but over time, she realized that they were only guarding their lies that were created over the centuries.

After understanding the prophecies better, Babe knew that Isa. 54 described the Barren woman and many would say that chapter pertained to the Bride of Christ. Even though they all connected, Babe decided that being the Bride of Christ would be better, because she wasn't content with this government and what they were doing and signs from the word of God, assured her they were up to no good. Why would someone just try to take over her life, without any regards to how she felt about it?

Literally Babe began to feel that they were trying to exploit her life. Babe felt good about China and she would contact the leaders of China via Facebook ,even though she couldn't speak Chinese she would look for the address to contact them though, she knew that if she vented on Facebook they would eventually find out about her public outcry, whether they heard from her or not is questionable, but she knew that many countries were involved and wanting to know what the outcome would be, but some of them were just like the idiots hanging over her head, all they wanted was for Babe to have a baby, Babe told China, they need help in America ,because God called her to help women understand abortion, via the Holy Bible, but this government has done nothing but tried to exploit her sexually and they were doing things, that wasn't of God. They were lying to people about what Babe was supposed to be doing, but all the men they would use, proved that they were some pimps trying to prostitute her, just like they are doing the single women, they started putting single women on a pedestal, like Mother Mary, so, knowing how the Catholics were, Bab e guess that's how it got started. Babe read where China didn't like the Catholics faith and they didn't like the Illuminati. China only had a few Catholic churches, and Babe read where most of the people in China jail, were protesters of abortion rights, Babe thought she needed to go there. Babe feared everywhere she turned society had this image, woman and man. Babe had that image once but when God called her and then the government started interfering, she didn't have that image, Babe wanted God and more of God and Babe knew that it was her choice, just as it should be for women in other countries. It's almost like the governments were trying to play reverse psychology on Babe, because they never cared about the message of freedom for women everywhere. They just thought they would redirect their message on her and she knew it would never work, not that way.

Women need to decide whether to have a child or not, yet these women are exploited and forced to have children just so the government can take and sell the children to the highest bidder. Babe knowing that this government was trying to do the same with her, made it all clearer, that she must rise above this so that women in other places could as well.

China was a power country, with the largest military alone with the most people in the world, so it was obvious why they had to limit the population, by making mandatory abortion. Babe had heard they had to exterminate a section of their country that wasn't thriving. It's called genocide. Thinking about it, other countries have been accused of the same thing.

A couple of years into Mr. Trump's presidency, there seemed to be one thing after another Babe sensed that anything, she said negatively at her home would get back with him, and she was tired of that also. It seems like an ongoing thing, with all of them and she didn't know how far back, but Trump was the only one that appeared to take everything personal.

Since Babe would fast every November before Thanksgiving Day, 2018 usually she would go the 21 days and sometimes, just liquids, she remembers the fast started off kind of crazy, she went to purchase some gasoline, and she was so anxious to get on with everything she had to do, after she purchased the gas, she drove off and was on her way home, that Babe forgot that she didn't put the gas in her tank.

Babe droves back into Quiktrip convenience store, and she told the guy she was on pump 12 and she paid for 20 dollars' worth of gasoline, and she forgot to get the gas before driving off, Babe apologized for her forgetfulness, and he assured her it was fine. The pump 12 was already used and he assigned her pump 9, after getting the gasoline, Babe drove off and then she started wondering if it was a sign from God since she had just started the fast. Simply because when Babe is seeking God, she had to be sensitive to numbers as well as words. The number 12 would always remind Babe of the 12 Tribes and the disciples and how he commissioned the disciples to go ye unto the world, then the 9 had really been a flag for women's rights, the scriptures using 9 they are involved with women's rights and flights, as well as abortion. Thinking about President Nixon and how he was the 37th President, also Amos 3:7describes a prophet from God. Then after thinking how Psalms 137 described everything with the immigrants, but the key verse was describing a full-birth abortion. Plan Parenthood was asking for donations because South Carolina was trying to withhold abortions after the 6 weeks. That's been an issue, but after the immigrants came and I had to look at that verse closer, then I began to understand the entire chapter, because before Babe ever knew what was going on, but now it all made sense. Babe fasts weren't that restricted as before, but she hoped to get back to the more serious kind of fasting, but the interference was always hanging over her head, she knew that whatever went on they would use it any kind of way they could.

The incident at the gas station, had Babe on page one and she felt God was still showing her about the abortion issue around the world. Babe felt it was time to confront Mr. Trump.

It didn't seem like it took long for God to speak, on the first day of the fast, and she knew that she would be writing to Mr. Trump again., she also begins to feel that something big was going to happen in 2020 and she wanted to warn Mr. Trump

After the Holidays, Babe was busy as usual, But right about Jan. 9. 2019. She remembers sitting down at her laptop and writing to Mr. Trump. She even titled the disk prophecy 2020, because for some reason, it seemed like God was going to be doing something big in 2020, because the year just had something about it. She knew it was a vision, but she couldn't put her hands on it.

In the letter she tried to be nice and polite while telling Mr. Trump that, He needed to stop supporting countries that wouldn't honor women rights, Babe also mentioned that the drugs situation is out of hands and they need to think about legalizing the drugs instead of using drugs to bait the poor people, while the politicians and presidents were putting the drugs out there. Babe knew that Timothy McVeigh was trying to bring attention to the government corruption when he set a bomb in front of the Alfred Murray Drug Enforcement Agency, because about that time, one of the presidents had move neighbors next door to her selling drugs, they were from Arkansas where the ex-governor and President lived. This letter was pretty intense as Babe warned the President that by the year 2020, they need to start putting Planned Parenthood into these countries, Babe repeatedly told him about the suffering of women everywhere and how her book tied in with the Bible, that letter spelled out a lot of things, and since Babe wrote him the letter in Jan. 2019. It was documented by others apparently. Babe also suggested that Mr. Trump wouldn't run in the next election.

Throughout the year of 2019, Babe would repeatedly make claims that God was looking for a perfect vision and it would be by releasing the captive's women free in other countries. The suffering of women in other countries was getting Babe's attention and for sure she knew that God was still edging her to confront Mr. Trump with the truth of God's word.

After Babe wrote the letter, she doesn't remember getting a letter, if she did it would have been a general email, informing her of general thing or a donation. Since she would tune in on the internet or television, she saw where President Trump was sitting with a group of men, referred to as the GOP, they were trying to be sarcastic about not being able to help other countries, sound like they were trying to say something about the letter she sent him. Then they started joking about women being raped. That really had Babe thinking, since she assumed that they probably paid the rapist she killed, they're paying men to rape women in these countries as well. Babe thought they really weren't helping many of the countries anyway, so why joke about it. Babe didn't see anything funny about it, it's like if they gave women a choice if they wanted an abortion, then the others would also have their choice as well, but the least they could do is give the women a choice. It seems like these people would know what to talk about when she was looking at them, because they had some kind of device that would inform them. and since the others were hanging over her head regardless,

Whatever he did, Babe did her part by informing him, but that's the last thing he cared about, it seems like he hated women, until it came to sex, and making them procreate any kind of way. Babe read where Mr. Trump was on Howard Stern's program talking, he thought about having an abortion, because of an adulterous relationship, landed him in hot water, but because the woman didn't want an abortion. He ended one relationship to get in another one, but the other one didn't work either, because that's typical when people are already in sin and only try to cover it up. It seems like if he was that pro-life, he wouldn't have admitted to that, sound like a hypocrite.

Trump had a way with the international policies, they already believe he was colluding with Russia; but now he decided to conspire with Ben Netanyahu, in Israel about a year after he was in office, they concocted something up, but it sounded like bribery. They wanted to move the United States Embassy from Tel Aviv to Israel. It seemed like they talked about 50 billion dollars, Babe thought it sounded suspicious to her later they found out they were selling the Ethiopian immigrants into slavery. Babe couldn't believe it, even T.D. Jakes had something on the internet informing people that was going on. We were told they were selling the women as sex slaves and the men were being sold for body parts, that was terrible, Babe thought Mr. Trump and his conspirator was trying to say something to her, because she had told them in a letter that she's not going to be their sex slave. Repeatedly, since she had known all the governments cared about was getting her married, or just having sex, hoping she would have children and Babe could tell by the men they sent, they weren't of God. Yet they just kept trying to direct men or if she had friends, they would start using them, it's like they would ruin the relationship before it had a chance to get off the ground. These were flags that made Babe realized that they thought they could pick up where they left off with slavery

After finding out that Israel provided free education and healthcare for their citizens, Babe thought, all that money and we don't even get any benefits like that. and to hear they normally send them 10 billion a year, but at least they do have legal abortions there. Babe remembers traveling to Israel over 20 years ago, she was concerned if they had legal abortions, seemed like they legalized abortion in 1978 they legalized abortion in the United States in 1973. After reading the Nag Hammadi Library, a collection of scrolls buried underground, discovered while some peasants were preparing the soil, the glass shattered and they were discovered in 1945. They were finally translated by a team of interpreters and were finally published in 1970. The Nag Hammadi Library was an awesome collection of biblical history, they were translated in New English, and they would openly state abortion but some people would overlook the truth in the Bible because of Old English translation

Babe also visited. Cairo, Egypt, she found out that they didn't legalize abortion and she read in the Nag Hammadi library where Syria would be destroyed and it was., Babe believe Syria and Cairo, Egypt was someone connected.

Nevertheless, Trump and Netanyahu seem to be saying that it was okay to have sex slaves. That was a dumb message to convey, although they might have wanted to justify slavery, and what the government did to the blacks, but it still wasn't right.

They sold the Ethiopian immigrants in Lebanon and a year after that an explosion rocked their country with so much damage that it took years to restore and some never was restored, over 200 people were killed. It seems like many things Trump was doing was just stirring up hatred all over again. He talked about making America Great again, but most of it was about hate.

Babe started warning people early that something was going to happen in 2020 because God wanted to clean the house and establish a perfect vision. She would sound like John the Baptist, when he would go through the people and social media to repent, for the kingdom of God is at hand. Babe thought she must have sounded a little crazy because she didn't know exactly what was going to happen, Babe knew that God was going to give her a sign Babe. thought, Lord, Babe sure hoped she wouldn't miss the sign because when Babe would tell people about the number game, they would ask her what she was drinking.

Babe continued working and stayed busy but later that year when Babe brother took ill, she didn't see that sign coming, JJ was the brother that worked at American Airlines and he had just reached his retirement age, and Babe thought it couldn't be, but it was devastating, because it seemed like JJ was the glue that kept the family together since they lost Josie years ago JJ was a momma's boy; but her mother's love is what might have been the reason why the devil was able to sidetrack him.

JJ must've been having problems with his eyes and knowing Babe's mother, she told him to get that checked out before it got out of hand, JJ went to the eye doctor and the doctor gave him a shot in his eye. Because the doctor reviewing the history of the family thought JJ had a case of glaucoma, because my grandmother did, not to mention that JJ was an organ donor, that made him vulnerable to every corrupt doctor out there. Lord, when Babe heard about JJ having seizures and how it had gotten worse, he couldn't go to work, because of these seizures, Joanie his wife would pay someone to stay with him and watch him so that he wouldn't leave in the truck and have an accident. Later on, Babe found out that JJ just had a pink eye and she was upset because she thought a simple antibiotic would have cured it, but JJ was naive and he would believe anything some of those Doctors would tell him. Babe had to tell him once not to take those diabetic pills, because she had suspicions about them.

A couple of months before it happened, Babe confided in JJ and asked him if she died to handle her affairs, and he said he would, but he tried to assure her that nothing was going to happen to her, but Babe told him she thinks these people would rather have her dead if she don't get married. JJ stated, why not just get married, and Babe thought, because she doesn't want to marry just because they want her to and not only that, they also seem to be playing God, thinking Babe got to do whatever they want... When Babe thought back to their conversation. She regretted ever involving JJ, they had a tendency to think Babe was suicidal, which wasn't correct, she just got tired of them trying to tell her what to do, when she felt that they didn't care about the world and what they were doing to women., she knew it would be some trap.

Babe didn't realize that JJ was as bad, until Mother finally told her about the seizures, Babe thought oh my God, all Babe could do was think about telling him to get some Adderall, a synthetic form of meth. Babe had heard that it was a strong medication that would help him focus,

But this was getting serious, and Babe thought, let me call him, as Babe dialed the number, he didn't answer the phone, so she left a message and told him, try to get a doctor to give him a prescription for some Adderall and to leave that Viagra stuff alone, because it could be the problem with his eyes. Babe had heard that they had an effect on the eyes as in blinding. Babe didn't get to talk to JJ, but she prayed he would get better.

A couple of days had passed, and Mother called Babe and told her that JJ had went to the hospital again and Joanie was waiting for him to recover, Mother said that Joannie was at the hospital for about 4 hours and when JJ came out of surgery Joanie saw him before she left to get some extra clothing and to eat. When Joannie returned, they informed Joannie that JJ took a turn for the worse, and they had no other option but to pull the plug because he would have been braindead.

When Mother called and told her that they lost JJ, Babe couldn't believe it, she thought Lord, it doesn't make sense, Babe didn't want to believe it but before we knew anything they were getting ready to make plans to travel to Texas, where JJ lived, and they would have a service and cremate him. But they had to wait about 2 weeks because they had to remove his organs, and it would be a 2-week process.

Somehow, Babe thought about her brother being an organ donor, and she thought she's glad she changed her mind about being an organ donor, the system wasn't like it used to be, some people are coming up dead with the organs taken, and then the slaves they sold for their organs, if America would do like China do, they wouldn't have so many Doctor that would allow a patient to die, just to get their organs, they are corrupt and Babe wouldn't put anything pass the government now days. China takes the organs from death row inmates, whether it's consensual or not, Babe was sure they make arrangement, but just to kill a person to take their organs is inhumane, but what does this country and the other countries know about humanity?

After realizing that Babe needed to do God's will before she could be an organ donor, she removed the organ donor off her license. It's something that is definitely questionable.

Since we could still fly on Babe brother flight status, they were planning on flying, Mother and Babe and Mother's close friend Betty, she also worked at the airline company and she made arrangements, Betty and Babe would be staying at a hotel and Mother would stay with Joanie for a couple of days even after the funeral, Candie didn't want to fly because she wanted to drive with her family. Mark had also planned on driving with his family, everybody had children and it would've cost them to fly. Betty didn't have children, so we could hang out, she got the hotel, and Babe rented a car.

Mother and Babe flew earlier, and Joanie picked up mother at the airport, and since Betty was going to join them later, she gave Babe the information for the hotel. Joanie dropped Babe off at the hotel and took Mother with her to her home. At the Hotel, Babe made arrangements to have the rental car to pick her up, thinking she could pick up Betty at the airport when she arrived later, and we could have the car for the funeral as well.

At the hotel Babe enjoyed some free time, her and the Lord and whoever these freaks are hanging over my head, Babe didn't understand how this government could do this, but Babe knew it wasn't God, they used it to whatever advantage they could, but now it seemed like they were trying to destroy her and her family, or what was left of her family

When Mother told Babe that JJ and Josie both died on the same day. Babe thought these idiots, thinking they have my attention now and it's not in a good way. All this time all they give a hoot about is trying to make her get married, so what, they could control that, Babe thought...

Betty got in about 8 P.M. that night at the DFW airport, Babe had some practice but not much driving in the Dallas traffic, it seem to be a little bite more congested than Tulsa, Babe finally made it to the airport, but Betty had a back-up plan just in case Babe didn't find the airport okay, but on the way back was a pain, it had gotten dark and Babe glasses were not up to part ,Betty Was upset because we kept getting lost, but we finally made it back in time to get some rest and apparently she had had something to eat. Babe was still sad, because JJ was her brother that she looked to, he finally found happiness and now he's gone Babe remember once his biological daughter was upset with him and she said, she wouldn't attend his funeral and Babe thought how she would know that he would die before them.

The next day, Mother saw Babe and Betty together at Joannie's house before the funeral, and we would follow Joanie to the crematory and funeral home. Babe had contacted JJ's children and they had planned on being there except for the oldest one that ended up in jail where he couldn't even get out for the funeral. JJ had 3 children from his first marriage, they had problems, because his divorce was a bitter one. One thing Babe learned not to get married nowadays because you have to. It seems like that seldom works. Especially if the parents that raised you for marriage didn't work.

Stacy and Simone, they were dressed to kill, real fashion plate nowadays, Stacy had moved back to be in Nebraska with her mother, she's the one that said they wouldn't go to JJ's funeral when he died Babe thought how prophetic, but they came, JJ tried to help Stacy adjust to living in Texas, but she was so close to her mother, it wouldn't work out and then she felt left out when JJ's step daughter wanted to do things for him, and she didn't want to be with them for special days. Either way when families go their own ways, it's sometimes a difficult adjustment.

We never were that close because JJ's first wife despises everything about JJ now, since he's the one that wanted the divorce.

At the funeral everybody drifted in, Mark and his family, Candi and her family were running behind and they didn't get to view the body, but Babe took a picture of him. To show her. Many of JJ's friends gathered to wish him off, it was awesome the picture Joanie selected to post at the funeral, JJ standing in the parking lot, waving goodbye to everyone. How appropriate that picture was so fitting, but still so sad, because we knew that we wouldn't be able to see him anymore.

Lots of good comments, but Babe just never had any words to share at occasions like this and she felt in due time, God would have her to be his mouthpiece, whenever it was time.

After the funeral, Betty and myself met back at Joannie's home and we ate a bite, and met Joannie's neighbor, who was nice enough to show us how to return the car back to the rental and then took us to the airport. She really was a blessing; she had a daughter that lived with her, but we didn't get to meet her.

Back at the airport, Betty was on standby, and Babe was able to confirm her flight, but such as it was, we had to wait for Betty to be confirmed. Luck was on our side, we both got back to Tulsa, just in time to get some good sleep. It was probably about 11:00 at night. Betty left her car at the airport, she drove me home and we broke even since she provided the hotel, and Babe provided the rental car even though she claimed we didn't need it.

At home, Babe had the 4 walls staring at her and she couldn't phantom what was behind them. Although she knew she could sense something watching her all the time, it was strange how they could do so, but Babe didn't fear what man could do, because she knew God was greater. Although she did get really tired of their presence, knowing they were of Satan.

Mother stayed with Joannie for a few days after the funeral and talked and promised to stay in touch. JJ had told Joanie that if anything ever happened to him to make sure Mother was taken care of. Before JJ died him and Mark had been fussing about my grandmother's house that Mother ended up letting JJ and Mark handle. It seems like they had been clashing before JJ died, because JJ wanted Mark to give Mother part of the money that he got for rent since it took the estate attorney too long to settle anything.

Babe tried to tell Mark afterward just let the tax default for about 3 years and then go and buy the property at the auction, since Mark had made an offer to buy it. Why not just give mother the part that would have been divided Babe decided to stay out of it she had enough to do with the rent house she still had.

It looks like the people were turning into mush, everybody that Babe tried to hire had already been informed by the governments, much nonsense, so Babe literally had to fix up everything herself and then every time she turned around, she was being scammed, usually by some foreigners. she. knew the Muslims didn't like her because they were in cahoots with the government; but some thought she was a challenge. Yet Babe didn't feel that any of them were a challenge. God didn't send her to play games with the men or the government they were using.

Babe was thankful that she had a sense of direction and to God be the glory for that. Several weeks after returning home, Babe fell asleep because she must've been tired. It must've been like a nap, but when she woke up at exactly 9:11, Babe glance over at her phone to see it light up and when she reached for it, it was the last call she made to her brother, actually it was a message she had texted him because he wasn't answering the phone. Babe thought she would leave a message.

The message she texts him was to ask the doctor if he could prescribe her brother some Adderall, thinking it would help him get focused, if she had been there, Babe would have given him a diet pill, to help him clear up his focus, then Babe also told him to leave that Viagra alone, because it could cause blindness. To seek out other sexual enhancers, that was of the natural elements. It suddenly dawned on Babe that her brother's birthday was on 9/11, and that message was if God was telling Babe to carry on.

God was still pushing Babe with the truth of his word, and Babe knew that because of that she would forever be committed to him.

Mother made it back about a week after the funeral, Joanie, gave Mother a lot of things that JJ had left, she brought some house shoes home and was going to give them to Babe, I took the house shoes home and left them at my home in my closet storage. I also got a coat that JJ had, but it was nothing like having JJ still there.

Everybody back at their own home, and mother still grieving because of JJ,, she must have fallen asleep in her chair when she fell over and they had to take her to the hospital, when she got out she had bruises so bad that Babe felt bad for her and decided to stay with her until she got her strength back, at the same time

Babe thought she would clean up the books and get them to the presidents, but the president we had wouldn't be a good president to send them to because he already proved he didn't care about anything but money.

2020 was here at last and we had an entire year to wait before we could vote this president out, it must have been the middle of January, when all hell broke loose. It was a worldwide epidemic, people were dying by the dozen and more, some kind of virus, they called NOVEL-19 CORONAVIRUS, wow, all of a sudden, it dawned on Babe, this was the sign. They even named the virus Novel, like the novel she was writing. Also, the prophecy letter was titled 2020 prophecy, dated Jan 2019. To think this is what God was showing her and she needed to let the countries know, and Babe immediately got on her computer and notified Mr. Trump this is a ransom note, if he didn't open all those abortion clinics and get ready to open more Planned Parenthoods, that God is tired of what they are doing to women everywhere Babe jumped for joy, and Babe said yes sir to God almighty, but it was going to be a showdown and she was glad to be on God almighty's side.

God did it, it seem like everybody that wasn't rooted in the word of God was being taken under with this virus, all of a sudden, the entire world went viral with this sickness, the president tried to blame China, but Babe recall way back and

2019 she told him to stop supporting countries that wouldn't allow women their choices. But him and the selected GOP were joking about it, and I thought. Okay. Then God tried to tell me about 2020 but I didn't know what to expect, some of the key Republicans that had already been sick with some form of cancer, they died off, too many names to even mention.

Planned Parenthood called me and asked me what was going on, and I told them I sent the president a letter and demanded that he open all those abortion clinics and I told him this is a ransom note, if they cannot plan on reopening more Planned Parent hoods in other countries God would continue to judge the world. They told me we were in this together. I thought that was nice, but they couldn't keep this government from harassing me and it still seemed like they were trying to break me. All the men that came on to me, were a waste of my time.

Many of my coworkers, were joking about me, talking about how people better start believing me now, I didn't know how or when God kicked it off but I knew this must be the sign they even called the virus "Novel," the book I was writing on, that was all the proof that I needed that the God's must've heard my cry. Babe knew all this time all this government was trying to do was create a diversion, Babe wasn't about to jump on the opportunity to be with any man because all they talked about was having a baby and Babe didn't want to promise any man that without God's approval, but just to ask her to have a baby, some didn't look like they could afford a child, all they wanted was the sex that went alone with them.

This President Mr. Trump was awestruck, he couldn't do anything but look bad, then they started talking about him encouraging people to drink Lysol, they must have seen the Lysol on my kitchen cabinet, and he started joking about stuff like that, this virus was no joke, everybody was looking at Babe as if she had something to do with it. Babe had nothing to do with it, she didn't know, she made several pleads to the Great Businessmen of the world, they might have concocted something up, because Babe wasn't going to fall for their lies about getting married, especially the way they are still treating women in other countries. They never changed; they just wanted to keep women in bondage to childbearing even when it wasn't of God. And even in America, many were upset with her because they had children because they loved having a family more than the word of God. One guy had the nerves to tell me that he wanted a family, but he did nothing to keep his family together, first sign of sickness he fell for the doctors lies and started taking diabetic medicine and talked about his brother that got killed by the street drugs, because someone spike the drugs and he died as a result of taking drugs that they spiked with something toxic.

Now knowing the government is just as much a part of the drug thugs, Babe hoped that God would make them legalize drugs as well, once she told the government, if Mexico could market their Corona beer, why don't they let them market their marijuana and cocaine, if the people could buy their drugs straight, they might put FDA out of business, all those chemicals FDA were using in some of the drugs, were leaving people at risk for the side-effects. Then Babe realized that they had named the virus Corona also, however it came together it was weird, but she couldn't have done it that well even if she wanted to.

This virus was going strong, and it was killing off people that we loved, and many were set back because everybody had to start wearing a mask, Babe thought about how they mocked Michael Jackson, but Michael Jackson had a big heart, the video he put together, "We Are the World. "Made Babe realize we are the world; we are not just America.

Rumor was that one of the billionaires that was big on computers, started talking about getting rid of some of the people in the world because many countries were just deplorable. Starting with Africa, On Facebook, a video was being circulated about it, although the man wasn't on the video, but they mentioned his name, and I thought, that could be defamation of this man's character if they couldn't prove it, so I wouldn't list his name, then I thought he might have done me a favor because as much as I hated to admit it, some countries were deplorable, but then again, some rich people were just hell bound like many people in America, that had been so blessed they didn't even think about the people suffering in other countries. They were happily blessed enough to even afford a few international adoptions, some of the adoptions didn't go as planned and they were thrown back into the pool and readopted, it wasn't a pretty picture what was going on with adoption, scams after scams were being reported. People were losing their money. The governments were replacing the bastard hood with the black-market adoption, but now God was in the picture and was upset that when President Nixon vetoed abortion, he didn't do it worldwide. Nixon also tried to legalize drugs, but the government was knee deep with corrupt leaders, even the presidents were putting drugs on the street, I know now because Reagan was the president when my sister was murdered and I calculate the years and he was the president at that time, although I didn't know anything about him until the book was completely finished. He put it in the family, causing me to lose my sister and when Clinton decided to bring it around again, I already had the idea to write that book that my sister mentioned.

With this pandemic still going on, the GOP were mad, talking about this isn't a laughing matter, because they were the only ones who saw me laughing and God. They had set up everything to make sure they didn't miss out on watching me every minute, what I was doing no matter where I was at, so if they were invading my privacy, it was their own fault. That's when I realized they knew every move I made, so they could set false fleeces up. Millions were dying and the numbers were still adding up, especially in these other countries where they abused women the worst, if it wasn't the pandemic, it was other problems. It seemed like those that opposed abortion were getting hit the hardest and then the countries in America, they only started trying to restrict abortion because the government or the Popes, had people thinking Babe was supposed to have children. Clearly misleading because, Babe didn't even want children anymore, it took them too long to see the light and now she knew she had to fight for the other women.

I felt sure this was the sign that I needed., but when grief and hardship occurred, it turned from bitter to worse, Texas was the number-one place of terror for most women, they started closing all the abortion clinics they could. I was furious, but it looked like the next year proved to be worse for Texas, because they lost power for over a month, people were dying because they had the worst cold storm, many of us felt it but not as bad as Texas. We were told that Texas never prepared the flaws within the State for infrastructure. All that time they were wasting time and money trying to make the women suffer by closing the abortion clinics and never thought about the state of their state. Another story caught my attention about Texas, was a single mother, had a baby and the baby had many medical issues, the baby was near dead anyway and they wanted to pull the plug, because they had spent a billion on the baby and it wasn't getting any better. The baby was only 3 months old. Yet the birth mother, grew angry and demanded that they keep the baby living because she was the only one that could make that choice. I thought about all the taxpayers that would end up paying for her costly mistake. Yet Texas was so full of bigotry toward women when it came to abortion, I thought let those congressmen and those GOP, refusing to understand the grace of God through abortion pay for it. I think they just didn't care unless it happened to their loved ones.

I didn't get to celebrate much, but I knew that drinking was too much of a problem, so I decided to get me some crack, ever since I experience that Master Blaster with crack cocaine, I thought forget the big bang shit, it had to be for idiots, that didn't understand their soul salvation. At first when I got that hit, I thought what was all the other crap I experienced when my brother-in-law was doing it, they must have put so much cut on the crap that people don't know what they were getting, I see why so many people are killed behind drugs, when I got that blast, I repented to God and then I thought why would I call it that, but now it's the time to be honest and let people know, that would leave a smile on your face for days, if that's what they say about sex, it was then that I realized that some men were intimidated by drugs.

Still didn't make any sense to me because any woman would be glad to please her man in bed after that, but simple-minded men couldn't comprehend, but that was only for those that could relate, sex was good just by itself when the couple knew each other and had that connection. But I hear of couples doing things together to enhance their sex life, if all men can talk about is erectile drugs, then that would suck. But it's not a shame to be selfish, because you probably don't want to share that feeling with anyone that you truly don't trust.

I would look at some of the forensic file's pictures and I would think, why would a man want to get a girl high, just to have sex with her and then kill her if she didn't consent, that seem to be a problem, so all the more reasons to get high on your own.

I will never forget a story Tank my cousin told me about his classmates, they were getting high together on some cocaine, probably, I'm sure, they engaged in drugs all night long, but when the guy wanted to have sex, she refused, he literally beat her to death, I thought my God, then I realized that, women that take advantage of men, using them to get high with and knowing full well that they are going to want to get laid, or have sex, I hated to say it but this woman must have pushed this man to that. That's one reason, it seemed like it was okay, just as long as you knew your surroundings and if it wasn't there, it wasn't worth wasting time or money, whereas when the neighbors, had moved next door from Arkansas, they set out to get high and nothing would stop them, I was glad that I didn't have to put up with them long. They got busted and then evicted and I wasn't about to let them move in with me, whoever the thugs were hanging over my head, seemed like they were trying to set me up with them.

After treating myself, I knew the freaks knew everything I was doing, but I thought I would rather them see this instead of me having sex with someone, because that would be dumb to have someone throw that up in your face, when you know it's none of their business.

It was bad enough when someone on Facebook would harass me about not supporting his cause after I did anything, and I thought who in the hell is this and why would I support his cause, I only spent 20 dollars and they act like that was a big deal, it's when the government was hanging around telling everything and anything I did. When they did, I would do it just to piss them off.

Here it was halfway through the year and as if the pandemic wasn't bad enough, the next thing we are hearing about is George Floyd, a brother that literally was put to death via a pig policeman, holding his knee on his neck until he couldn't breathe.

Even when someone tried to help, I thought WTH, I immediately suspected the brother was doing or had done or was a frequent drug user and to my surprise crack cocaine. Such a merciless killing, as the story got out, it was said that Floyd had went the store to purchase something and the merchant told him the 20 bills was counterfeit, Floyd left the store and just hung out in front of the store, shortly afterwards a policeman came up to him and confronted him, but the policeman and Floyd had worked together at a nightclub, meaning to me that the pig knew that Floyd did cocaine. But nevertheless, that shouldn't have made any difference.

It began to seem like a setup because, the Muslim merchant, didn't have to call the police and later it was found out that the 20-dollar bill wasn't even counterfeit. Talking about putting the world on edge, then we had the protesting and the riots, someone on Facebook had the nerves to say it was because of him doing drugs. I thought, so what maybe we should all be doing drugs, then I began to wonder if me doing drugs set it off, then I thought about what happened when Whitney was killed, they say it was an overdose, but rumors were that her stuff was tainted with something. If I'm not mistaken when Whitney died, I had been a friend that was making meth, and I would hang out with him, but I never was into meth, but I thought surely, they weren't using this to teach me a lesson, because it didn't make any sense to me that they would do what they did to someone else because of me and what I was doing. Lord, this was getting the best of me, the entire world was on edge, people rioting all over the world behind what happened to Floyd. I though what the hell is wrong with this government, drugs are really a form of birth control, and they are too stupid to understand, that Floyd didn't want any more children, so drugs were his way of trying to have a good time without endangering others. I believe the Muslim merchant had to be in on it, because they are notorious for hating everybody that didn't abuse women, like some of them did. I begin to think after 9/11 the government started letting some of the foreigners into the country just to scam other citizens. Because lot of that stuff was going on.

Ever since I started writing the book about drugs, I thought it was my right to experience drugs, in order to tell the people in honesty what drugs were really like. One vacation, I had gone on a cruise and found out that I could get drugs over the counter without needing a prescription, in New Mexico. It took me by surprise, I found out at the spur of the moment, but I thought I would take advantage of the opportunity, a few things I got, and I was glad because some time it would cost you a copayment at home than the amount of the drugs. But since I didn't have the kind of insurance that I once had I thought this is really good.

But another time I decided to take the trip and I decided to see how easy it would be to get some cocaine. I was on the cruise alone, and enjoying some time reading and writing, then we stopped at one place and then the other, I was able to score easily, but I could tell the first town, the taxi was sketchy, like he was trying to backstab me, because we didn't speak the same language. So, I scored, and I immediately headed back to the boat, because while I was looking around it looked like their local policeman had his eye on me, I didn't buy much, but 100.00 at each place that I went.

Then we headed to another island which would be the last before heading back, and I scored. This guy was cool, he was white and we could relate better with the English, he asked if I wanted to do anything with him and I knew not to, I asked him about the drug cartel, and he told me that the drug cartel protected them, because they didn't step on it; I managed to slip it in my hiding spot and got on the boat without any problem, someone in a wheelchair, it looked like they searched them high and low.

After passing security, I got to my room and took another toot. I knew I was going to save it until I got home and frankly it wasn't enough to be busted by, but you know the laws can change at any time. I knew they had followed me on many vacations, but this one they couldn't wait to tell. Before I got off the cruise, I noticed some people looking at me, one guy had his wife or somebody and had the nerves to look directly at me and tell me to get married. I thought who the hell is this idiot, I didn't know him, but they would always know something about me, but they didn't know me. I could feel eyes all over me and I thought what the hell, these idiots better not get me in trouble over this, it's none of their business anyway.

After the cruise was over, I decided to ride the bus back, because Betty had got me a pass and it seem like the flight didn't come through on the way to the cruise, I would've missed my flight if I didn't come out of my pocket and charge a flight with my credit card, it might have been different coming back, but I decided to just catch the bus. While I had my stash tucked away, I could still feel the stares, whether they let me get away or not, it was a long ride back to Tulsa, from Long Beach, California, but when I finally got back, I was anxious to cook it and try it out.

What a waste, I thought, I didn't know how to cook anything, it had been 30 years when I dated Curtis, and he would cook it with my brother-in-law. I thought I had done something myself, but it was a disappointment, and a waste even more of a disappointment when everybody was throwing it up in my face. I thought I couldn't believe these idiots. I went ahead and admitted that this was supposed to be a little research with some adventure, but it looked like the spoilers were at it again, I couldn't do anything without them, trying to find something. I hate that I didn't get the rock, that the guy said he could have sold me. But that was history.

After what happened to George Floyd, I thought that was just too much, the next time I return to Mexico, I joke about getting it rocked. The next thing I know Breonna Taylor was getting her door kicked in and shot over 8 times, with her boyfriend. I just couldn't believe it, I thought, surely it wasn't because of what I had confessed to. This girl was innocent, and she was a hard-working independent woman. Disgusting to think I had anything to do with it., Lord, I just kept thinking, that they didn't have to die that way, neither one of them. Guilt of what I did, made me think that' don't make sense. But the president that we had was up to no good. It seems like he was instigating things, and they wouldn't reveal where the order came from and it appeared to be hush-hush. But to think they did it to teach me a lesson.

Why put me on some guilt trip, because if the government is crooked, it's because they are like that, Breonna Taylor's death set off another spark of fire, a few blacks were coming up dead also, cities were being raided and business being vandalized. The president wanted to send the military to kill them off, that's what most of us thought.

The mayors in these big cities, they refused the president's help, because they would rather see the stores vandalized than to see people killed, even though there were a few people coming up dead. They couldn't pinpoint their deaths. Now with this coronavirus, right in the middle of everything, it seems like maybe God would have to do something about the drugs as well, Babe knew that after Trump became president, he also became the target for hatred among races. I tried not to take it personally, but I just knew they were trying to tell me something, but I couldn't comprehend these senseless killings. Half of the people I knew were being used by the government, one guy that I had started using to help me finish the rent house, he was white and I like his work and his prices wasn't too high, but after the government started filling him in on my life, he thought I would consider him as an interest, I thought not on his life, he was about as ignorant as Trump, telling me that only black people did drugs, as if I would believe that lie.

However, it did seem like, every street drug that white people used, they would take them and make them synthetic so that the white people could buy them over the counter. Like the meth, became Adderall, and Newt Gingrich passed a bill that would allow an antidote to be sold over the counter, that when people that shot drugs up in their veins, if they overdosed, they could give them an injection to counteract the overdose.

Yet, they would get on my nerves trying to talk about crackheads, I looked at it this way, many of them were crackheads, because whatever they told them it was like they had a crack in their head and they would fill them with all kinds of lies, pretty much like the abortion scenario. I started smacking off on Facebook, telling the e-vape cigarette maker, that they ought to try to put crack cocaine in one of those e-vapes. I started being honest about it, because it seems like a need to educate the people was more important than trying to stereotype others. It's like to me, they didn't want people in the bedroom while they were having sex, so why would I want the government hanging over my head telling everything I did?

They didn't care, some of them thought it was a joke, I remember a late-night talk host, joking about how they love to see me mad. It was like nobody cared about nothing but getting a good laugh, but they knew they wouldn't get to see me have sex with anyone and that made them really mad.

My birthday was coming up, but it never was a big deal, we never had birthday parties when we were growing up, but now with the connection with the Bible, I would notice something indirectly would happen, sometimes bad, I remember someone tried to blow up the Statue of Liberty around my birthday. It was long time ago and I thought even then they were trying to blot out liberty. A bit of history I didn't know was the original Statue of Liberty was black.

Just after making that remark to someone, I thought, my luck that someone would break in my truck, and steal my monthly income holdings, I knew the government was wayward, but this time it was just too low. I thought I would wait a day or so and see if I had misplaced my things, or they would reappear, I know when they would play hide and go seek with my keys, sometimes I would find them and other times I wouldn't. Who in the hell would be low down, but it looked like I could tell that Trump didn't like me at all, he was set out to break me one way or the other. I regretted that I didn't' call it in immediately, but for some reason I thought they would have a change of heart. Nothing doing, when the credit cards started calling me, I knew then they were serious, and they wanted to destroy me. After calling the credit cards and my checking account with the bank since my checkbook was in the truck also, I knew they were stalking me everything I did was on radar, they didn't like the idea that I wouldn't date and I would aggravate them if I did drugs, but that's none of their business, I used my diet pills as a form for depression, because they were getting on my damn nerves.

It seems like Babe got a general message from the White House from Mr. Trump, on that same day as if he wanted me to know that he sent me a present, just not what I wanted. It was getting more and more annoying that they could do what they wanted and just kept on without regards to what they had done or who they had hurt, even though it would have been difficult for Trump to do these things personally, he knew all he had to do was give the orders, when you think about how leaders can throw their weight around just like that, it makes you wonder. Thinking about Vincent Foster, an aide that was under President Clinton came up dead and they said he committed suicide, talking about no end to that kind of corruption, and to think they may never see judgment until they leave this world.

To some degree, many will live out a life of blessing and prosperity, but the scriptures still inform us that it's harder for a rich man to enter the eye of a camel, than to enter the Kingdom of God. I thought for him to send me an email on the same day, I guess they really did get a kick out of seeing me upset, wow, to think that our government had nothing better to do. Yet you knew that many hadn't even consider anything in the Bible, they were going by tradition. Or by the Catholics teaching and since the Illuminati was the one that did all the sorcery and witchcraft, that was going on in my life. It didn't seem to get any better. Well, I knew they couldn't make me get married, and I knew that I couldn't change my stand because it was too plain to see that women were still suffering in other countries.

As a matter of fact, it seems like when my brother died, Trump sent me a letter, letting me know that there could have been a connection with that as well. They talk about how many people that one president had killed but, the FBI, CIA and the Illuminati, were the ones helping them, they had no morals whatsoever. Someone sent me an email and told me that the government sucks, as if they needed to remind me.

To me it seems like they wanted to pick up where they left off with slavery and I didn't feel the connection. I surely didn't feel like putting on a porn show for whoever was watching at all, it seems degrading to say the least. Now this lie they conjured, about me supposed to be having children, then they threw in marriage. I once thought maybe they knew something I didn't know, but now Babe know that since Rev.12:17 talks about the devil and how he went about seeking to devour the woman other children, if she had any, well, that's enough for me to know that this government is nothing, but the devil and they don't want to help me, they want to devour my other children and since I know that God gives me choices, I decided that if I don't want children, there's nothing they can do but make them look like the devil that they are.

It's like I feel, after dating an atheist, and how he blamed God for everything, actually the Bible tells us that Satan is the God of the world and since the government has people believing all those lies, they fit the description of the devil. Already doctors are allowing people with my name to die, it's not a coincidence, so why would I trust the doctors already telling people that they can put a toxic substance in a surrogate mother, who said they wanted a surrogate, I don't want children because now I know how evil this government is. I wouldn't trust a government still trying to force me into childbearing, when it's none of their business. That's why I might as well stand for the women in third world countries because they are trying to do me the same way.

Babe told this government from the very beginning that she's not their guinea pig. She meant it. To me there's nothing worse than passing down problems into your children life and Babe wouldn't chance it now for sure, the men that only want sex weren't of God anyway, so she didn't feel that she wasn't missing anything.

Another election year was upon us, and Babe was ready as the next person to move on with a Democrat, we had had enough of the nonsense, and most people thought that the president elect was the cause, it was terrible when we realized how bad the country was divided. Confederate Statues were being destroyed, Babe was learning a lot by all of this, even though she took a class in Black History, she never it was that way, yet Mr. Trump would support anything or anybody that would go alone with him, and I must admit most of them were just hiding behind their lies, just like him. Babe was told his father hated blacks and wouldn't rent to blacks, also he supported most hate groups like the KKK.

Babe was astonished to find out so many blacks support him, but many were bribed into it, it seemed too easy to sell your soul to the devil, and now I know that slavery was started to delay the truth about abortion. Many thoughts Babe would try having children but government, only made me leery about even dating. Some of the people that crossed my path, would tell me that they were always told through the slave master that abortion was murder. Now Babe believed that was the agreement when they bought the slaves, so the government would pay them for having slaves and it was call repartition.

You had to believe that this was the worst joke against humanity, but they had so many people still believing that all conceptions were of God, so they made the best of any situation. Then I realized that the Government and the FDA were just as much responsible, since some of the doctors were prescribing medication that caused birth defects and even though it wasn't intentional in many cases, they still did it. It was a part of the business aspect of the medical professional.

Back to the election at hand, Mr. Trump was so sure that he would win that he started telling people we could extend the terms instead of 8 years he was talking about more and I thought that would be terrible, because we would definitely be stuck with the worse if that happened. He had the nerves to tell people that he did more for the Christians than Jesus did, I thought, in what way, because he thought by making women have children they didn't want, the world would be full of rejects, and they would have the upper hand. Because of the man-made laws, you cannot tell whose of God, but God knew, and he would surely judge those that would come against his word.

With the pandemic and the riots all over everybody knew that the presidency was putting things on edge. A few Democrats were running for president and most of them were good no matter what, Bernie Sanders, had some great ideas, Elizbeth Warren, etc. While listening to Elizabeth Warren, I heard her say something about forgiving a sexual predator or sexual pervert. I wondered which ones, the ones they used or the government themselves?

Regardless, Babe still had a keen eye on her winning until her and Sanders clashed about something, when all else failed it looked like some Republican turned Democrat, that was making a good impact, because they turned his votes over to Biden. Next thing Sanders bailed out and endorsed Biden as well. Since Biden was the vice president for Obama, everybody started looking at him, he was our only hope, now I begin to see how things were going, the Democrats that were running, even though they knew they wouldn't win, they were loyal enough to endorse the best person and it began to seem that all of them knew, they would do anything to get that tyrant out of the White House. Even Elizabeth Warren, endorsed Biden.

After Trump elected a new Supreme justice after Ruth Ginsberg, succumbed to the cancer that had plagued her over the years, we all missed her dearly, but she fought a good fight, for women's rights and the whole scenario for human rights, she wanted them to not elect her replacement until the next presidency, but Trump wouldn't honor her last dying words because he was all about the Republicans. He hired some young replacement, that vowed to reverse Roe vs. Wade, and all shit hit the fan again, I'll be damned, why cannot these people leave the women rights alone and this was a woman, talking about women being submissive to their husbands. I thought what the hell does that have to do with running the country.

It was obvious that Trump thought she would be able to bail him out if the votes were too tight. After Biden heard her threats, he vowed to make abortion a law of the land. When I heard that I jumped for joy and I pushed Bid like never before, I believe that's what God wants anyway, "We are the world. "As Babe I thought about the song that Michael Jackson sung, when they all got together to raise money for the lost and dying worlds. Babe knew now that this COVID-19 had to be a sign, thinking about how Michael Jackson would wear his mask before we even had this pandemic, everybody thought he was just a freak, but

Michael Jackson's wisdom was far more than the average person and then they tried to make me look like him, by way of his flaws that the world tried to come against him for. I thought Michael shouldn't have never paid those people, I thought my childhood experience as a babysitter, left this government blowing an incident out of place. But I'm wondering how they would find out something so irrelevant that they could make people think I was some kind of freak, as much as I loved children and had cared for them. It's like they were fishing for anything they could use to try to make me look like the enemy.

Most people that really knew me, knew that it was all just too far-fetched. Nevertheless, I had people using anything they could because they had their children anyway it happened, and they didn't want to know that there were consequences even if they were happy, healthy and everything they wanted. But on the flip side to the coin, they had a lifetime of working out their salvation with trembling fear. If there were any consolation to that. Just knowing the Bible better made me accountable to live better and share the truth of God's Word, or I would be accountable for lying to the people like the false leaders and teacher and I knew their final destination would be the lake of fire. I knew that I would do anything God Wanted me to, because it was him, I live and moved and had my being.

When Joe Biden proclaimed making abortion a law of the land, I thought, God bless this man, also after the blacks that were haphazardly killed behind drugs, Kamala Harris, started talking about the drugs and the problems they had with them. She was running with Joe Biden as vice president. Kamala Harris used to be in the law enforcement, and she knew the laws were unjust, but what can you say, when you are in Rome you do as the Romans, it's easy to take a blind eye when you need your job and it's just not that easy when the laws have corrupted the lands for so long. But those drug-provoked riots had the entire country on edge. I thought, surely, I didn't cause them because of my testimony regarding drugs. Thinking back to Whitney, if this government had anything to do with that, it's like a slap in the face and the truth needs to be told, I know I was flirting with drugs then also to piss them off, but if that's how they retaliated I got news for them, then with Floyd and Breonna, how are they teaching me a lesson, by killing innocent people? Babe just heard that Breonna Taylor's family settled for 12 million dollars, Babe thought if anything, all that did was robbed the states that it occurred. But that jackass of a president we had, looked like he was stirring things up, he promised if he didn't win for the second election, he would start a war. Babe thought that's a chance we would have to take, because he wasn't getting anywhere that way.

The closer it got to voting, the more Babe prayed, I feared if this man won again, all hell was going to break loose, hell had already broken loose, but he was glad to welcome it, he had tried to start a war a few times with the other countries, but was unsuccessful, and Babe thought Thank God, because most of them that start a war and it assures them to run longer, how stupid can that be. When the journalist from Iran was murdered, our president was laughing and well-wishing them, because he was mad because he thought all journalist were the root of evil, because they were exposing the bad guy, now that should tell you what kind of person he was.

President Trump was so confident that he was going to win, he had already planned to stay another 4 years because most presidents do, but when the votes were tallied up, it kept proving the winner was Joe Biden. President Trump disputed all the states that he could and then claimed they beat him, I thought, now that's the pot calling the kettle black, after he stole the election from Hillary, now he wouldn't accept it.

Talking about big baby brat, he started threatening his own party and some of the idiots were right along with him, they wanted him to win as much as he did. But when Babe heard some so-called prophet say that Trump would win, her heart sank. Then he asked the people to pray the will of God. She dropped to her knees and reminded God of his word for women and others, and

I knew that it was God's will that these women would know the love of God and that the only way we could heal the land, is to start with exposing corrupt leadership.

After Trump raised much hell and had them to count the ballots over and over in some states, still came out in favor of Biden, some got more votes for Biden, Biden beat Trump by a landslide, it was wonderful, we could all rest at ease, we knew that Trump's days were over in the White House. I knew that Trump's agenda to close the abortion clinics made him the devil and all those that went alone with him were defeated. But I knew that battle wasn't over. I knew that I had to revise the books and make sure that President Biden and Vice President Kamela Harris receive them, I knew that President Biden was a Catholic, but he was a pro-choice Catholic, for that reason, I had to pray that God would open his heart after reading the books to do what he said he would do. Make abortion a law of the land.

One of the biggest billionaires in America, must've gotten upset with Babe drive to give women choices around the world, so it was said that he started talking about doing something about the overpopulated countries and he thought that they should start with Africa first, because many of the people there were deplorable. Babe thought whether he knew it or not that only justified abortion, there are deplorable people everywhere, we can start with the governments that's making man-made laws, and frankly Babe thought many people are just as hell bound as deplorable, and they don't know the difference. Because it wasn't making any sense to genocide a country that wasn't thriving when they never gave the women a choice. Many women being raped in these countries where they were forced to have rapist children, now they still trying to do that in some states in America. Babe would always speak out when she saw and knew corrupt government was behind it, the red states, would truly burn in hell because they were always coming against the women's rights, even in Oklahoma, the governor enforced a law that would prohibit the women from having an abortion unless they had an ultrasound first. Babe thought that's only to help crooked doctors get rich, while the women struggled with trying to pay the bill, since the last government wouldn't fund Planned Parenthood. About that time is when Babe realized that it doesn't matter if the heart of the fetus is healthy, because the brains were being damaged by the FDA drugs. Many of the cases of autism were being connected to the FDA drugs. Some of the depression medication the Doctors were prescribing to the women during pregnancy were being passed on to the unborn and most women should know to never take any medication other than herbs when pregnant. A strong feeling that insulin was damaging the unborn brains because of the gestational pregnancy and how the Doctors were giving these women insulin and the unborn was being affected. Insulin is a synthetic drug that can damage the brain of the unborn. When Babe asked a nurse, she claimed that women should take care of themselves better and, what's worse, the women dying from complications from the blood sugar or the child being born with autism. That's dumb there's another option and Babe knew it, when they go to nursing school, they don't even teach them about herbs, they insist on pushing the FDA drugs because it's their way of supporting their career and the hell with God's natural drugs. Most of the FDA drugs are man-made, they put God drugs on the street and bait people with them to increase the prison population. Then they make money through the Prison stock. Corrupt bastards, anybody that invests in prison stock, God ought to send them to hell anyway. because the schools need that money. They are capitalizing off the innocents of poor people, when they are in there for drugs. and the ones that should get the death sentence, they spend life in prison, while the prison stock increase and the taxpayers are paying, while they should've been executed and used their organs to be harvest instead of killing people just for their organs

After hearing about what Ben Nate yahoo and Trump did before he left the office, Trump.

Before Joe Biden was even inaugurated, Argentina the largest Latin state, had legalized abortion, it's happening Babe thought, God does answer prayers, Babe knew we would be fighting an uphill battle with the drugs, but she knew that if God said Rev. 22:2: "Do not destroy the trees for the leaves are healing for her Nations," Babe was ready for another fight. Not to mention, drugs were a bigger problem than abortion in many countries. They had people dying in overcrowded prisons, because of drugs. If God hadn't called Babe to prison ministry in the beginning, she wouldn't not have known how serious the problem was. But Babe knew that she would have to fast like never before. Too many people were dying and then made to look bad, because they look at it as a sickness, whereas God was trying to show the people that many drugs were a form of birth control, also when Babe experienced the master blaster, she knew that if people were taught how to do drugs, they could probably eliminate many surgeries that were killing the people in the long run that were dying behind complications from the surgeries. and could be the solution for many people, but as long as they are being tainted and put on the streets to kill people, because they want people abusing sex and women instead, all the governments have always been more concerned about increasing their population, hoping for a better economy, but they fail to realize there's a time to kill and a time to heal, and when God ordains abortion for an untimely pregnancy, his word overrides corrupt government.

Psalm 58

Yet corrupt government uses the fatherless to become victims of sex trafficking and worse, God knows the intent of evil men. Also, the flip side to that theory, is the wormwood prophecy in the book of Revelation, the wormwood prophecy is describing sex as the worse sin imaginable, but since wormwood is really a toxic plant or herb, now we all know how they can take poison from a snake and make an antidote for the snakebite. Ironically that's what God is saying about drugs. Sex is symbolic of the worse drug out there. because it produces idolatry, children are redeemed from their parents' sins; but if they aren't taught and follow the same way. The legacy of sin must be redeemed.

If Babe had listened to those doctors telling me that diet pills weren't any good, she might have failed for those anti-depressant pills that were killing people. What about *Prozac Nation,* a book written by a woman that was prescribed Prozac, unfortunately she died a while back, Babe really didn't read the book, but it looks like many of the pills they prescribed for depression were making them sleepy, or worse Babe hated being sleepier.

After reading an old encyclopedia about diet pills being used for depression, Babe decided to go with the diet pills, she started taking them as a teenager because she was overweight, but later in life, she would get back on them and when God called her Babe realized that she was being bombarded with the devils it was then that she realized that the diet pills had cocaine in them and, many times she would use them for the energy. They would suppress her appetite, and they would also work as a pain aide. Now, Babe knows why some doctors didn't want people taking the good diet pills, because they know that the good ones, would increase the immune system, when she found out the military would give them to the men on the battlefield, Babe's thought why not people that's on the battlefield for life. Life is a battlefield within itself.

As they prepared for the inauguration, a riot proceeded at the White House and Lord only knows who would attack the White House, one police officer was killed, and several people were injured. They had to call in the Air National Guard, Babe guess when Trump said he would create a war, he did just that. Now the world is on the edge again, but with all the people coming against Trump Babe could put that behind and look for better days in the United States of America worldwide if God has his way. As much as Babe loved America, she must agree with Jesus, we are the world.

It didn't take long before weed dispensaries were popping up everywhere and Babe knew before long women would read the book about herbal abortion. And they wouldn't need the government telling them what to do with their body, and as far as the Doctor's they were found in the dark. And since all they wanted from Babe was a baby, she knew not to trust a man for just that.

Chapter 19

Worldwide Conspiracy

While it seemed like the world was on the edge with the immigrants trying to cross the borders even though the president told them to wait until their asylums had been cleared, everybody wanting to blame the President for not controlling the border, but it seem like the border have always been a problem Babe did all that she could to stay business, hoping it would avoid wasted relationships, since that's all the government was doing, trying to push her into a relationship. Babe knew that if they could they would redirect her from what God had truly called her to do.

After taking a back seat to the world problems, it's was obvious things were getting out of control, it seemed like the man-made wars between Russia and Ukraine.

Never ending and the Russia President Putin even hinted about the Ukrainium's being drug addicts, Babe thinking what the hell would that have to do with anything, but before it was over he was drafting young men to fight, they were so blind-sided about the drugs, they didn't know that the kids were taking a hallucination drugs called salt. That only defeated them in their attempt at war. Babe had heard about the American government giving men the diet pills phentermine when in combat and when they needed them. Those were the pills that Babe had lost weight with in High School, and every now and then she would resort to the diet pills for depression, then she found out they were good for blood sugar, because it seem like all of a sudden more people were dying behind diabetic related sickness. After working in the medical profession many years Babe begin to question many things, she saw how many people were being put on that medicine, next thing you know they were removing s toes and legs and it made Babe quite leery; Especially after hearing a documentary that a white female Doctor had conducted. This white female Doctors claim they're putting some black people on that medicine that didn't even need it, next it was the Indians and before long, they were putting anybody they could deceive because Medicare and Medicaid would eventually pay for it even if they didn't need. Next thing you know they would say blacks were at high risk for being diabetics, and Babe thought, sure if they didn't suspect anything, but listened to the Doctors, that were only misleading them.

Babe started as a nurse aide, and later became a med-aide, but she had to question, much of the medicine, because the high blood pressure medicine was like a necessary thing, but when

Babe found out they were putting people on several different types of blood pressure medicine, then they would end up being sick from all the medicine.

Next thing you know they would end up on dialysis because all that medicine messed up their kidney. After finding out that some of the Doctors, never resorted to herbs or natural healing remedies, Babe just wonder what was wrong with the herbs, since God created them for the healing of the nations. When questioning a nurse about an herbal medication called Echinacea, Baby question the nurse and asked her if she knew anything about it, after she admitted that she didn't Babe askes her, why don't they teach them about herbs. And the nurse responded by stating the Doctors claim they made the organs to appear darker. That made Babe wonder.

Speaking of organs, it seem like the pandemic bought on a demand for organs and while, people were trying to avoid the pandemic, Some of Israel immigrants were being sold into slavery in Lebanon, The men were being auctioned off for their body parts and the women were being sold as sex slaves. Leaders without moral, It was happening from Israel to Lebanon, After the one American President gave Israel 50 Billion dollars, that must have sweeten the deal for sure. Because shortly after Trump lost the coming election, it didn't take long before Israel and

Hamas was fighting over in Gaza again. Hamas attacked a concert in Israel and took them by surprise.

Now we have another man made war, and it don't look like they want to cease fire anytime soon with either one. Israel was killing any and everything that got in the way, Hamas had killed about 1200 from Israel, and Israel had killed so much more, that everyone was afraid it had turned into a genocide. People were upset that Israel wouldn't cease fire or nothing else. They eventually moved into other areas, and even though many wanted the wars to end. The Prime Minister of Israel didn't want to stop until all the hostages had been release.

It seem like all it did, was created a diversion from what was really going on in the world, even the Russia, President suggested that they make the women in prison to procreate and replenish the land with more people, Babe just wondered, if that's why they were fighting, just to make women believe if the men could fight in the war, the women should feel obligated to replenish the earth. It seem very twisted after hearing this leader speak this way, because they weren't just killing innocent people they were destroying the country. After seeing the results of devastation behind the war, it didn't seem like they would ever be equal. Because some of the Russian soldiers were rapping the women as well.

After the death of JJ, mother remind Babe that Josie, died the same day and while fasting around the same time, it was mentioned that John F. Kennedy was assassinated the same day. Babe never thought about it until now, to know that a President was killed on the same day that she lost her sister and brother. Babe was only 7 years old when the president was assassinated. Now it seem like there were some kind of connection, Babe, never thought about it until she realized that they all died in a bad way, even JJ, should've still been living, but since he was an organ donor, it seem like the Doctors didn't care about saving him because they could get more money using his organs.

Googling information seem to be a way of life for Babe, after realizing that knowledge was only a few steps away with cellphone technology, technology have advanced enough for even poor people can have access to the knowledge God wanted them to have. Within minutes Babe had found out that the conspiracy that John F. Kennedy wanted to reveal was that all these countries that didn't want women to have choices, were in on the deception. Alone with the drug cartel, how they used God drugs to fatten their wallets, while the FDA produced that synthetic medicine that was killing people in the long run. It didn't take long for Babe to understand the Presidents of the United States were no different than the drug cartel, after finding out about Reagan, and there may have been more, but since

Reagan is dead, Babe thought it would be safe to expose him. Even though the movie "Made in America, was the making of the America Conspiracy. After finding out that President Reagan was no different than the drug cartel, opened Babe's eyes to the reality of what was really going on, It seem like they did a bait and switch with the real drugs in order to use God drugs to create crime and criminals. Then to find out they were making money off the prison stock, just left Babe with great remorse, knowing that many people would fall into worse crimes after a jail sentence, or worse some wouldn't make it out alive. Especially in some of the third world countries prison.

It was so bad in some of the third world countries, they would place women in prison if they had a miscarriage, and many were left to die in the prisons. The word of God would always seem to tell it like it was, after Babe realized that President Nixon vetoed abortion, and he was trying to legalize drugs, but they were making too much money using God drugs to bait people into prison and crime, she could see why they ostracized President Nixon, But by Nixon being the 37th President, and to understand Amos 3:7, Babe knew that Nixon was trying to do the right thing. However now the America Conspiracy have become the Worldwide Conspiracy because to know that drugs were never supposed to be illegal. It seems like you can read the Bible and read over all the facts until one day, when you search and seek out the truth, then God will show you in his word.

While reading the book of Revelation, 22,2, Babe was alert to read about the tree of life and their fruits. It seems to be saying something about drugs. As Babe read the scripture. "Do not destroy the trees, because the leaves are healing for my nations. As Babe read over the scripture it seems like she had hit the jack pot, knowing that the leaves they were talking about was the marijuana and the cocaine leaves. These are the drugs the governments were baiting people into crime by. It wasn't long before Babe was writing the President to inform them, she was going to write a book about drugs and expose the government for all the people they had led down the wrong road, by deceiving the world about drugs. Babe realizes that she had discovered something awesome in the Bible and as she continued to seek God, the Bible revealed even more about drugs. As Babe begin to search for more scriptures , a song came to her, it was an old song they would sing. The song was about blowing the Trumpet in Zion, Since Babe had taken on the name of Zion, as her email name, she begin to reveal more things in the Bible about drugs. Google was amazing, it was a thesaurus, as well as a concordance and dictionary all in one. It was awesome to have knowledge at your fingertip. After using google to verify part of the song, It was interesting to know that it would tie in with the book of Joel.

As Babe investigate the scripture, it was only natural to read all 3 chapter. It was astonishing that the first chapter included a scripture that proved that drugs were never supposed to be illegal Joel 1 Talks about the drunkard, and how he should leave the wine alone and go to the vine. Babe couldn't help but understand that Joel was referring to marijuana or cocaine, because they both have leaves. In that same chapter Joel was comparing the apples and the pomegranates. Then Babe remembered the old saying about the apple a day keeps the Doctors away. It seem like the Doctors didn't want people to be healed, they just wanted them coming back to them because they depended on that money, Even though there are good Doctors, It's like the book of Job revealed. Job 13:4 How the physicians were worthless. After reading the book of Job, Babe felt for sure that Job was an abortionist, because of the scriptures he referred to the widow that he saved from her spoils. Back then they referred to an untimely pregnancy as spoils.

The book of Joel had captivated Babe's attention, especially when she realized that song came from one of Joel's books. They rushed to the city they ran on the wall, Great is the army that carries out his word. After reading the book of Joel, Babe knew that she was a part of that Army that would expose the truth of God's word. Her involvement in prison ministry, reminded her how many people would go through hell because of this conspiracy to keep people ignorant about drugs. As Babe continued reading the book of Joel, she noticed the 3rd chapter, revealed judgment of the nations. Which listed none other than Palestine. Babe thought that's what's going on now, with all the upheaval about ceasing the war, because the Palestine's were losing more and more every day. No one like what was going on over there, but even the leaders that tried to intervene. The PM of Israel wouldn't cease fire, he continued killing because of the hostages, even when some of the hostages were being killed by friendly fire.

As Babe summed up the 3 books of Joel, it seems to connect drugs in with the wars, and Babe felt a little baffled, wondering how would people understand this, then she remembered something a client told her, the drug wars were keeping the older people from getting their drugs, she felt this way because she had recently been in a rehab facility and they were notorious about not giving her the pain medication that she desperately needed. Babe knew that to be a fact, because she remembers working at some of the places where the med-aides were stealing the drugs right out of the cart or either they were switching some of the narcotics with the regular pills if they were shaped the same way. Babe thought maybe she had a point, then Babe remembered what Putnin stated right before they went to war with Ukraine. Referring to them as drug addicted, when that didn't make any sense. Yet the young men he drafted into the war, were losing the battle by taking the wrong drugs.

Ever since Babe lost her sister, then to find out that they killed Whitney Houston with tainted drugs, Babe became somewhat rebellious, knowing that the government kept putting them out there. It seemed only natural to give them a taste of their own medicine, since they were putting drugs out there, why not, "Babe thought, Knowing the Presidents were no different than the drug cartel. Then to hear them talk about drug dealers ought to receive the death sentence. How many times did Babe have to hear that before she ended up writing the White House Government? It begin to offend Babe to think that the government could get away with putting drugs on the streets while they increased the penalty for those that did them. They were no different than the drug cartel. Just to think about all the people they were tainting their drugs, just to teach them a lesson. How would they learn if they were dead and gone. Babe couldn't help but remember Whitney Houston, last word, "She was going to see Jesus". I truly believed she would see Jesus after dying. They talked about how bad Whitney had gotten with the drugs, but it still didn't seem fair that they would kill her off like that. Babe had been flirting with drugs and she saw nothing wrong at the time, because it was her way of pissing the fed's off. Babe never thought her habit was that bad, and sometimes she felt herself doing them just to piss off the devil, knowing that she didn't have time for a man, because the imps hanging over her head was bound to figure out how to use them, so it was just safer to do drugs.

After realizing that the government was moving drugs into the neighborhood, Babe just sit back and realize that they must be trying to set her up, and she begin to write the books about drugs, so she needed to play alone with them. After finding enough in the Bible to stand on, she knew it was time to prove the word of God was right and how loving God is. It didn't take long to stumble upon the book of revelations and as complicated as it appeared to some, Babe knew that the spirit of God would reveal to her the truth, to convey to others. In the book of Revelation, the 8th chapter, it talks about the wormwood prophecy. As Babe read over that chapter, it seems like it was saying something about drugs and sex at the same time. Babe knew the Bible talked of symbolism in explaining the things of God. Now knowing that wormwood in actuality was symbolic of sexual sin, but actually wormwood is an herb and a very toxic herb, they don't recommend that they have children or pets near this herb because it can be fatal. But the flip side to the coin is that they have extracted the herb using it as an anti-cancer medicine. If people could understand this, why not understand, that many drugs can also work as a form of birth control, even if a person would rather do drugs instead of having sex.

Babe couldn't help but to think about an audio tape of Natalie Cole. Listening to Natalie experience in Las Vegas, but unfortunately the hotel caught on fire and since she was on the high rise end of the Hotel, they advise the customers on the high end of the hotel, to remain calm and to put wet blankets by the doors to keep the smoke from entering the room, causing then to suffer from smoke inhalation. Natalie was with her body guard, as they struggled to remain calm, Natalie's body guard suggested that they make love because if they were going to die, they might as well have a good time while they could.

Babe could only imagine what Natalie was going through. Without thinking twice, Natalie pulled out her drug paraphilia in shot a dose of drugs in her veins, I don't remember what kind I think it was heroin. Whatever it was, she appeared to be cool as a cucumber. While her anxious body guard had to figure out how to calm himself. They got through the fire just fine, but years later her body guard died due to some of the smoke inhalation he was affected by. Natalie eventually had to have a kidney transplant from the drugs damaging her kidneys, I think if Natalie had a Doctor that cared or even knew that she could've preserved her Kidneys by taking a potassium pill from time to time, she probably wouldn't have damaged her kidneys. But most Doctors try to frown on people that do drugs, because they would rather them taking their drugs. While most people are killing themselves slowly over the effects of alcohol. That's why Joel, was telling the drunkard to leave the wine and go to the vine. It makes you wonder if that's why many people didn't have any other choice but to do alcohol and it made more alcoholics out of them. But it makes you wonder if the conspiracy did involve people that would be force to drink alcohol, simply because alcohol is easier to get then the other drugs especially since they just made marijuana away available with a green card.

Alcohol kills more people then drugs, the problem is they can take the time and care to teach the kids how to have safe sex, but at the same time, they will not help people to understand the importance of tempering themselves from drinking too much alcohol or using drugs When according to the wormwood prophecy, Drugs might be better in the long run because people cannot commit idolatry with drugs. Maybe that's why drugs were made illegal, because some religions don't believe in birth control. When common sense teaches you somethings, people get pregnant when they don't take precaution, but they want to blame the woman no matter what. One client was pretty bad with cancer and he had a colostomy bag for his feces, since he didn't have any children he could tell Babe, that women should use birth control and he didn't believe in abortion. Babe was always in trouble for discussing things with the clients that got upset over everything she said, but in reality they were just a part of the Antichrist that was doomed for the worse fate of hell.

This client was so self-righteous, that Babe could see she couldn't get through to him and she figured why bother, some people are content with being stuck on stupid. And even though he was surviving, his time would be limited on earth because he was slowly dying of cancer. Babe cleaned his apartment once a week, and he was filthy, he wasn't supposed to smoke cigarettes in the apartments that he lived in but he did, Babe thought the job was getting old, and then the fact that some of these people that Babe tried to reach out to were the very people complaining about Babe talking about the government. While Babe knew she was making the best of her situation at the time, she looked forward to moving on because it was too many people that needed services of some sort, but apparently most people envied Babes calling and knew that they would and could rat her out for the dumbest and most minuet issue. The government love having that power over Babe, even though they hated her, she had become like John F. Kennedy to them, they didn't want John F. Kennedy to expose the conspiracy so they killed him, but with Babe, they knew the prophecies were strong and fearful to many.

The Bible explicitly told the told the barren women, that know weapon formed against her would prosper and any weapon formed against her God would judge, Isa. 54 begin to be a scripture that Babe could stand on, and she stood on it to the point, she didn't even want children, but the government was so busy telling the world stuff that they didn't know themselves, leaving Babe pissed off at men that only wanted her to have children. One neighbor told Babe that he wouldn't have to pay child support if he had a baby by Babe, this upset Babe as him and his friend joked about their mamma babies, Babe just knew the government was misinterpreting the word of God just to make men come on to her any kind of way. Like the Mexican neighbor that was helping her neighbor remodel their home, after getting to know Babe, and introducing Babe to his youngest daughter, he started hinting around about his daughter wanting a baby brother or sister, Babe thought, He must be crazy, he had 7 kids by 3 different women and now he thinks Babe would have a child for him, talking about crazy. It was getting crazy because Babe knew the government was telling men that because that's what they had planned for this woman all alone, When Babe thought about how they bought her people over to the United States in the worse way, now to think that all those people had to submit to the unjust laws that the government created just to undermine the women of the world, because after they did what they did to the slaves, women around the world were nothing but sex slaves to some governments, Babe thought hell to the no.

Even though Babe knew the governments were only trying to use her for their own demented and disgusting reason, Babe had a way about it, because she knew it would probably buy enough time to expose them for all the other shit they were doing in the name of corrupt government. Babe knew they killed John F. Kennedy because men then and some men now don't women to know their place in the world. Babe had a slight advantage over Kennedy, they were lured by Babes femininity and they would try to seduce her into a relationship if they could but Babe knew that the men couldn't be trusted because it looks like they knew how to play people in the name of their country. Babe was glad and thanked the veterans for their service, but Babe also knew that many were blindsided and lost their soul because they didn't put God first.

Around the worlds, war was going on and Babe thought it was just a diversion to keep people mind off the real problem, which was about the rights of women and men, that needed to pardon for the crimes of drugs that were never supposed to be a crime. America took the lead, first President Busch then President Obama, begin to pardon the men and women that had been imprisoned behind drugs, People would laugh about President Busch and how he joked about smoking marijuana and enjoyed it, whether Obama did drugs or not he begin to pardon as many behind drugs as he could, if their drug offense didn't lead to something worse like murder. To hear about women dying in prison in these 3rd world countries behind abortion, only stirred up Babe even more. Babe knew this was the conspiracy President Kennedy was trying to warn America about, but they killed him hoping that the conspiracy theory would never be known. But Babe knew she would take the torch and run like hell, because she knew that if all the martyrs had to die, she would be glad to go alone with them instead of watching the world go to hell in a handbasket without fair warning.

The deeper Babe got in the word and the truth, the less her friends would go alone. An old time friend that Babe had worked with for many years would frequently agree with Babe about the rights of women but after retirement, they couldn't keep in touch as much and she was later influenced by her only son and husband, whom she loved dearly, they were very much a big part of her life, Bette only had one son and she haphazardly had him and made the best of the ordeal, and Steven her husband had a child under the same circumstances and he love his son even though he didn't raise his own son, but he was still involved with his own son as well as helping Bette to raise her son. Thomas her son turned out to be the delight of any child, but that stigma hung over his head, "That if he had never been born." Babe begin to pick up on it like it was obvious that people like that wanted to put themselves over Jesus, and even though Bette used to always agree with Babe about women rights, now all of a sudden, she's going alone with the orange blob that only wanted to take away the women rights for good. Babe couldn't understand Bette's reason to side with people that wanted to put adoption over abortion, creating another reality check. Babe thought adoption was a lot like surrogacy, until the Pope tried to rule against surrogacy, for whatever reason it still seem unfair. Surrogacy got complicated when people started changing their mind about thing before the deal was sealed. Like the one couple that wanted twins, but when the surrogate only conceived one they wanted her to terminate the conception and they would start over with someone else. The women didn't want to terminate the fetus, that's one of many problems that developed with surrogacy.

When Babe realized that many of the School terrorist were adopted or they had some underlining problem that triggered them to kill off massive innocent children. Babe had to steer clear of all the lunatic that would rather pass their problem down through adoption, rather than just abort and return the unborn back to God. Babe had proof now that God was the author of the scriptures that advice the sinner to return the unborn back to God that the sinner would be saved. Psalm 90:3. Babe was convincing that Bette was going the way of Balaam the false prophet in the Bible, that tried to bewitch the people of God into have children any kind of way that it happened. Babe thought many cases of adoption was okay, whatever the reason, but some of them were only passing down their problems to others in an unsuspecting way and then they would rebel and take their anger out on the world, killing innocent people.

Like the Sandy Hooks incident, how the kid had one of the extreme cases of autism and his mother was taking him to target practice, later he killed his mother alone with twenty-six other innocent children that didn't deserve to die that way, as they were televising the story, Babe, saw a few businesses that she could identify with, a street called by her last name. Then the other kid that went off at Parkland Florida, killing his classmates, he was pass off through adoption, and suffered from some underlining problems. Many that are diagnosed with the extreme autism, don't find out until they go off on some terrorism attack and it's too late to change things then.

Babe noticed that most of the kids that went off into violent rages and created a hostile environment for others, were abused and neglected from the point that nobody cared about these kids and even if they did get the right attention as some did, no one knew they would create havoc on the world by killing up a bunch of innocent children. After everyone knew of the hatred Texas had for women, by closing all the abortion clinic, one governor was fired by President Obama, but they continued until they got another one that was just as hateful and ignorant. It wasn't long before a young man that had been raised by his grandparent, begin to feel the rage of all that they had taken him through, his mother passed him off to his grandmother and this young man was feeling anger, remorse and hated the fact that the government didn't care about these children after they were forced into the world to be denied the love and care of a real family. Yet they expect these children to carry on like everything is normal. Its seem like in Uvalde Texas, a town that even sounded like Babe's first name, but all of this was overlooked, because people think they can pass their mistake down to others when even others don't care or they cannot do any better than others in raising wayward children. Solomon talks about it would be better if people weren't born if they cannot have a proper burial, even if they had 100 children, but didn't have a proper burial. They would've been better off being still born, the same as saying they should've never been born. There's no way a proper burial would entail killing themselves or killing other's in the battle of their own life or others. However, when our men are caught between the crossfires and have to fight for their countries, they are granted a proper burial, but many question their fate afterwards, but if they go on to serve God in honor of their country. God and the country allows them a proper burial, but that's not the case, when people are killed by the officers in the line of fire and their bodies lay wait for a burial in the land of the homeless or unclaimed bodies.

Yet the truth of it all is that many people have been born this way and will continue to be born straight from the pits of hell, if women are forced to have children they know in their heart they cannot afford and the child is only going to be put out there for the wolves to use through the system, because many people know they can get a welfare check for many of the children, they will take the money, but not care about the welfare of the child, then the child will turn on the world the way many have done via terrorist attack.

Now back to the wars, it's almost like the book of Thunder mentioned, how this feminine order being described in this book, would create wars, Babe felt in her impression that she was the feminine order of Thunder, because that book was a conglomeration of all the books in the Bible that connected the Ethiopian daughter to the barren woman as well as Kings daughter. Even how the book of Thunder went through the process of reincarnation, when she spoke of her being her mother and father and brother, as weird as it sounded, Babe knew that this figure had lived through a series of lives and could connect to something much deeper than the world could grasp. While trying to understand the book Thunder, Babe had to relate to the number theories as well, since this book was discovered in 1945.

Knowing that both books Isaiah 54 and Psalms 45 described the Ethiopian daughter, even though Zephaniah 3:10 mentions the Ethiopian daughter, despite those numbers don't match, the main prophecies describes both numbers transposed equaled 9 the number connected to the eternal message of eternal life. Babe hoped that she would be a peacemaker in pursuit of her calling. But in understanding the book Thunder. It states that she is peace, but wars have came because of her. Babe knew that many governments were on to her and her calling, many of their countries refuse women the rights to choose. Babe knew they had to be in on the conspiracy, because most of their citizens became the immigrants of the world, fleeing these countries, because the conspiracy only created a bigger problem down the road.

The leader of Russia made disparaging remarks, even though he started the war with Ukraine. First he called them drug addicted, next thing you know his remarks about women in prison procreating to repopulate the world. When women in prison shouldn't be made to replenish the earth via of being raped by the soldiers or guards, Babe realized that this man alone is connecting the prophecies in the book of Joel together whether he knew it or not. After Babe understood Psalm 137 describes the immigrants coming across the border, and how even the 9th verse described a full birth abortion. Babe knew somehow, she could prove that the drug was connect to the man-made wars, simply because of the Russia leader that made all those offbeat remarks.

Looking back at Russia history, Babe couldn't believe that they allowed legal abortion, before many countries in the United States. In 1920 the Soviet government legalized abortion. In 1922 martial rape was made illegal in the Soviet Union. Labor law also assisted women. This was verified by Wikipedia. Now it seems like over the years they have tried to reverse and stem the laws behind abortion. Babe felt that since her calling would bring out the worse in the government, many have tried to create more havoc. Especially since her own government seems to only think that Babe should be trying to make some effort to have children, they don't seem to really care about the testimony of truth. Which is the offering Zephaniah 3:10 is referring to. Babe thought that it really would be a miracle if she had children, because she was told that she couldn't and since the government only cared about her making some effort, they thought she would be the slave they had created when they bought them from Africa and made them procreate. All it was doing to Babe was turning her off of the entire notion. She loved children, but she saw no need in having any at this point, because it took too long for the governments to understand that women aren't just about having children that they don't want. Too many scriptures refer to God being better than the children of men, referring to the untimely pregnancies women would be forced to carry because of the conspiracy.

Since Babe was on to the truth way back in 1993, she knew that Israel had legal abortion and to know that Russia had it way before them, only makes Babe realized that they got upset to know that she would bring the offering of truth that many men didn't want to hear about, so they started in on the war on women. Even though the wars are out of control, they are still trying to make war on women because they cannot relate to the truth of God's word, and since Babe haven't made some dumb effort to even try to have a child. They want to take it out on other women. Which will only provoke God to bring judgment down on all of the countries that would rather put the unborn over the word of God.

Much research and study proved that the Johannine theory was substantial in understanding the consequence behind sexual sin. Even though the promises of God would forever bless the world and the people that served God. There was also this possibility that men and women both will jeopardize their eternal blessings if they continue to be ignorant of the truth. Another book that tied in with the Bible was the Gospel of Truth, found in the collection of the Nag Hammadi Library, because when John wrote in the book of revelation that the spirit says to come, John knew that by now people should know that the spirit of truth would show them all things and since Babe real name meant True, this is the offering that Zephaniah spoke of when he mentioned the Ethiopian daughter would bring the offering of God. Yet the government knew this all alone but they wanted to enforce procreating no matter what, When Babe thought about her diagnosis, how she wouldn't be able to have children, yet the government doing nothing but telling men that she should bear children and by now, Babe thought, who would want them the way they have proved to be nothing but idolaters, they brainwashed the slaves and made them bare children, hoping they would keep the legacy going on. But Babe knew that she wouldn't want children the way they were making a big deal about it. Because too many women were suffering behind the same thing. Even when couples have children, they grow bored and leave their families for all the wrong thing, but many will raise their children and see the pride of their product when they commit to the things of God.

Babe knew that things were happening that threw her off guard, now the government had her attention and they knew she wouldn't settle for a man just to satisfy them. When her closest friend start changing on her, but she was only one person, but it seems like since she made a good life for herself, it made Babe think they might be on to something, but she couldn't go by that alone, Babe knew other people out there hadn't already committed the unpardoned sin and they wouldn't sway in their beliefs and the rights of others no matter what.

One of the publishers, would try to avoid Babe because she would speak of abortion openly, and it didn't take long to see these people were wasting her time, then one of Babes friend that she would hire to do work from time to time He claim that the same publisher left him a text, as if they wanted him to come on to Babe, Babe knew this guy was only a friend that she would hire to do work and he wasn't interested In her that way, so Babe didn't understand why they would reach out to him, nevertheless Babe eventually left this publisher and ended up with the current one. However, many things happened because they seem to be delaying things, sure enough after Babe mother went into the nursing home, that set Babe back also because they end up putting Babe in a rehab, simply because they needed time to move the paper work for the transition. Babe mother wanted to die in the nursing home and Babe wasn't alright with that, but after they put Babe in the rehab Babes hands were tied.

All it took was a slip up, and that slip up was bound to happen, with Babe remodeling her mother's house, One day Babe had forgot that she had left the gasoline in the house and when the hospice administrator came to visit, she smelled gasoline Babe was dumbfounded because she forgot about the gasoline that was used to get some stains off the floor with, and she had left it in the house. Mother's friend had been over earlier that day and she never mentioned it, nor did Babe smell anything that cautioned her, but when the administrator came by that morning and got a whiff of gasoline odor, it threw everything into a panic frenzy. Next thing that was happening was the fire department, came alone with Mesa, to take mother to the hospital to be checked. Within minutes they had turned a completely beautiful day into a war zone it seems like.

While the administrator acted like the house was on fire, Babe tried to assure them, that nobody even smelled gas until they came, they acted like Babe mother was in imminent danger, while they opened all the windows in the house to aired out, they questioned Babe about what kind of medicine did she take, all of a sudden they had turned the table on Babe and the police where there to take Babe to the rehab to be checked over also. Babe couldn't believe they had taken a completely beautiful day with promises of getting things done and turned it into a disaster from hell. They even put cuffs on Babes hands and escorted her to the Rehab, if Babe had known anything could happen like this she would have taken off and came back after everything was over. But Babe had to be there for her mother.

As they rushed Babe's mom off to the hospital to be checked, they were planning on taking Babe to a Rehab without her having a clue of what was going on.

They came up with some scheme to keep Babe in the rehab, until everything was official that Mother would end up living the last days of her life in the nursing home. Babe was so upset knowing that it was nothing she could do while in the Rehab. Babe would keep her diet pills around to fall back on, because it got to where Babe didn't trust half of the Doctors, after seeing so many people put on medicine they didn't need and to see them die behind the drugs that would never cure them.

Dealing with rehab was a nightmare, because Babe was forced to be there, she didn't have any other choice. All Babe could think about was how long she would end up staying there, she had let a couple move into her house, hoping to rent it out, but she had repairs that needed to be done, but nothing was getting done, while Babe struggled with the fact that she was in Rehab against her will and there was nothing she could do about it.

After the weekend came and past, Babe was still in rehab, but at least she was finally able to see some kind of Doctor, after they talked with Babe as a team, the Doctors, told Babe that she needed to leave the diet pills alone because they were making her manic, Babe thought they were wasting her time telling her that because she knew that she wasn't manic, and if she appeared that way, it was because Babe knew that the government was using everybody to play her crazy, even the couple that had moved in

Babe's house, they smoke marijuana like it was normal, every time Babe would see them, she could smell the marijuana before she entered the house. But now Babe wouldn't be able to tend to the repairs while in rehab, Babe was also concern about the roof that had a leak, the addition that Babe had put on had a leak and just being in rehab was taking a toll on everything Babe was trying to accomplish. All Babe wanted to know was when she would be able to get out, but they had some long drawn out plan. Steps and stages to talk to different people,

They started Babe on some of their medication, for depression and bipolar, and then they tried to say that Babe was schizophrenia because she was upset that they could hold her against her will. Compared to some of the people there, Babe was very calm, some of the people were there because of a court order and they were loud and displayed violent behavior, because they were there against their will also. Even though Babe was upset, all she could do was cry, when she thought about what her mother was going through, Babe felt terrible thinking that all because she left that dumb gasoline can in the house they blew it way out of order. Babe called the Hospice agency while she was in rehab they questioned Babe sense of responsibility, making Babe feel even worse, thinking all of this over a stupid can of gasoline that wasn't that big of a deal. Because mother nor Babe nor Betty could even smell anything. Babe begin to wonder if it was all a set up because mother had been upset about the remodeling and then she wanted Babe to stay at home more instead of working on the weekends. Babe had thought to use her great niece to sit with mother on the weekends, but mother didn't give Babe time to even resolve anything.

Nevertheless, all Babe could do was worry about things that wouldn't be done, while she was in Rehab. Babe had to take injections and she didn't like them, and before long her acid reflux started in on her, she was vomiting up the food, because she needed her heart burn pill, Babe would take them at home, because her love for coffee, taught her that somethings came with a price. Finally, they gave her something to combat her heart burn, a week had past and all this counseling wasn't getting her closer to leaving, then after about a week, they told Babe that she would have to talk to a judge that would allow her to leave after she consented to her rules. Babe was desperate to leave, and all she wanted was to get out of there, hoping she could keep her mother from staying at the nursing home, but after Babe talked to her mother counselor through the workforce agency they allowed, Babe was told her mother finalized everything she could and it was official that the nursing home would be Babe's mother final resting place.

Mother was on Hospice at the house, but it was the kind of hospice that they didn't pressure her with the medication that would slowly kill her, Mother condition wasn't getting any better, she couldn't walk and she had a weakness on one side of her body, mother missed JJ so bad, that sometimes she would cry thinking that she wish it would vet been her instead of JJ. Babe would just listen to her and cry with her, but apparently it wasn't God will for mother to die before JJ.

Still at rehab, and week 2 was coming up, finally Babe would have a chance to talk to some judge about the orders she would have to adhere to. Babe was anxious but didn't know what to expect. When she finally met with this judge via televised video, the judge gave Babe some orders to go by, and Babe didn't like the orders at all, the judge told Babe that she wasn't supposed to have any drugs other than the ones they gave her in rehab, no alcoholic beverage and she would have to continue their rehab through Copes a clinic for Adult Behavior. Babe would have to meet monthly for another 6 months after they released her. Babe hated the orders and thought all this hell they had put her through. Babe knew that if she didn't agree to the terms, they would keep her even longer. Babe agreed to the terms so that she could get out and finish up with the repairs and check on the welfare of her mother.

Getting out was like a fresh breath of air, Babe had so much unfinished business, but all she could think about was seeing her mother. After rehab it seem like Babe wasn't talking clear, and her gait was sluggish, Babe had to get a job and get one as soon as she could because she knew that mother had a mortgage and now Babe would be responsible for paying all the bills and the utilities. First thing first was to visit mother, she was in a nursing home that was close by, Babe used to work there through the agency she was working through. Going to see mother, gave Babe some peace and knowing that she was okay and on the other hand, to see her at the nursing home, depressed Babe knowing that Babe couldn't do anything about it. Babe was so depressed that even going home made no difference, Babe missed her mother immensely she took over her mother's room because she had opened up the other room where she put the addition on and there was a slight leak, Babe cousin had been helping her with some of the repairs but he seem to be wasting her time and money when he tried a few times to repair the leak from the inside then later he looked at the roof again, but about time Babe decided to reroof it, since she just used roll roofing. Babe decided to let another friend reroof it, the cousin got all upset because she let the other guy reroof it, but it appears like she had already wasted money on her cousin and he hadn't fixed it right, and since this other guy wasn't of the same political beliefs they were the cousin got all upset. Babe was tired because it seems like he started acting childish about things and Babe didn't have time for it.

Finally making a trip to the nursing home, refreshed Babe for a minute, because she could see that her mother was at peace and she was happy, Babe tried to put on a happy face to help her mother feel better about it all, but deep inside Babe grieved because she had to stay at that hell forsaken rehab just to get her mother in the nursing home. It was difficult talking to Mother because of what the effects of Rehab had left on Babe. Babe knew her mother was behind it all and she had to grin and bear it, because Babe knew the only thing, she could do now was to make her mother comfortable where she was at. Babe told her mother she would try to get a job at the nursing home where she was at, but since Babe was still with another agency, Babe thought she would just pick up more hours, but Babe wasn't working out well with the agency because they were sending her to nursing homes. After rehab Babe had lost weight and she could barely talk, the injections they were giving Babe had her sluggish and stiff, and the agency questioned whether Babe could even do the job anymore. Babe had got out of practice with charting and Babe would walk around like a zombie, Babe thought it had something to do with the injections she was getting and Babe didn't like them. After rehab Babe had a difficult time speaking and her gait was stiff. and her speech was slurred not to mention that it looked like she was stiff, when she told the agency she wanted to work, they could tell by the way Babe talked that they couldn't understand her and they didn't want to put her on a job. Babe panic thinking, she was losing her ability to speak, eventually she realized that her dentures weren't fitting her good because of the weight she lost, she started using the adhesive more when she wore her dentures. Then Babe had 4 teeth on the bottom that were loose and she would have to have them repaired or pulled and to think about pulling them only meant she would have to pull the others that were still there, in order to be fitted for bottom dentures. Babe knew she would have to have a total of 12 teeth pulled out for dentures.

Visiting mother at the nursing home, made Babe think maybe she could get a job at the nursing home where her mother was, but after having a difficult time trying to work with the agency she was already with, Babe knew that it would be too touching to see her mother around the clock at the nursing home, so she found a job doing home health care. They kept her busy, so busy that Babe was getting overtime and paying the mortgage and catching up the bills. But the pain of seeing her mother was somewhat draining because after working long hours from the other job, Babe still managed to see her mother a couple times a week. Babe was upset about being in rehab, but she couldn't let her mother know, she was the only one visiting alone with Betty. Candi had turned on mother and refused to even visit her at the nursing home, When Babe would visit they would turn the conversation on Candi. Somehow Candi grew upset with mother when she went to the nursing home, because of some black art figurine dolls that Candi ended up with, but mother wanted Betty to have them, Candi refused to give them to Betty and then she refused to even visit mother at the nursing home as well. Babe was torn between the 2 of them, Babe knew that mother needed someone to walk her through this process and she realized that Candi wouldn't be there, Betty and Sandra, Babe's sister-in-law to brother Martin. Who was now struggling to live himself, because he had prostate cancer.

Martin told them in the early part of the year that he had cancer, and Sandra, his wife was taking him to chemotherapy treatment. Babe was out of the picture, because since she had moved in to help mother, they had been to themselves.

Now Babe was visiting mother at the nursing home, Mother seemed bright eyed to see Babe knowing that she was her mother's ray of sunshine. Babe would think about that song. You are my sunshine as she looked at the sign that hung on her mother's wall, because at some point Babe mom had become her sunshine, but now to see Babe visiting her mother, she became her ray of sunshine Babe didn't know how long it would last, but she knew that seeing her mother gave her strength to carry on. Shortly after JJ died, it seems like Martin Babe's last brother left living ended up with cancer, it was heart wrenching enough that mother had to deal with the death of JJ, but Martin took everybody by surprise, Martin came over one day and everybody noticed that he was losing weight and just didn't look like himself. Finally, Martin had to confess to mother that he had cancer, mother was still grieving from JJ death, but now to know that Martin had bladder and prostate cancer, Sandra Martin wife had been taking him for chemotherapy treatment. Mother was still at her home when she found out that Martin had cancer, so Babe was taking care of mother.

November 2022 Mother moved into the nursing home and she wanted Babe to think she was just fine, but after falling out of the bed a few times, Babe knew that her mother was slowly slipping away. They gave mother a nice size bed, much bigger than the one she had a home, but she never fell out of the bed at home, and Babe knew it was out of her hands. She looked at how they got her mother up, Babe mother had some height on her and Babe knew that she couldn't get her mother up without the Hoyer lift at home, but they would get her mother up without the lift and Babe would fringe, when her mother asked her to help her while they were getting her up. Babe never tried to get her up without the Hoyer lift, but they wouldn't use the Hoyer lift until her mother kept falling out of the bed.

Babe felt so helpless, but she knew it was nothing she could do, Sandra was busy caring for Martin, so basically it was Betty and Babe caring for Mother. Betty was better than her own sister, because Candi probably just didn't like the nursing home scene, but she still never visited and Babe was upset about that.

January 2023 Martin passed away from his cancer, his body was so weak from the chemotherapy they were giving him, around the same time Martin died, it seems like Babe longtime friend sister in law had cancer died also, she talked about all the people they were treating for cancer, it was like a revolving door for the Doctors, but the patient were the ones dying like flies. Mother had to grieve for Martin in the nursing home, At least Babe and Candi attended Martins funeral, Babe had just recently gotten out of rehab, so Babe was like a stiff neck and she could barely eat or talk, Babe remember how she couldn't even enjoy the dinner after the funeral because of her dentures and just getting back to being normal. Sandra really tried to give Martin a nice memorial, she had a fifteen course meal and all that food and Babe couldn't even enjoy it. Babe didn't get to grieve Martin, because it was all together with everything else. The rehab, and then mother being at the nursing home, Babe began to feel numb about it all, she was forced to attend monthly visits at the outpatient clinic for the rehab. Babe had rules and she knew that she didn't want to ever go back to rehab, so the court order would be for six months and Babe had to commit to it, even though they told Babe no diet pills, Babe couldn't wait to ignore those orders, because it was like they had put all these sicknesses on her and she knew they were fabricated and she knew all she wanted was to get back to being normal.

After Babe put some of her weight back on she begins to talk normal, and eventually she got off the injections they were giving her. Because after they tried to charge her 700 dollars for the injections, she knew she wouldn't pay for them because she never wanted them anyway, they eventually gave her the pills which was equivalent to the injections they were giving her, but she never took the pills. It seems like every month Babe made her visit, they would give her some other drugs that she was supposed to take, Babe was just counting down to when she would end the court order, because she knew it would all be over in May and she knew she would never go back. She would comply with the court order, but after that Babe had had enough. She was upset that they could make her comply with something like that and when the date arrived when she was finished. She vowed to never return. Babe knew that was how they recruited patients, but Babe never had a mental problem and she saw no needed in seeking their help.

It was mandatory that she made that monthly appointment, and it took a while before she could convince them that she didn't need that injection, it seem like the injection was making her stiff and sluggish. But eventually, she had completed the court order and she threw all the pills they had given her away and resorted back to her diet pills occasionally. Babe had seen to many people depending on Doctors and before long they needed them because of the side effects some of the medicine was creating.

After the court order was done, Babe had more time to visit her mother at the nursing home, Babe had struggled with accepting her mother but as time passed, she tried to understand. Babe found a classmate that helped her with the remodeling of the house. He had the house looking very well and with the overtime Babe was working she was able to pay him gladly. Now all Babe had to do was tend to her mother's need. Sometimes Babe mother would be calling for her at the nursing home, she thought Babe had taken a job there, because Babe had told her that she would try to get a job there, but Babe wouldn't have qualified after rehab, because she lost her job with the agency she had been working with because she couldn't keep up with the pace of the nursing homes.

Babe was working some long hours and after a 16-hour shift, she decided to visit her mother at the nursing home. It was late, and when she got there, Babe mom was sleeping in the wheel chair, and unable to wake from her sleeping, Babe was afraid that she could be dead, but Babe had found her mom sleeping deep when she was home, she called hospice and they were upset because her mom was still breathing, but Babe just feared the worse since she knew it was bound to happen. At the nursing home Babe found a nurse to check her mother, but the nurse wanted to seem concern, so they called EMSA to take Babe's mother to the hospital, Babe was tired and knew the day had already been long so she was going to go home, When Babe tried to leave she noticed she had a flat tire from earlier when the construction was going on at the resident home she worked at. After realizing that she had a flat tire, Babe decided to call Betty, mother's longtime friend, Babe waited on Betty and then they went to the hospital to check on Mother. The Doctor check out mother and knew she was doing fine, but he decided to put mother back on hospice, since they discontinued it when she went into the nursing home. Babe and Betty finally left the hospital and Betty took Babe back to the nursing home where she would wait on AAA to fix her flat tire before she could leave.

One of the employees saw Babe waiting and asked her if she needed any help, but Babe told her AAA was coming, while waiting the employee talk of how fond they were of Babe's mom and hoped she was okay. Babe felt good knowing how well they liked her mother at the nursing home. AAA finally arrived and Babe finally got her tire fix and headed home, it was late but she knew that she had a full day and thought, at least she knows her mother was find. But Babe feared that now that the Doctor decided to put her mother back on hospice, they would execute the orders before longs, when Babe mother was at home, she wouldn't give her any medication that would terminate her life. But now Babe knew this would put them at the crossroad, and all they could do was to wait.

The nursing home would try a combination of drugs to help the tremors, but eventually they had to give her the morphine, when mother was in and out of consciousness, Babe would visit her, Babe wanted more than anything to let her mother know how sorry she was and how much she loved her, the house was finished but it would not make any difference now, since they started administering the morphine, it was like she was on a journey to leave this world. Mother would recognize Babe, and she would smile to assure Babe that it was okay, but Babe couldn't bear to see her that way, with tears in her eyes, Babe would tell her mother how much she loved her and with stammering speech mother would utter the words back. "I love you". It was all that Babe could do was to smile back and rejoice over those last words of love that mother gave her back, Babe would leave shortly after that, knowing that she could be at peace just to know that her mother was dying with the assurance of her loving and being loved.

It was a gradual process, but before long the morphine would take effect and she would soon succumb, and it was over. Mother died peacefully that September 8th of 2023. Babe was left with getting the burial and the obituary ready, Candi finally came to see mother, a couple days before it was all over.

Mother had already finalized her funeral and most everything was taken care of, Sandra, Betty and Babe met at the funeral home. Since Sandra had an insurance policy she needed the death certificate. Sandra was supposed to pay for the closing of the casket and Babe didn't know that mother still had to get a gravestone for her. The funeral was at Betty's and mother church, they were 7 Day Adventist, all went well, she was properly put away, JJ wife had helped with mother's burial arrangements after JJ died, JJ left instructions to put mother away nicely, JJ wife did just that, but she didn't make it to the funeral. But she enjoyed the obituary they sent her after the funeral. Candi made it to the funeral and her kids was with her, but her husband Stephan wasn't there, Babe wondered why Stephan wasn't there, Candi said that he was sick. After the burial of mother, it wasn't long before they found out that Stephan had cancer of the lungs and Candi was in for a downhill battle with Stephan sickness.

Months after the burial of mother, Sandra was in a bit of a tumultuous situation with the insurance, they wouldn't honor the policy because her name wasn't on the policy and they were looking for the next of heirs to grant the insurance money to. Babe knew that she would help Sandra in any way that she could, but they had been talking with Candi about it and come to find out they said the next of heirs would be entitled to the insurance money that Martin had had over the last 12 years on their mother's life, Candi was struggling with the sickness of Stephan her husband. Candi had already told Babe that they would be sending the insurance money to them and Babe thought what the hell happened, Candi had already planned on using the money for herself since their car had broken down, shortly after finding out that Stephan had cancer.

After submitting the paperwork, it wasn't long before they were sending Babe and Candi the money, after they made some adjustment because of the late payments they adjusted. It all happened so fast, Mother was buried in September and within months they found out that Stephan was going for treatment, they had waited so long to find out that I had spread over his body. The following year Stephan died in January and Candi cremated his body, without a service. At that time the insurance money came in and it really blessed Candi because she needed help with the burial of Stephan and they also needed to get transportation. Sandra thought they would send her the money, but they divided the money between Candi and myself. Babe called Sandra and thanked her for the insurance money, and she was highly upset, and Babe told her that Candi said they were the rightful heirs since her name wasn't on the policy, Babe wanted to help Sandra out but after she acted so rude when it came to the closing of the casket and then the thought that Babe would've had to get a burial stone for her mother after it was said and done. Sandra was really upset that she didn't get the money, but Babe knew that Candi needed the money more than ever because of Stephan's death.

Even though Sandra was upset that they gave Candi and Babe the insurance money, Babe told Sandra that at least she ended up with their grandmother's house and Candi didn't get anything, Babe was okay by not getting her grandmother's house because Babe had her own place and a rent house that she had to get rid of but Candi was always in need of something because Stephan didn't work, and Candi had to care for her grandchild that had autism. Babe wanted to help Sandra, but she knew that it was bad blood, sometimes because Sandra thought Babe should have given her rent house to her nephew, who she barely even talked to.

Babe and Candi was thankful for the blessing to receive the insurance money, neither had expected it, and after all were said and done, Babe could focus on finishing the book. The publisher was more than ready to help, but after Babe mother went into the nursing home and the visit to rehab, delayed Babe even more. At the publishing company one agent that would call Babe more frequently than anything, all of sudden Jack the agent was gone and Babe, was looking for answers, she knew that the government was still in the picture, but Babe decided that she would move on as if she didn't know about anything other than trying to finish the book. Another agent tried to fill in for Jack but because he spoke broken English and Babe wasn't interested In just friendly conversation, which it was beginning to seem like with Jack, so for a few months, the book laid dormant because the other guy that did the editing was on medical leave, eventually they introduced Babe to a female agent, and it seems like they could relate to many things, just like Jack, he agreed that abortion should stay legal because many would need the service and having a safe and legal environment would make the difference for women that needed that.

Finally, they could focus on the completion of the book and having the assurance of other women made all the difference in the world. Even though they would bump heads Babe was willing to be wrong just to get everything done right.

As the world turned around the globe of chaos, more wars were on the brink, While Babe tried to understand the Bible connection to the war, she couldn't help but think about the prophecy from the book of Joel. Even though Babe realized that the last chapter of Joel, revealed that God's drugs were being used to bait people into crime. Then the 2nd chapter would reveal how the army of the Lord should reveal the conspiracy of drugs and the last chapter of Joel would tell of Judgment upon the nations. Described the Headline, + 3rd chapter even talked about

Palestine, although different translations referred to Palestine as Philistine and we all know about how David slew the Philistine. All the blood shed was described as the Terrible day of the Lord. Babe also remembered the immigrants from Israel how the women were sold in Lebanon as sex slave and the men were sold for their organs. It seems like Joel was saying the same thing when it talked about how they cast lots for Gods people and how they sold a girl for wine that they may drink and a boy as payment for a harlot. It seemed to be a type of what was happening during the wars. Many were hating on Israel for all the killing and Babe didn't know what was really going on, because most Christians would stand by the Bible because the Bible states that whoever helps Israel, God will help. Babe didn't like the fact that Palestine was being torn down, but after reading about some of the terrible things Palestine would do to their women, and how they hated the LGBT people, Babe wondered if God wanted people to understand that if God couldn't open their eyes one way, he would find another way to reveal his plan for the rights of women.

On the other hand, Israel was a champion for the rights of women and they stood for justice for those that couldn't defend themselves. People of LGBT background was protected by the laws of Israel. Since Babe main objective was to open the eyes of people everywhere about the rights of women, Babe couldn't help but think these wars would do things that Babe could only pray for. It wasn't long before Israel and Iran started war among each other and Babe thought Iran was just another country that didn't care about the rights of their women. Many were still upset with Israel, but the book of Joel claimed the victory for the children of Israel, no matter what, the United States kept supporting Israel and they also supported Ukraine, because these countries were once the underdog, but they both respected and love their women as the Bible tells them. While the other countries put the rights of the unborn before the women and now Babe thought it was appropriate to call anyone that didn't respect the rights of women were the branch of the Antichrist. Even if they proclaimed to be Christian, Babe knew they wouldn't honor the rights of women and God endorsed abortion, when he sacrificed his son for their sins.

Many could see through the leader of Russia, since he started the war and made all those arrogant remarks about women and drugs, he would be the connection between the war on drug as well as the war on women, it's obvious that he didn't care and to let their soldiers impregnate innocent women while they were at war, proved that they didn't care and if the leaders made wars only created wars for women, then No wonder God will bring havoc on men that only thought women should replenish the world, just to kill them off with man-made wars.

All the countries were they forced women to populate their country only to become an eyesore for their country when the men fled and left the women alone to raise children they never wanted and was raped and made to have only to become an eye soar for their country, while their country do the unthinkable by genocide of that country. Yemen genocide their women and children that was left desolate by men that fled the country after they populated their land with the seed of the rapist. 58.000. Women and children were bombed to death at the hands of evil and wicked men that didn't care, while they never reflected on the women that became martyred because their rights were violated when their leaders would rather go alone with the conspiracy to keep women pregnant and uneducated while they pollute the world with the seeds of the adulterer. Yet their God don't understand the teachings of Jesus Christ when he told the Daughters of Zion to fear not.

The conspiracy that these countries played into will bring them down now, because they fail to understand liberty and justice for all, and If Israel is a champion for women rights, now I beginning to understand why God tells us that whoever helps Israel he will help. Many people that's for Israel, don't even know that Israel is for women of every color and every creed, but through the turn of the century this will open the eyes of even the wayward Christians and become revelation that they refused to accept before because the light had blinded them. Lord only knows when the wars will end, but if the evil doers insist on fighting for no reason, surely the point will be made eventually. That women aren't going to replenish the earth even if they kill them all.

Appendix

Most of the verses used from the Holy Bible were from the King James Version, and some New International translations were also used. The Nag Hammadi Library was referenced in some writings because this collection of scrolls discovered in 1945 in Cairo, Egypt, indicated that after the ascension of Jesus, he stayed with his disciples for forty days afterward, teaching them and showing them the ways of the world as opposed to the things of God. Several books have additional warnings of fornication and how to avoid and shun it.

The *Secondhand Third Epistle of John* by Judith Lieu and edited by John Rich—this book used in this novel proves that the same problems exist during the days of Jesus' ministry. They also revealed too that the process toward acceptance was not a linear one but was made up of many strands; more importantly, they showed that the question of whether some parts of the New Testament are more central than others has been a consistently recurring one and that their avowed purpose lies elsewhere, leaving room for further interpretation. Also, it emphasizes on the Johannine Christianity, which is based on the teaching of Jesus Christ by the apostle John. Clues throughout the Bible give directions for eternal life, and the name given to John's writings,

"Johannine," bears the meaning of eternal life as well. The meaning of the number 9 has an eternal message, which is what the resurrection of Jesus Christ is all about.

John Rich was instrumental in editing some of the Nag Hammadi and the Gospel tradition as well.

The Lost Books of the Bible (Testament 1998 ISBN -0517-27795-6.) The Lost Gospel of Peter, The Forgotten Book of Eden (Alpha House 1927, ISBN 0-517-30886-x, ISBN 1-56459-636-2. The Psalms of Solomon, Testament of the Twelve Patriarchs.

www.ingramcontent.com/pod-product-compliance
Lightning Source LLC
LaVergne TN
LVHW042244070526
838201LV00088B/9